The Reiki Man

The Reiki Man

Dominic C. James

BOOKS

Winchester, UK
Washington, USA

First published by O-Books, 2011
O-Books is an imprint of John Hunt Publishing Ltd., Laurel House, Station Approach,
Alresford, Hants, SO24 9JH, UK
office1@o-books.net
www.o-books.com

For distributor details and how to order please visit the 'Ordering' section on our website.

Text copyright Dominic C. James 2009

ISBN: 978 1 84694 413 0

Design: Stuart Davies
Illustrations: Denis Fraser

Printed in the UK by CPI Antony Rowe
Printed in the USA by Offset Paperback Mfrs, Inc

We operate a distinctive and ethical publishing philosophy in all
areas of our business, from our global network of authors to
production and worldwide distribution.

For Donald Thornton

Acknowledgements

Special thanks to James, Jo, Laura, Liz and my dad for reading the initial manuscript and keeping me going with their enthusiastic comments; the team at O-Books; Denis for all his help and advice over the years, and his invaluable assistance in the marketing of the book; Dani, Digger, Jon, Nana, Paul and Wags for their encouragement; Alex, Martin, Rob and Tom for their constant ribbing; my family; and everyone at JT's in Banbury. B, Casper and Ellie.

Books that have proved helpful for information:

Reiki The Ultimate Guide: Learn Sacred Symbols and Attunements Plus Reiki Secrets You Should Know - Steve Murray.

Essential Reiki: A Complete Guide to an Ancient Healing Art - Diane Stein

Author's note

Reiki - Universal Life Force Energy

Modern Reiki originates in Japan and is used worldwide as a healing practice. At the heart of Reiki are the sacred symbols that connect the practitioner to his or her energy source. There are four main symbols used in traditional Usui Reiki, with a total of twenty two in use in other forms of the art. It is said that another 300 symbols exist, and that they are hidden in a temple situated in either Tibet or India. The symbols will only be released by the monks that guard them when the human race is ready. Nobody knows what these symbols are or what they do. Until they are released we can only speculate...

Prologue

The study was silent save for the soft ticking of the grandfather clock. Henry Mulholland closed his laptop and sat back in his chair. It was three o'clock in the morning and he was beat, yet his head still swam with numbers. He poured himself a generous malt whisky and lit a cigarette. Closing his eyes he breathed out a sigh of smoke. It had been a long day. The markets were still volatile, as they had been for weeks, and on top of that he had spent most of the day negotiating with the GMB union over the closure of the steelworks. His offer had been more than fair but they were becoming greedy. Maybe if…

His train of thought was suddenly interrupted by his subconscious.

Henry opened his eyes and focused back on the room. The atmosphere had changed. He couldn't put his finger on it but something was different. He felt cold and the back of his neck was starting to tingle. He tried to take a drag of his cigarette but found himself unable to move his arm. In a panic, he tried to move each limb in turn. It was no use: he was totally paralysed.

"Don't bother trying," said a voice from behind.

The man walked slowly round to the front of the desk and stared hard at Henry. He was Oriental and dressed in black from head to toe. Henry tried to speak, but found that too was impossible.

"I'm going to release you now Mr Mulholland. When I do, I want you to stay still and quiet. Only speak when I ask you a direct question. If you understand and are willing to comply, blink three times." His voice was calm yet commanding.

Henry blinked three times. The man made a zigzagging motion with his right arm and Henry felt life come back to his body. He stubbed out the cigarette which had nearly burnt down to his knuckles.

"I've come for the box, Mr Mulholland. Where is it?"

Henry looked quizzical. "What box?"

"*The* box."

"I really don't know what you mean."

The man made a sign in the air and immediately Henry was paralysed again.

From his trouser pocket the man drew a six inch stiletto blade. He leant over the desk and pushed it to Henry's throat.

"Mr Mulholland, I will not hesitate to kill you if I don't get what I want. I suggest you think very carefully about this."

He slowly withdrew the knife and put it back in his pocket. From the desk he took a notepad and pen and drew a symbol. He released Henry again and held the symbol in front of him. "The box I'm talking about is made of wood and is covered in symbols, this one," he pointed, "is larger and is positioned directly in the centre. Now again, where is it?"

Henry shook with fear. Beads of sweat ran down his forehead and stung his eyes. He had no idea what the man was talking about.

"I...I...don't know. I have no box like that," he stammered.

"I thought you might say that...Very well."

Without another word he paralysed Henry again and drew the knife. The blade entered Henry's heart with surgical precision and he died instantly: eyes wide with horror and helpless as a newborn kitten. The man put his mask back on and crept out of the window into the shadows of the night.

Chapter 1

It was dark and it had started to rain. Stella Jones braked swiftly and took a hard left into the lane that led up to Addington Hall. Since the call had come through her mind had been in overdrive. How the hell had someone breached the tightest, most modern security that money could buy? There were no scapegoats, there was no-one else to blame, the buck stopped with her.

She pulled up to the gatehouse and was greeted by the sight of squad cars. A young policeman strode up to the car window and she whirred it down.

"Evening Madam," he said politely. "What is your business here?"

"Stella Jones, head of security," she said, and flashed him her ID.

He carefully scrutinized her pass, and when satisfied he wandered out of earshot and spoke into his radio. Thirty seconds later he was back at her window.

"Ok Ms Jones, the boss says you can go up."

She drove slowly up the driveway and parked behind the mass of marked and unmarked cars that had gathered on the gravel frontage: Henry Mulholland was a well-connected man.

The ornate front doors were wide open and the entrance was barred by crime scene tape. Another young PC was standing guard and Stella strode briskly up to him, ID in hand.

"Stella Jones, head of security," she said.

The PC radioed his chief, and a minute later a smartly-dressed, portly, middle-aged man came across the entrance hall to the door. He was Stella's old boss. His name was David Brennan and he was the head of Special Branch (SO1).

"Hello Stella," he said warmly.

"Hello David, what are you doing here?" she said, pleased to see a familiar face. "I didn't think this was Special Branch's territory."

"Strictly speaking it isn't, but the PM wants this dealt with quickly. They were good friends, as you know."

Henry Mulholland had been friends with the Prime Minister, Jonathan Ayres, since university. They had both studied philosophy, politics and economics at Oxford. They were joint owners of three racehorses, one of which was favourite for the Cheltenham Gold Cup. Well, they had been joint owners - now one of them was dead.

Stella and Brennan climbed the grand sweeping staircase, heading for the upstairs study.

"What have you got then?" she asked.

"Not a lot to be honest," said Brennan, slightly downbeat. "The killer came in through the window and left the same way. No fingerprints, no nothing. Forensics has swept the room minutely, we may get a few fibres or a hair if we're lucky, but I'm not holding my breath. Highly professional job, may as well have been a ghost."

"How did he manage to get in? This place is wired up like Fort Knox."

"Good question. The gatehouse guard can't remember a thing, one minute he's awake, the next - nothing. Same with your man in the CCTV room."

They walked into the study. Stella's eyes immediately fell upon Henry Mulholland, sitting bolt upright with startled eyes. He looked like he'd been frozen in time. Perfectly mummified save for the dried blood that stained his Saville Row shirt.

"Odd isn't it?" said Brennan, seeing the look on Stella's face.

"That's an understatement," said Stella. "Surreal is what I would say."

"Yes, surreal is a better word. No struggle, no resistance, he just sat there and let himself be stabbed. Can't quite get my head round it."

Stella carried on staring at the body: Henry Mulholland, 43

years old, billionaire businessman and philanthropist, sportsman and playboy, drinker and gambler, gentleman and scholar; the last of a dying breed. Henry Mulholland; dead.

Brennan produced a baggie from his pocket. Inside it was a piece of notepaper. "I said we have nothing, that's not strictly true. We do have this," he said, handing it to Stella. "Mean anything to you?"

Stella looked at the symbol on the paper. At first she stared blankly at it but then a hint of recognition hit her brain. She was sure she had seen it before, not here at the house but years previously; another time, another place.

"No, what is it?" she said, not wanting to get Brennan's hopes up.

"I don't know, but it was on the desk in front of him when we got here. Seems reasonable to assume that it was either him or the killer that drew it. It's really the only clue we've got."

"We've got a bit of a mystery on our hands then, haven't we?"

"*Our* hands?" Brennan looked across at her with quizzical eyes. "I hate to point this out to you Stella but you are a civilian, and have been for a few years."

Stella bowed her head dejectedly. "I just thought I might be able to help out. I've been here for two years now and I probably know more about Henry's life, private and business, than anyone else. I could be very useful."

Brennan sighed. "Well I suppose you could assist us with our enquiries, as they say. Just remember The Official Secrets Act is for life, you're still bound to it."

Brennan liked Stella. He'd liked her ever since she was transferred to Special Branch as a wide-eyed young constable. There was something about her that had set her apart from her contemporaries. She had a natural feel for the job, and an animal-like sixth sense that had made her ideal for close protection. Brennan had nurtured these raw talents and she had become one of his best and most trusted operatives. He had been extremely disappointed when she left to work for Henry Mulholland. Although he understood that the money must have been a huge carrot.

"Shall we go and get some coffee?" suggested Brennan. "It looks like you could do with one."

Stella took a quick glance in the study mirror. She looked a mess. Her eyes were puffy, her dark, shoulder-length hair was loose and bedraggled, and the black sweat suit she'd grabbed off the bedroom floor was twisted and crumpled. She looked more like a drug addict than a security chief.

"Yes let's get some coffee, we'll go to my office."

Her office was elaborate and traditional, in keeping with the rest of the house. Brennan was impressed. "You've certainly done all right."

"Yes, not bad is it."

She made them both some black coffee and they sat down on opposite sides of the large walnut desk. Brennan looked old, Stella thought. It had been two years since she'd last seen him; he looked like he'd aged a decade. His bright keen eyes still shone through but his face was ashen and drawn. The pressures of work had caught up with him.

"So let me get this straight," said Stella. "Someone put two security guards to sleep without them knowing, disabled the entire security system, climbed through the study window, killed Henry, and then disappeared without a trace. What about the dogs? Did none of the staff hear them?"

"The dogs were asleep as well, just lying there on the lawn.

The staff heard nothing."

Stella's head hurt. "No-one could have done all that on their own."

Brennan nodded. "I agree. Somebody's lying. Probably one of the guards. If not that, then one of the staff has drugged them. Either way the killer's had help from the inside. Must have done. We'll know more when the blood tests come back."

Stella gazed out of her office window. It was now 7am, and daylight was starting to creep through the drab December sky. Some holiday, she thought. She was due to fly out to Mauritius at 3pm that day; Christmas away from it all. Two weeks of lounging on white sandy beaches being waited on hand and foot. Two weeks of doing nothing and thinking nothing. A dream getaway. The dream would have to wait: she was going to get to the bottom of this, with or without Brennan's blessing.

"Any idea who'd want to kill him," asked Brennan.

"Can't think of anyone offhand. He was pretty much well-liked by everyone he met. Could be a jealous husband I suppose - he was a bit of a rogue where ladies were concerned. Didn't seem to care if they were married or not, they were all fair game."

Brennan gave her a knowing look.

Stella answered the look with scorn. "No - if that's what you're implying. Our relationship was purely professional. He flirted a bit occasionally but I made it very clear where my boundaries lay. He accepted it - end of story."

Brennan laughed. "Ok, ok… No need to be so touchy." He'd been winding her up, he knew very well that Stella wouldn't compromise her position in that way.

"Anyway," said Stella regaining her thread, "I'm pretty sure that symbol's behind it, not some love-crazed man."

There was a knock on the door. Stella beckoned the knocker in, and a tall, muscular, suited man with blond hair entered the room. He was in his early thirties, Stella guessed, and he was good-looking in a pretty boy way. He nodded to Stella and smiled.

"Hello Jennings, what have you got?" asked Brennan.

"Not a lot sir, just thought I'd let you know that the initial blood tests are clean."

"Nothing?" said Brennan, bemused.

"None of the usual drugs sir, no. They're going to test for some of the more obscure ones but it'll take a while. This afternoon at the earliest they said."

"Any news on the symbol?" asked Brennan hopefully.

"Not yet sir, we've got people trawling the Internet at the moment."

"Ok, keep me updated."

Jennings left the room.

Brennan turned to Stella and shrugged. "Well this is all fucked up then, isn't it?" he said.

"Yes it's all fucked up. Dogs, guards, laser trips...everything!"

Brennan eyed Stella thoughtfully; she was holding something back. "You've seen that symbol before haven't you?" he ventured.

"Maybe...How did you know?"

"I've been studying body language for over thirty years. I worked with you for five of those. I can tell when you're on to something - your left nostril twitches. It twitched when I showed you that symbol."

Stella laughed. "I should know better than to hide anything from you, shouldn't I?"

Brennan pressed: "So about this symbol."

"To be honest David, I just don't know. I've seen it before but I can't quite place it at the moment. I'm sure it'll come to me, I just need a memory trigger."

"Ok, no problem," said Brennan. "Just relax and take your time, there's no point trying to force it. Just let me know when you remember."

There was another knock on the door and Jennings came

9

bursting in. "We've found it sir!" he said excitedly.

"Found what?" asked Brennan.

Jennings caught his breath. "The symbol sir, we know what it means."

"Well go on then, spit it out," Brennan demanded.

"It's an ancient Japanese symbol sir, from some healing art called Reiki."

"Oh, ok. But what does it mean?"

Jennings paused nervously, as if embarrassed by the answer he was about to give. "God is here sir, it means God is here."

Chapter 2

Yoshima stared aimlessly at the cracked motel ceiling. The whore was snoozing happily beside him. It was good to get it out of your system. A kill was a kill: it was exhilarating, mesmerizing and yet not soul-fulfilling. There had to be some release afterwards. £200 was a cheap 'no questions asked' release. It would be even cheaper if he killed her, but then he would need another. It could go on ad infinitum. Best to pay the £200 and be done.

Unfortunately it had been mission unaccomplished. Nothing good to report back with; apart from the death of the pig, the greedy Western pig. Why couldn't these ignorant bastards keep their noses out of strictly Oriental business. Weren't they happy with their money? Couldn't they find sanctuary in their mindless capitalism? Obviously not. No, they had to keep searching for 'something else', some unfathomable answer that they strived for. Acupuncture, feng shui, yoga. Everybody wanted in on the bandwagon. There was no respect for the thousands of years of history that had made all these practices possible. All the West wanted was to take the knowledge and treat it as a transient symbol of their spirituality. The lazy man's way to enlightenment!

He grabbed the cell phone out of his mini kit bag and locked himself in the bathroom, out of earshot. He dialled the number that was committed to his memory. After two rings someone somewhere picked up.

"Hello," said a voice, in Japanese.

"Hello, this is Ghost," said Yoshima.

"Go ahead Ghost. The line is clear."

"Suspect questioned but the item was not in his possession."

There was a pause at the other end. "Are you sure?"

"Yes," said Yoshima. "I am certain. The man was not lying. I know people, I can see through lies. He had no knowledge of the item whatsoever."

"Ok, Ghost. Proceed down the list as planned."

After taking a cold shower Yoshima felt refreshed. It had been a long night but there was not yet time for sleep. He was still too close to the murder scene for comfort. The whore would provide a good alibi if needed, but it was best not to need it. He relied on stealth and secrecy.

The whore was up and dressed when Yoshima emerged from the bathroom. She was attractive but in a dirty way, certainly no Geisha. If he'd had the time he would have fucked her again. Time, however, was pressing and he would have to take a rain check.

"Are you off my dear?" said Yoshima.

"Yes," said the whore. "Unless you want to go again that is."

"A tempting offer, but I'm afraid that I have an important meeting to attend. There is no rest in the financial world."

"Your loss."

Yoshima got his wallet and counted out three hundred pounds. "Here's your money plus extra for your trouble…and of course your discretion."

The whore took the money gratefully. A couple of grams of charley, a few cocktails, perhaps even some food. It was going to be a good day.

The whore left and Yoshima made ready to get going. He had got her to check in the previous night so as not to be seen. She had paid cash so there was no need to check out. He hadn't been there. The whore had seen him of course, but what was she going to say: just some kinky Jap businessman looking for a bit of rough sex, he was there all night. What did he look like? They all look the same to me, would be the answer.

Chapter 3

The Angel Inn, Peckham, was a 'spit and sawdust' establishment. It had chairs, it had tables and it had a bar. Its only concession to luxury was the fantastic Wurlitzer jukebox that stood proudly luminescent in the far corner. It was a drinkers' pub: no women, no children, and no wine or cocktails. If you liked beer and shots and rock then it was the place for you, if not then you could always try the wine bar down the road. The punters ran it for themselves, the name above the door was just that - a name. Wild and uncontrollable, fierce and legendary, it was home to the Devil's own.

Stella stood uncomfortably in the street. Jennings had volunteered to go into the Angel and make some enquiries. She wasn't happy at having been landed with a chaperone, she was quite capable of looking after herself, but as Brennan had pointed out - she was no longer a policewoman; and officially she was still under suspicion as an accessory. Jennings wasn't too bad anyway, perhaps a bit eager and keen to please, but a good bloke nevertheless. Whether he had the ability to handle himself in a dive like the Angel, she doubted very much.

Within a minute of entering the pub Jennings was back out again; not walking but flying. He landed without grace on the pavement next to Stella.

"All under control then," she laughed.

"Yes, very fucking funny," said Jennings. He pulled himself to his feet and dusted his suit down. "They're not exactly a welcoming bunch in there. Are you sure this is the right place?"

"This is the address I was given by his brother. It makes sense as well - what better place for an alcoholic to live?"

"I suppose so," Jennings agreed. "But I don't see why we need the help of some down-and-out booze hound. How's he possibly going to further the investigation?"

"I don't know, but I've seen that symbol before and it's got something to do with him. And anyway he's not just some idiot drunk, he's...well he's just him ok."

"Ok, ok, enough said," said Jennings seeing the look of pain in Stella's eyes. "So how do you suggest we get in there?" he asked.

"I think perhaps a woman's touch is needed in this situation," said Stella. "You aren't going to get very far flashing your badge in a place like this. Law and order mean fuck all to these guys. I'll bet the local police never set foot in here: too scared. You wait out here for me."

Stella strode confidently through the door. The bar was busy but not heaving. The rank smell of stale beer and cigarettes hit her almost immediately, and she tried desperately not to make a face. Heads turned. Her smart dark blue trouser suit made her look like a high flyer from the city, not the sort of woman who would walk into the Angel. Appearing unfazed she squeezed in between two barflies and waved a twenty pound note at the barman.

"Pint of lager and a shot of tequila please," she ordered.

The barman, a bearded lunk, looked bemused but went and got the drinks.

As she waited she felt like the whole pub was staring. The jukebox played on but all voices were hushed. She stared straight ahead, acting as naturally as she could. The smoking ban appeared to have eluded the Angel so she pulled a pack of B&H out of her handbag and lit one up. When the drinks arrived she ignored the lager and downed the tequila in one swift movement.

"Another one," she said, gesturing at the empty shot glass.

She scanned the room quickly trying to gauge who out of all these apes was the Alpha male. If she could lock on to him then she might last longer than five minutes. There were plenty of likely suspects, every man in there looked like they could rip you limb from limb. They ranged from short, muscular and psycho-pathic to huge, muscular and psychopathic.

Unable to make up her mind, and with her bladder bursting from the long drive, she took the opportunity to make a trip to the toilets.

The ladies' room, such as it was, stood to the right-hand side of the bar. The unhinged door was chipped and cracked, and the skirted icon was hanging upside-down. Inside it was no better. There were two rancid cubicles, neither of which had locks, and the feculent floor was covered in a year's worth of scum and grime. The one consolation was the provision of toilet paper. Stella gritted her teeth and entered one of the cubicles.

A minute later she was about to exit when the sound of music from the bar grew briefly louder and then deadened again. Someone else had entered the toilet. Stella froze. Her heart hammered away in her eardrums. There had been no sign of another woman in the bar. She crouched as low as she could and craned her neck down to get a view of the floor outside. There was no-one there. She got to her feet and inched back the door. The room appeared empty. Perhaps someone had just poked their head in.

She exited the cubicle and went to the hand basin. After a bout of pantomime chugging the tap eventually produced some water. Before she could rinse her hands though, a sturdy arm had grabbed her round the neck. She tried to break free but the hold was too tight. A knife waved in her face.

"Don't struggle or I'll cut yer·face," said a clammy voice.

Stella lifted her leg and kicked back hard into her assailant's shins. He grunted but held firm. He moved the blade towards her right eye. "I told yer not to fuckin' well move. Any more trouble an' yer lose yer sight. Understand?"

Stella gave a strangled "Uh huh".

Keeping his arm round her neck and the knife at her eye, he grabbed her handbag from the side of the basin. Then he loosened his hold and made to escape.

Instinctively Stella turned and let fly a kick at the back of the man's legs. It wasn't a hard strike, but it was enough to send him headfirst into the ground. She made a lunge for her handbag. The attacker flipped himself over and swiped at her legs. She fell to the floor. After a brief struggle she found herself pinned to the ground with the knife at her throat.

The man lowered his head to within inches of her own. His face was skeletal and cragged; his eyes were wide and popped; his breath was fetid. He pressed the knife hard against her throat.

"Yer shooda jus' let me go," he whispered with menace. She felt his free hand groping at her belt. She felt sick and helpless.

The blade still tight to his victim's throat, he fumbled and tugged at her trousers, slowly inching them down. Stella lay still, waiting for a split-second chance to throw her attacker off. It didn't come. He moved his hand towards her thigh. Angry and resolute, Stella braced her body for an upward surge. If she died, she died; this wretched snake was going to take more than her life.

As she prepared for her thrust the toilet door burst open. Before she could grasp what was happening she was free, and the would-be rapist was lying on the floor beneath the hand basins. Above him was a bear of a man with 'United Bikers' emblazoned on the back of his leather jacket. He had wild black hair and a beard that could house a family of crows. He gave Stella a stern look and motioned for her to leave. She straightened herself up, grabbed her handbag, and did as he asked.

Back at the bar she tried to steady herself. Her hands were shaking and her eyes were fit to burst. She took a large gulp of her lager which, thankfully, was still there, and ordered another shot of tequila. She pulled out a cigarette and sparked it up with a tremulous flame.

"Are you alright luv?" slurred one of the barflies.

"I'm fine," she said flatly. "I just need a drink." The tequila arrived and she downed it swiftly.

"Good girl," said the barfly.

Stella ignored the comment.

The biker emerged from the toilets, muscled the barfly along, and stood next to Stella. He gave her an ambiguous look.

"Thank you," she said. "That could've been unpleasant."

The biker said nothing. He continued to stare.

"Would you like a drink?" she asked.

He nodded and pointed to the Guinness tap.

"I'm Stella by the way," she said, feeling uncomfortable with his silence.

"Oggi," growled the biker. Then he took her arm and said, "Now Stella. Come with me."

Stella stiffened slightly and looked up at him. His eyes were blank, unreadable, neither filled with menace nor kindness. What did he want?

Oggi sensed her trepidation. "Look, it's ok. I'm not going to hurt you. I know what you want. I know who you're looking for. We need to talk in the back room, it's quieter; not so many ears." His accent was surprisingly public school.

Even though he'd saved her in the toilet Stella was still wary of the giant biker. But she needed information. If he was telling the truth then it was a good lead. If not, well, best not to think about it.

The back room was sparse and dimly lit. In the middle there were a couple of NF louts playing pool on a table that had seen better days. Oggi gestured for them to leave; which they did obediently. He then led Stella to a rickety table in the far corner, and they sat down on the equally unstable chairs. Stella lit another cigarette and took a swig of her lager.

"Ok then Oggi, who am I looking for?" she said.

"Stratton," he said and looked at her hard. "You're looking for Stratton."

"How do you know?"

"For a start, you came in just after that poncey squealer who was poking his nose about. Two strangers in the space of five minutes is rare in here."

"Well why didn't you throw me out as well? How do you know I'm not a copper?"

Oggi smiled and took a gulp of the Guinness that he'd brought with him. He wiped off the milky moustache and continued. "I don't know but I recognize your face."

Stella was confused. "How do you recognize me, I've never been here before in my life. And I certainly don't recognize you. I'd definitely remember you."

"I've seen your photo: Stratton had a photo of you in his wallet," said Oggi.

Stella's eyebrows' rose. "Stratton had a picture of me in his wallet. I don't think so."

"Well, believe it or not, he did. I saw it once, just before he...." Oggi stopped mid-sentence.

"Just before he what?"

Oggi thought for a brief moment. "Just before he burnt it."

"Oh," said Stella, slightly hurt but not surprised. "Anyway, how do you know so much about Stratton? I didn't think that you guys associated with non-bikers."

"That's a bit of a sweeping statement isn't it? We wouldn't get very far in life not talking to anyone but bikers. I do understand where you're coming from though, we're not renowned for our great sociability. As for Stratton, well, let's just say he's a good friend and I owe him one."

"Ok, but where is he?" Stella pressed.

"To be honest, I don't know. Lenny the barman said that he saw Stratton leave via the back door at about half nine this morning. In a hurry he said. Had a rucksack with him. Told Lenny that he'd be back in a couple of weeks. Looked really stressed according to Lenny, which is strange because Stratton never stresses about anything. I've tried his mobile but it's going straight to answer phone." He paused. "I'm worried about him."

Stella took the information in. Oggi was right: Stratton never worried about anything. What had happened to make him leave in such a hurry? Could it be related to Henry's death?

She picked up her mobile and dialled Jennings who was still outside. She let him know that she was alright and asked him what time the press had broken the news of Henry's murder. Sure enough, as she had guessed, it had been around nine am. She told Jennings to go back to the car and wait for her and hung up.

"Is there any way of getting into his flat upstairs?" she asked Oggi.

"I think there's a spare key behind the bar, but I don't really like the thought of poking about in his flat. He's a friend. Whatever's up there is his business."

"Fair enough," said Stella. "But it seems like the logical option at the moment seeing as we can't get hold of him. Unless you have any better ideas of course."

Oggi shrugged and they went to get the spare keys from Lenny. At first he was loathe to hand them over, but a stern look from Oggi helped oil his conscience.

Stratton's flat was neat and uncluttered. It was a studio with polished pine floorboards and minimal furniture: a far cry from the half-assed drunken mess that Stella remembered from the days when they lived together. Searching the place was not going to take long.

"What are we looking for?" asked Oggi.

"Anything really. An address, a name, a phone number. Whatever you can find," said Stella.

Within fifteen minutes they had covered the whole flat. Drawers had been opened, furniture had been moved, and cushions and mattresses checked under. No clues.

Stella stood by the breakfast bar and thought hard. Was Stratton on a mission to find someone or something, or was he running away? Running scared from whoever got Henry. If it was the latter, where would he run to? Where would he be safe?

Oggi interrupted her thoughts. "What's all this about anyway Stella? Why are you so keen to find Stratton? You're obviously not here for a social call. From what I can make out, you two aren't exactly the best of friends any more."

"No we're not, and the last person in the world I want to see is Stratton. But I think he might be able to help me with something important. I can't tell you a whole lot more - it's classified information."

Oggi mumbled to himself, obviously dissatisfied with Stella's curt answer. However, she was no longer paying attention, her eyes had been drawn to a small painting on the kitchen wall. It was a watercolour depicting a thatched cottage, and it gave her an idea as to where Stratton might have gone.

Chapter 4

Scott Grady was an UFA, he joked that it stood for U Fucking Asshole. In reality it meant that he was an Unaffiliated Field Agent. He was a gun for hire available to any government department that wanted him: CIA, FBI, NSA; they had all used him at some point or other. Unaffiliated meant untraceable. Whenever there was a job to be done, and it was too dirty for their own hands, they would call Grady in. His ID and cell phone number were known only to a select few, namely directors and deputies; and you wouldn't find him on any database. To all intents and purposes Scott Grady didn't exist, just another faceless black guy making his way through a nondescript life.

His latest secondment differed from the norm. Two days previously he had received a call from a Mr Sharlo Miles, purporting to be from an organization called the National Institute of Paranormal Studies (NIPS). According to Mr Miles, NIPS was government funded and had close links with the security services. Grady had taken Mr Miles' number and said that he'd get back to him: it all sounded like a load of hokum. After ringing deputy director Bob Tobin at the CIA, Grady realized that Mr Sharlo Miles was on the level. He called back and they arranged to meet the next day.

The Screaming Chicken on route 66 was the designated rendezvous. It was a place that Grady often chose to meet people. In the middle of nowhere, it afforded a good view of the highway in both directions. The booths were private and the service friendly but not intrusive. It also served the best steak he'd ever tasted.

Sharlo Miles had been twenty minutes late. Grady hated tardiness but was used to it from the chiefs. Miles was Caucasian, late fifties and thin and bald. After ordering two steaks and two beers they had talked.

"I'm assuming that you've never heard of NIPS before Mr Grady," said Miles.

"You assume correctly Mr Miles."

"What do you think we do?" asked Miles.

"I guess you study ghosts and shit like that. Don't you?"

"Well that's a small part of it. We look at everything that is beyond normal scientific explanation. Things like telepathy, telekinesis, clairvoyance and the like. All the stuff that the scientists have no answer to."

Grady had seen some of these so called psychics exposed on TV. "It's just a load of tricks and nonsense isn't it?" he said.

Miles laughed. "Of course there are a lot of frauds about making money out of the weak and vulnerable. They tend to be the showmen, very clever, very resourceful, but ultimately grifters. There are, however, people in this world who appear to have certain, shall we say - supernatural gifts. You won't see them on TV or at the local theatre. Everyone I've met with real ESP shuns the limelight; they have too much respect for their abilities. They're scared that if they profit from their talents then they might lose them. A reverential bunch."

The beers arrived and Grady took a swig.

"Ok, so what do you want me to do? It's hardly international espionage is it?"

"Well you wouldn't think so would you? But back in 1943..."

Grady cut Miles off mid-sentence. "Whoa, hold on there Professor. Let's just cut to the chase here. I don't need any goddamn history lessons I just need to know what you want done. Usually when I'm called it's because somebody needs finding and / or bumping off. Which is it?"

"Somebody needs finding," said Miles. "Somebody and something."

"Ok," said Grady. "I'll find them."

Now, two days later, Grady was in London. He sat quietly in his rented green Focus and pondered his next move. The blond cop was no longer standing outside the pub, but the girl was still in there. He recognized her from a photo in the mark's file and guessed that she was there to find him. Grady hoped that the girl would lead him to the mark. He cursed himself for losing his man on the subway earlier on. Things were getting complicated; too many people, too many variables.

Ten minutes later the girl walked out of the pub and headed down the road. She stopped after a hundred yards and got into the blond-haired man's car, a blue Lexus. After a brief exchange of words they drove off. Grady sparked his engine and followed them.

Chapter 5

Jennings drove calmly through the staccato evening traffic. He was used to the city streets and the inevitable gridlocks. There was no point getting flustered, it was just the way it was. Stella sat quietly beside him, seemingly deep in thought. She intrigued him greatly and he wanted to know more about her, but the circumstances dictated professionalism.

"So, what makes you think that he's hiding out on Exmoor then?" he asked.

"Just a hunch really. But it's where he always used to go to clear his head. It's a little cottage in the middle of nowhere. It's an ideal place for someone who doesn't want to be found," said Stella.

"And you want us to go there now?"

"Yes I do. We can't waste time. We need to find out what's going on."

"But it'll be almost midnight by the time we get there," Jennings protested. "Surely it can wait until the morning. I can't imagine he'll be going anywhere soon."

"Maybe not," said Stella. "But we need to get on the trail of the killer ASAP."

Jennings decided not to argue any longer. He knew that she was right; the problem was that he was tired. He'd been up since four in the morning dealing with this Mulholland shit and he needed a break. His brain was all over the place and his eyelids were heavy and lethargic. Even the cool breeze from the open window wasn't helping. He reached into his jacket pocket and pulled out a brown plastic pill bottle.

"Can you open this and pass me a couple of tablets please?" he said, handing the bottle to Stella.

"What are they?"

"Just some stay awake pills. A kind of Pro Plus."

"Are they legal?" asked Stella.

"Well you can't get them on the high street if that's what you mean. They're standard issue for the intelligence community though. I believe the CIA developed them - some sort of Benzedrine based compound I think. Whatever they are, they do the job."

Stella passed Jennings two pink capsules and he swallowed them with a swig of mineral water. The effect was almost immediate.

Within a couple of minutes his eyes were once again wide and bright, and his mind was back in focus. He was also starting to feel the enhanced confidence that was a benign side-effect of the drug. His body tingled with enthusiasm and he was now looking forward with relish to the task ahead. It never failed to amaze him how two small tablets could make such a vast difference to his frame of mind.

It was nine o'clock when they finally broke free of London and hit the M4. A motorbike accident on the Chelsea Embankment had put them back by at least an hour. Stella had been attempting to have a power nap but the constant stop-start of the traffic had made it impossible.

Instead she had been thinking about Stratton and what she was going to do when she saw him again. It had been nearly five years since they'd parted and her last memory of him was not one she cared to dwell on: a broken man he had been; wallowing in a heady cocktail of alcohol and self-pity; crying and begging her not to leave. She had been physically sick as she walked out of that door. It had broken both of their hearts. At the time though, it had been the only option: his alcoholism and roller-coaster mood swings had torn her apart. Self-preservation had taken over before she too drowned in his whirlpool of depression.

As if echoing her thoughts, Jennings spoke. "What is it with you and this Stratton guy anyway? You seem to be worried about him, and yet I'm sensing reluctance."

"It's complicated," said Stella. "We have a lot of history."

"Fair enough," Jennings conceded. "But from what I can make out it's been about five years since you've seen him. It's a long time to be harbouring feelings for someone - he must be one hell of a guy."

Stella was silent and her eyes briefly glazed. "He was once," she said eventually.

"Sorry, I didn't mean to pry," said Jennings honestly.

Stella regained her composure and put her pragmatic head back on. "That's all right. Don't worry about it. This is a serious case and you need all the information you can get. He could be a suspect for all you know."

"Do you think so?" he asked.

"No, of course I don't. But having more information about him isn't going to hurt so I'll give you a brief rundown...Do you mind if I smoke?"

"Well, technically it's illegal given that this is a works vehicle. But I won't tell if you won't."

Stella lit a B&H. "Stratton was born in London on November 8th 1975 to middle-class parents. His father was a trader on the stock market and his mother, who was of Oriental origin, kept the house. He grew up in the Home Counties and at an early age it was noticed that he was exceptionally intelligent. He was sent to a special school for gifted children when he was six years old but he hated it and his parents took him out. After that experience he refused point blank to be educated anywhere except for the local school with his friends. And so that's how it was until he'd taken his 'A' levels in which he got four 'A' grades: pure maths, English, history and physics." Stella paused. "Do stop me if I'm going into too much detail."

Jennings laughed. "Not at all. It's like having a report read. I'm impressed."

Stella took a deep drag on her cigarette and carried on. "He went to St Peter's college, Oxford, where strangely, considering his scientific bent, he studied theology. He got a first and was encouraged to stay on for his doctorate but he was bored and left education. He stayed in Oxford where he drifted about doing bar work and generally enjoying himself. There were no money worries as he had a substantial trust fund that had been released on his 21st birthday. Drink, drugs and women were the order of the day and he enjoyed all three in equal measure. Then all that changed when he fell in love with a beautiful young police-woman…"

Jennings smiled. "Who was that then?"

Stella grinned and continued. "We lived in Oxford for a while but when I got into Special Branch we moved to Greenwich. By this time he'd spent most of his trust fund and was having to look for work. He drifted in and out of temporary jobs but couldn't really stick with anything; he was lost really. In the end he was just sitting around the flat all day drinking himself senseless. It got to the point where I didn't want to go home. His mood swings were becoming increasingly erratic and he spiralled out of control."

Jennings interrupted. "Did he ever hit you?"

"No; never. He's not like that; even when he was completely out of it I never felt in any physical danger. He was cruel with his tongue, not his fists. Although he hurt me so much emotionally that maybe taking a punch would have been less painful. Every day he chipped away a little bit of my heart. It was more than I could bear watching this brilliant, beautiful man self-destruct. I made up my mind that I had to get out to save myself. It was the hardest thing I've ever had to do. I walked out and I haven't looked back."

"So you haven't heard anything of him since then?" asked Jennings.

"Not really. He kept trying to contact me after I left but I changed my mobile number and that was it. I had to be single-minded even though I missed him terribly."

"All sounds very sad," said Jennings sympathetically.

"I suppose so," said Stella and lit another cigarette.

Jennings left Stella to her thoughts for a while, sensing that it was politic to do so. She had shown him a certain vulnerability in her words, belying their perfunctory delivery. This was a woman who, out of necessity, had methodically built a stone wall around her heart. Once violent emotions were now brushed aside with seemingly casual ease. And her previously inseparable heart and mind had drifted apart; co-existing in a practical state of detachment. But Jennings had caught a fleeting glimpse of the sadness that she bore deep inside, and guessed that she wasn't as impervious as she would have liked.

"Do you really think he's going to be able to tell us any more about that symbol and what's going on?" asked Jennings, breaking the silence.

"If anyone can then he can," said Stella. "It's too much of a coincidence that he did a runner this morning for a start. And that symbol was on the front of a tatty old book he had around the flat. I remember because he was always very secretive about it. It was handwritten in some ancient language, probably Sanskrit or something like that. He seemed to understand it though, or the majority of it. But I'm pretty sure that there was some of it that he didn't get. I could always tell when something was bugging him: and that book definitely bugged him. It was almost like an obsession at some point, he would just sit staring at it for ages with a puzzled look on his face. He was like that. He couldn't let anything go until he understood it completely. He always had to have an answer. A 'thirst for truth' is what he called it - I called it neuroses."

"How do you know that he has any answers now?"

"I don't, but he's going to know a hell of a lot more than we do."

Thanks to fast driving and a clear road they made rapid

progress. By 10.15pm they had reached Bristol. Jennings needed the little boys' room badly and so they made a pit stop at Gordano services. Stella got out of the car as well, to stretch her legs and catch some fresh air. Inside the service station it was relatively quiet. The steady flow of daytime custom had given way to the trickle of late evening. The fast-food outlets were getting ready to close, and the newly-arrived graveyard shift were on the wrong side of a long and torpid night.

Jennings strode briskly to the toilet and whizzed to the urinals, almost bumping into the gawky teenager who was busy mopping the tiled floor. The youth muttered something but Jennings was on a mission and couldn't be bothered to take the kid to task. Two minutes later he was at a hand basin and looking at a pale, drawn, version of himself. Even his miracle pills couldn't disguise the physical signs of exhaustion. He washed his hands and splashed his face with cold water and took another tablet. After drying himself with a paper towel he walked out.

Whether it was tiredness or preoccupation he didn't know. But by the time he saw the man as he rounded back into the corridor it was too late; they collided. The man was black and smartly dressed in a grey designer suit. And he was extremely apologetic.

"Jesus. I'm sorry man; I wasn't looking where I was going. What a dope," the man said. His accent was American. Jennings guessed New York.

Jennings pulled himself together. "It's no problem, it was probably my fault anyway."

"No man, it was definitely me. My mind's elsewhere," he insisted.

"Well whatever. No harm done is there," said Jennings and walked off.

The man smiled to himself and went into the toilets.

Jennings got back to the car and found Stella stubbing out yet another cigarette. It was a habit that he found unattractive in other women, but with her he could forgive it. They got back into the car and drove off; oblivious to the tiny transmitter in Jennings' pocket that was now monitoring them.

Chapter 6

The beast sat upright and alert, his sleek black coat glistening in the pale radiance of the moon. Whiskers twitching, he sniffed the cold night air hungrily, hoping for the scent of prey. But his friend the wind was absent tonight, and the sweet smell of the moor was all that greeted his nostrils. It was two days since he had eaten and the thought of that last juicy meal was now in his mind; he might have to chance another visit to the ambrosial utopia that lay just a mile away from where he now stood. It was a big risk: the last time he had nearly been caught by the man with the gun. But the potential reward was also great: a whole sheep could keep him fed for at least a week.

He decided very quickly that he had no option. Wildlife on the moor was scarce at this time of year and he needed to eat. He started off at a smart trot, his huge paws bouncing lightly off the brisk dewy turf. He came to the top of a rise and stopped to survey his surroundings. The farm was directly in front of him, only half a mile away, but his gaze was drawn to his left side. In the distance he could see a light. A light he had not seen for many moons. The sheep could wait, he had to investigate.

Onward he bounded, his long loping stride devouring the ground. All thoughts of hunger were banished from his mind. He focused on the light and hoped that it meant what he thought. Had his friend really returned? He had waited so long for him to come back that he dared not believe it was true. A lonely existence it was on the moors, constantly on the move, hiding from the men who knew he was there but could never catch him. Companionship was a luxury not afforded to the life of the rogue predator, and although it was seldom that he craved it, it was nevertheless a welcome gift. The nearer he got to the little cottage the surer he was that his friend was there: his sixth sense told him so. There was a psychic bond between the two of them that had existed since they had first come into contact with each other. That had been in the summer three years previously and he remembered it well. He remembered sitting in the hedgerow watching the man curiously as he performed some sort of ritual in the back garden of the cottage, moving and twisting his body into strange positions. His aura had glowed pure white and the inner peace that he exuded was hypnotic and infectious. The beast had stayed out of sight, but he was sure that the man was aware of his presence.

The beast had remained in the hedgerow even after the man had gone back inside; he had felt compelled to. He had watched the cottage way into the evening, feeling that he had to be there but not knowing why. His patience had been rewarded, when, just after sundown, the man had reappeared in the back garden. In his hands was a huge slab of meat that he had proceeded to set down but ten feet from where the beast lay hidden. Hands together, he had bowed his head gently towards the beast and had gone back inside the cottage. The beast had come out and sniffed the meat cautiously: it was cattle. And, satisfied that it was good, he had eaten his fill.

This had continued for the next few days: beast watching man and man feeding beast. Eventually on the fourth day the beast decided it was time to show himself. Creeping slowly out of hiding he entered the garden and approached the man from behind. The man was in the middle of his daily routine, and if he was aware of the beast he didn't show it. The beast moved ever closer, finally stopping about twenty feet to the man's left, just in his line of sight. Still the man carried on, engrossed in his own world.

It was not until he had finished his routine that the man turned his head toward the beast. He eyed the beast with a smile, his bright green eyes beaming with wonder. The beast held his gaze and let out a small roar. By now a normal man would have either run or gone for a shotgun. But not this man; this man was calm and unafraid, as if he were embracing the beast's enormous muscular power, and drawing it into himself.

The man moved slowly toward the beast, his arms hanging loosely and unthreatening by his side. The beast sat still, undaunted by the advancing man. Their eyes were still locked and both knew that there was nothing to fear from this encounter. When he was close enough, the man held out his right hand and laid it gently on the beast's forehead, and a calmness that he'd never known before enveloped the beast's innate visceral psyche. The power emanating from the man's hand was incredible and the beast's mind leapt wildly, as if transcending both space and time. Then the man let go his hand and the beast was back in the garden. And ever since they had been connected by a deep-rooted understanding and telepathy that endured beyond the physical world.

These thoughts occupied the beast's head as the cottage loomed before him. As usual he took the back way, and eased himself through the gap in the hedge that was just wide enough to accommodate his frame. The illuminated window was downstairs on the right, just as he expected. And he trotted up to it keenly, placing his front paws on the sill and staring into the living room. Sure enough, his friend was there, lounging in the easy chair reading a book. He signalled his presence with a friendly roar. Inside the man smiled to himself, and put down his book, and went to let the beast in.

"Hello Titan," said the man, greeting the black panther warmly as he opened the back door.

Titan let out a loud affectionate purr and brushed against the man's side. Then he got on his hind legs and nuzzled him. The man fell backwards under the weight of the unwittingly forceful feline, but he wasn't scared, not in the slightest. He just lay there laughing as the panther's head nestled below his chin.

"Okay Titan, that's enough," he said after a brief and playful wrestle.

And the panther let him up immediately.

On the kitchen sideboard was a large uncooked leg of mutton. The man had purchased it that afternoon, knowing that the beloved cat would be stopping by. He presented it to Titan who accepted gratefully, and set about demolishing the joint messily on the terracotta tiled floor.

The man watched thoughtfully as Titan's power-packed jaws ripped the meat apart, his pointed teeth scything through flesh and stringy sinew alike. It was an awesome spectacle to behold, and he knew he was fortunate to have this animal's trust. There couldn't be many people in the world who would be allowed this close to a killing machine like Titan, he thought. He closed his eyes and breathed in hungrily, bathing himself in the dangerous glow of primitive crimson energy that filled the room, letting it wash over him like a warm surf, and empowering the beast within.

He felt like he'd been away from the cottage for too long. He missed the fresh country air, and he missed exploring the moors and woods with Titan at his side. It was down here, far from the selfish commotion of urban life that he was most at peace. Inner tranquillity came easily in the back of beyond: there were no smog-filled roads packed with cars and buses and vans; and neither were there grey and dirty sidewalks, occupied by nameless, faceless, lemmings with flailing elbows and an acquired contempt for humanity. The simple charm of rural life made exercising self-discipline seem effortless. The only problem was the solitude: solitude was both his friend and his enemy. As much as he enjoyed the idyllic isolation and the verdant views; he missed the company of people just as much. Whether they were good people or bad people, tall people or short people, fat people or thin people; or whether they were black or white or multi-coloured, he would thrive off them. It was the energy that he loved, and his entire being drew upon it with voracity.

For the moment though, he had had enough of people and

was quite content to spend the next few weeks in hiding. Would it just be a few weeks though? He wasn't sure how long it would be, and he wasn't even sure who or what he was hiding from. Maybe he was being paranoid, and Mulholland's death had nothing to do with their shared family histories. Only instinct was persuading him of the connection: there were no cold hard facts to support it. He only knew what the news report had said: that Mulholland was dead, possibly murdered, and that the police were investigating. He needed more details and the media were providing very little. For now he would have to sit tight just in case there was a link.

The man returned to the living room, and Titan, having eaten his fill of mutton, followed. The open fire was starting to fade so the man added a couple of medium-sized logs and stoked it. The embers spat and crackled back to life. He sat down in his favourite black leather chair and watched the flames dance lightly above the newly-lit wood. Titan lay down near the fire and readied himself for a post-dinner catnap.

The man reached for his book on the side table, but instead his hand hit upon the slim, rectangular, form of his mobile phone. He picked it up and realized that it was out of power. He retrieved the charger from his rucksack and plugged the phone in. After half a minute the message alert sounded its single beep, and he dialled his voicemail. There were two new messages, both from Oggi. The first was just a general one asking him where he was and if he was ok. The second one was more interesting and very surprising, he listened to it a couple of times to make sure he'd heard correctly.

Stella Jones was the last person he expected to be looking for him, albeit in an official capacity. He wondered what she could possibly want. Oggi's message had been brief and lacking in detail: he'd simply said that Stella and another copper had been trying to find him and that it seemed important, there was no mention of why. Perhaps she had been assigned to investigate

Mulholland's murder, she was after all in Special Branch, or had been when they parted. But that didn't explain why she was trying to find him. There was no way she could know about the connection between him and Henry, only a handful of people did; and he was pretty sure that she wasn't one of them. Still, whatever was happening, his stomach could feel the steady offensive of big trouble coming his way, and he would have to deal with it.

A good sleep was what he needed. He would phone Oggi in the morning and attempt to track Stella down; there was nothing more to do tonight. He left Titan snoozing by the fire and made for the bedroom.

Halfway up the stairs he heard a growl from the living room. He went back down and saw that the previously dormant panther was now upright, his ears keen and alert. Titan trotted to the small drawing room at the front of the cottage and the man followed. He kept the lights off and looked out of the window. At first he could neither see nor hear anything, and thought that the cat was imagining things. But after a few moments he espied it: about half a mile away he could just make out a set of headlights, advancing slowly down the weather-beaten track that led to the cottage. It was gone midnight now - so it wasn't the local cub scouts on Bob-a-Job week.

He let Titan out of the back door and turned off all the lights, and keeping out of sight he sat in the front room and awaited his untimely guests.

Chapter 7

The rock-strewn dirt track was beginning to narrow considerably, and Jennings was finding it increasingly difficult to navigate the harsh terrain. He needed a 4x4; the Lexus for all its comforts was not built for the countryside. He was not in the best of moods anyway. During the last hour the inbuilt SatNav had guided them to five dead-ends, and number six looked like it was on its way. Stella had been no help either. It was her misdirection that had got them lost in the first place. Tempers had flared and words had been exchanged. And so the car was now engulfed in a stony silence, broken only by the sound of the underside hitting pointed protrusions in the earth.

The headlights fell upon a small hand-painted sign at the side of the way. Jennings stopped and read it. It stated: 'Beware of the Beast.'

"Beware of the Beast," he said aloud. "What the hell does that mean?"

"It means that we're on the right road," said Stella. "The cottage is about 300 yards on the left."

The cottage was surrounded by a tall thick hedge. The only space for parking was a grass verge on the opposite side of the track. Jennings stopped the car and killed the engine. He leant over to the glove compartment and produced a torch.

"Come on then," he said. "Let's take a look."

They approached the cottage through the tall archway cut into the hedge. As they walked through, disappointment hit them: there were no lights on. Jennings shined the torch over the vacant windows.

"Looks deserted to me," said Jennings with just a hint of annoyance in his tone.

"Maybe he's gone to bed," said Stella optimistically. She walked up to the front door and knocked loudly, and when there was no answer she repeated the motion. Two minutes later there was still no sign of life.

"Heavy sleeper is he?" said Jennings.

Stella was determined not to give up. "Look, I'm sure this is where he would come. Let's go round the back. I know where he keeps a spare key to the back door."

Jennings begrudgingly agreed. There was nobody at home; he was certain of that. But he decided to humour her for a bit longer. Secretly he wanted to get out of there as quickly as he could, and not just because he thought that Stella was wasting their time. The place was giving him the creeps. Perhaps he'd seen one too many bad horror movies, but there was definitely a menacing atmosphere out there on the moor. Ever since childhood he had disliked the dark, although he couldn't remember specifically why, and in the middle of nowhere he liked it even less. Vision was his friend and blindness his enemy, that was how it had always been. And now, even with his flashlight, he felt blind. He was sure that he could hear rustlings and scratchings emanating from the ominous thicket that surrounded the cottage. But every time he shone the torch at the suspect point, he saw nothing.

Stella noticed Jennings' edginess. "Bit jumpy aren't we?"

"No, I'm fine," he said manfully. "I just thought I heard something in the bushes, that's all."

"It's probably the Beast of Exmoor," she said. She raised her arms menacingly above her head, and laughed a diabolical laugh.

"You're very funny. Ever thought about stand-up?" he said. "But seriously, what is the Beast of Exmoor?"

"Just what you would call an urban legend, or in this case a rural legend. It's supposed to be a large black cat that stalks the moor killing and eating livestock. It's generic. Bodmin and Dartmoor have their own beasts as well. I'm surprised you've never heard about it. Every few years they drag it up on the telly: some West Country weirdo claiming to have seen the alleged Beast, or, better still, captured footage of it on some grainy amateur video. It's usually in the light bits at the end of the news, along with cats on diets and dogs that play football."

"Oh right," said Jennings, feeling a little stupid. "So what's the sign on the road all about?"

"Oh, that's been there for years. Stratton's grandfather put it there. It appealed to his sense of humour."

The gap between the side of the cottage and the hedge was filled with tall unkempt grass and weeds and brambles, and Jennings was slow in negotiating their way through the muddled foliage. Stella had wanted to take the lead but he wouldn't part with the torch. She thought it was a show of his male pride, and didn't realize that it was purely nyctophobia. And so, after more stumbling and cursing than was necessary, they made it to the relatively well-kept back garden.

At that moment Jennings heard a distinct rustle in the bushes, and he pointed the torch to where the sound had come from. He was greeted by a pair of brimstone-yellow eyes that sat upon a large dark figure; a catlike figure. Jennings froze and almost stopped breathing. The figure turned and sloped off out of sight.

"Did you see that?" he said heavily.

"See what?" said Stella.

"That animal in the bushes over there," he said, pointing his finger wildly.

Stella looked over. "I can't see anything," she said.

"Well it's gone now hasn't it, but it was there a second ago. It was a huge cat with big yellow eyes."

Stella sniggered. "Oh really. Don't you think you're imagination's running a bit too wild. There are no big cats out here, it's just a myth."

"Well I saw something. I know that."

"It was probably just a fox," she said.

Stella asked for the torch, and Jennings reluctantly handed it over. She walked up to the stone birdbath that stood central in the garden, and rummaged around in the gravel at its base.

Searching by torchlight was tricky but she eventually found what she was looking for: a medium-sized smooth grey pebble with sporadic white markings. She opened up the fake plastic pebble and drew out the key that was hidden inside.

"Lucky he still keeps it in the same place," said Jennings.

"I suppose so," said Stella. "But there's no reason for him to move it. Crime isn't as rife out here in the sticks."

She tried the key in the back door. The lock was old and stiff and she struggled to get it to turn, but after some frantic wiggling it finally clicked. She opened the door carefully and reached for the light switch to her left. The hallway was thirty feet long and stretched from the back door right up to the front entrance. The kitchen and staircase were on the left-hand side as she looked, and the living room and drawing room were on the right.

She entered the kitchen and turned on the fluorescent strip light. There were two pans and a plate drying at the side of the sink: someone had used the kitchen that evening. On the floor, on top of some blood-stained newspaper, was the leg bone of a sheep. It had been completely stripped of its flesh, and the embedded grooves indicated that it had been gnawed viciously by incredibly strong jaws. A large dog perhaps, she thought.

"Well someone's been here," she said.

"You're right," said Jennings. "But where are they now?"

They walked across to the living room. The fire was still smoking and the embers glowed red. There was a large green rucksack leant against a black leather chair, and a book open spine side up on the adjacent table. Alongside the book was a half drunk cup of herbal tea, and next to that was a mobile phone on charge.

Stella picked up the phone and checked for text messages: there was only one and it was from the voicemail centre. She rang the voicemail and was greeted by the familiar educated tones of Oggi.

"This is definitely Stratton's phone," she said.

"If that's the case, then where the hell is he?"

"I don't know but he can't be far away. Maybe he's gone for a walk. He used to do that a lot at night."

They searched the rest of the house but found nothing, and decided that the only thing to do was wait. Stella went back to the kitchen. She returned three minutes later with two steaming cups of strong black coffee, both sugarless. Jennings grabbed his eagerly; itching for a hit of caffeine. Stella got the fire started again and threw on a couple of fresh logs, and they sat quietly for a while and sipped their drinks.

"Why don't you check out his rucksack?" said Jennings. "There might be something of interest in there."

"If he doesn't turn up in the next hour then I will do. Until then we have to assume that he's coming back," she said. "And anyway I don't really want to be snooping about in his personal belongings, it doesn't seem right."

"And I suppose breaking and entering is?" said a cheerful voice that wasn't Jennings'.

Stella's stomach began to turn: she knew that voice; it was one she couldn't forget. She had been mentally preparing herself for this encounter all day, and thought that she would be okay. Yet now the moment had arrived, she was far from okay. Her brain had suddenly turned to scrambled egg, and her limbs were beginning to feel uncomfortably numb and independent. The past: their past, flashed through her mind in an instantaneous blur: the good times and the bad times, the arguments and the shared laughter; it all span round in an irrational kaleidoscope of liquid thought.

'Pull yourself together,' said an inner voice. 'Pull yourself together…. Now!' It repeated. The internal struggle came to a swift head, and then, just as quickly, it abated.

She steeled herself and turned her head towards where he stood, in the doorway. He looked just the same as he had done when they'd first met. His scissor-short jet black hair was still loose and unruly, and his defined, slightly Oriental features, seemed to be defying the laws of both time and gravity. His skin, once pale and wan through drinking and smoking, had flourished, and it now glowed with a healthy blush. And those eyes, she thought, as she stared into them for the first time in years. Those bright green smiling eyes that danced and dazzled with mischievous delight. They were as boyishly infectious as ever, and yet they seemed to have grown older and deeper and wiser at the same time. "Hello Stratton," she said neutrally.

He looked into her eyes, and she saw a fleeting spasm of pain cross his face. Then it was gone. "Hello Stella," he said, "how are you?"

"I'm good thanks, a little bit tired though."

"Well you would be, it's one o'clock in the morning. A bit late to be snooping around people's houses. And who's this?" He gestured toward Jennings.

"This is Jennings," she said. "He's a detective with Special Branch."

"Hello," said Jennings, and nodded courteously.

Stratton reciprocated and said, "Well that's the pleasantries out of the way then. Now what can I do for you? I'm assuming this isn't a social call."

Stella thought for a minute. In normal circumstances she would use a 'softly, softly' approach to gain trust, and also to stop the subject from finding out more than they needed to know. But this wasn't an ordinary situation, and Stratton was no ordinary person. If she tried any psychological manipulation with him, he would see through it straight away, and most likely clam up. She knew from past experience that the only way to deal with him was with complete openness and candour. He was an honest man and he expected complete honesty in return.

"Well actually Stratton, we really need to pick your brains. Jennings is working on a case, and there's only one piece of evidence. I think it falls into your line of expertise."

"Oh yes, and what's the evidence? A bottle of Jack Daniels?" he quipped.

"No," said Stella, ignoring the comment. "It's this." She produced a piece of paper with a copy of the symbol on it.

Stratton took the piece of paper and gave the symbol a perfunctory glance. He appeared unimpressed. "It's just a Reiki symbol. 'Cho Ku Rei' it is in Japanese. Roughly translated it means 'put all the power in the universe here'. It's fairly common, any Reiki website or practitioner could have given you that information. Why did you need me?"

Stella felt slightly foolish, but persisted. "I just remember seeing it on the front of that little brown book you used to have. You know the one I mean don't you?"

Stratton nodded.

"Anyway," she continued, "I just thought that you would be more informative than any other expert or website."

"Okay Stella. Cards on the table, you tell me more about the case and I'll help you as much as I can. I need context so that I can hit upon the points that are relevant to you."

"No problem, we'll tell you everything," she said.

"You can't do that," Jennings protested. "It's classified information. And you don't have the authority to divulge it. Remember you're a civilian."

Stratton looked confused. "A civilian?" he echoed.

"Yes Stratton, a civilian. I'm not with Special Branch any more, I'm in private security. It just happens that our paths have crossed on this particular occasion. If you let me explain you'll understand. And you," she turned to Jennings. "Why don't you just let me tell him? Trust me, he won't say anything, and I'm sure it'll help us out."

Jennings begrudgingly relented. He was none too keen on telling Stratton more than he needed to know. He was also beginning to get slightly peeved at the respect that Stella was giving to her ex. After all, he thought: the guy's just a glorified drunk.

After Stratton had made them all another drink (coffee for Stella and Jennings, fennel tea for himself), he sat down in his chair and listened intently as Stella went over all that had happened.

His expression remained impassive throughout. Both Stella and Jennings watched professionally for signs of agitation: a flicker of the eye; a twitch of the lip; a raised eyebrow, but there was nothing. If he knew anything he certainly wasn't letting on.

"Mmm, interesting," said Stratton after Stella had finished. He took a casual sip of his tea. "And you say that there's no sign of drugging or force used on any of the guards or dogs?"

"That's right," said Stella, "the lab confirmed it this afternoon. What do you think?"

"I think that there has to be an explanation, but..." he paused briefly, thinking how best to put his point across. "But I think you may have to start considering unconventional means in this case."

"What do you mean by unconventional?" asked Jennings.

"Exactly what I say: unconventional," he said emphasizing the last word.

Jennings grunted: he was becoming increasingly irritated by their laconic host. Stratton seemed to have a total lack of respect for him or his job. He was an officer of the law for Christ's sake! Most people, even innocent ones, got slightly nervous when speaking to a detective. But not Stratton, oh no, he just sat there like he was talking to some fluff-haired, snot-nosed, primary school kid. Who the hell did he think he was?

At that moment Jennings realized that he was getting worked up beyond reason. It wasn't Stratton's demeanour that was annoying him, it was something else: something he didn't care to admit to. He calmed himself down and put his cop head back on.

"Okay," said Jennings. "Why don't you start by telling us a bit more about this Reiki shit?"

"Of course," said Stratton, and began. "Reiki is an ancient healing system in which the practitioner lays his hands on, or just above, the recipient. The modern version was started in Japan in the late nineteenth century by Dr Mikao Usui, a Tendai Buddhist priest. It is said that he wanted to learn how Christ had healed the sick. With this in mind he went to Mount Kurama (horse saddle mountain) and meditated there for 21 days, with only water and a tiny amount of rice for sustenance. At the end of his meditation he was close to death, and that is when a light hit him and he had a vision of mystical symbols. These symbols attuned him to the energy of the universe and form the basis of modern Reiki. Reiki Masters now use these symbols to attune their students. The symbols are drawn in the air by the master and enter the student through the crown chakra at the top of the head. The student is then able to draw on the energy of the universe to heal himself and others: Reiki roughly translated means 'universal life force energy'," he paused briefly. "And that's it really. I could go into more detail but it would only bore you," he added, seeing the look on Jennings' face.

"Sounds like you've been watching too much Star Wars to me," said Jennings.

Stratton laughed. "Yes I suppose it does sound a bit far fetched, but you did ask. And I've given you the salient facts, as I see them."

"I appreciate that," said Jennings, "the problem is that I don't see how it helps us. No-one is going to commit a murder over a load of mumbo jumbo: not in Britain in this day and age. Henry Mulholland was a businessman, not some voodoo priest."

"No, he probably wasn't some 'voodoo priest' as you put it. But his killer must have been looking for something," Stratton countered. "Whether Mulholland had this thing or not, the intruder certainly thought he did. And yes, people who believe in that sort of thing will commit murder if the prize is big enough. History is littered with slayings over religious and spiritual artefacts. The Greeks, the Egyptians, the Romans, the Mayans: every civilization since time began up to the present day has had mortal arguments over objects of supposedly divine provenance."

Stella, who had been sitting quietly and letting the boys be boys, decided that a fresh input was needed: Jennings clearly had a closed mind on anything non-secular, and it was holding the discussion back. "Ok," she said, "let's assume that he was after some spiritual artefact. What could it be? And why would Henry have it?"

Stratton thought for a moment. He was pretty sure that he knew what the killer was after. In fact he was beginning to suspect the identity of the killer.

There was only one way that Addington Hall could possibly have been penetrated in the manner described, and as far as he knew, there was only one person in the world who could have done it. He didn't know the man but he had heard rumour of him on his travels in Tibet. In one of the temples that he visited, the monks had told him about a Japanese man with apparently supernatural abilities. This man, an expert in the martial arts, could stop an opponent in his tracks without even touching him, they said. Stratton hadn't believed a word of it at the time, but the longer he had spent in that strange and deeply mystical land, the more he came to believe that it might, however ludicrous it seemed, just be possible.

There were ancient practices and rituals that still continued in the Orient: basic ideals that had gradually disappeared from the rest of the world, as mankind surged ever onwards in its pursuit of scientific and technological advances. As the manipulation of the visible world had progressed rapidly, so the ability to harness the power of the unseen had been all but forgotten.

Stratton had learnt a great many things out in the East, things that had changed him irreversibly. He no longer saw the world in the same light as Stella and Jennings did, and he knew that he would have to be careful in his approach with them: if he told them the truth as he saw it they would probably cart him off to a nuthouse. Guards and dogs disabled by what they would call magic, they wouldn't go for it. As for the killer's intended plunder, he would just have to come clean with them; he needed their help just as much as they needed his.

"Well," said Jennings impatiently. "What do you think they were after?"

Stratton made for the door. "I'll be back in a minute," he said. "I've got to get something from upstairs. Something that might explain what this is all about."

"This is getting weird," said Jennings when Stratton had gone.

"I guess so," said Stella. She was non-committal.

"All that stuff about 'life force energy', the bloke thinks he's fucking Yoda or Merlin. This is the twenty first century; we're not living in the days of King Arthur."

"I know we're not. But at the moment he's your best lead, and from the look of it he seems to have an idea about what the killer was looking for. All you've got to concentrate on is finding out who did this; forget about the rest of it, take it all with a pinch of salt if you like. Just keep yourself focused on the end result, because that's all that matters."

Jennings sat back like a scolded child. She was right of course: all that mattered was catching the killer. He could ignore all the fairy stories and go with the cold, hard, feet on the ground, facts. This is what he told himself, and his brain repeated it over.

Deep down inside him though, there was another voice, a voice he was trying desperately to suppress, the voice of his instinct. His protestations and scorning of Stratton's ideas were based on one thing, and one thing only: fear.

Ever since he had turned up at Addington Hall that morning he'd had an uncomfortable feeling in his stomach: there was something just not right. This sensation had grown throughout the day, and now, isolated on the desolate moors it was stronger than ever. And then there was Stratton; calm and unflappable Stratton.

Was this guy for real? Did nothing faze him? He had an apparently impenetrable air of serenity that lit the room; he was a contented man; a man at one with himself; and, most unnervingly, a man who Jennings could quite believe had access to a much higher power.

Stratton reappeared two minutes later. In his right hand he was clutching a red, A5-size, bound notebook that had seen better days. He sat down and opened up the ragged tome.

"What's that?" asked Jennings.

"This," said Stratton holding up the book, "this is a transcript of a tape recording that my grandfather made ten years ago, a few months before his death. It's basically his life story. Most of it is just ramblings about his childhood etc. But there is an interesting bit about his time in the army during the Second World War."

Jennings let out an involuntary groan, and then quickly apologized after realizing his faux pas.

"Don't worry, it's relatively short and painless, and it'll be very informative..." He stopped and looked over at Stella. "That is if you're awake."

Jennings gave Stella a nudge. Her head was down and she was starting to snore. "Wake up sleepy head," he said.

Her head jerked back up and her eyes opened. "Sorry, it's been a long day."

Jennings got out his bottle of pills. "Have a couple of these."

He handed her two tablets and she swallowed them with some cold coffee.

Stratton thumbed through the notebook until he arrived at the relevant section, and slowly and clearly he began to read.

Chapter 8

Transcript of Stratton's grandfather's tape recording:

On the 20th February 1942 I was in Rangoon, Burma, a lieutenant serving with the Duke of Wellington's regiment, or the 'Dukes' as we were known. The Japanese were attacking fiercely and a three-day battle ensued. It was one of the most frightening times of my life. The Japs were all over us. They had attacked swiftly and without warning, and we were totally unprepared.

By the 23rd it seemed like the whole of Rangoon was aflame, it was total and utter carnage. The Japs were dropping bombs all over the city, and the smoke ridden streets were filled with civilians and soldiers alike; all trying to stay alive, and all trying to escape the mayhem. Bloodied bodies lay strewn on the ground unheeded by the evacuating hordes; the acrid atmosphere was almost unbearably noisome and sticky with death; and mothers stood wailing for lost children, unable to make themselves heard above the reverberating sound of gunfire. We were beaten and the only thing to do was retreat.

By the evening the Japanese had taken the entire city. Myself and my dwindling unit of men were positioned at the end of one of the last remaining bridges over the Sittang. We were armed with two machine guns, and we tried to hold back the enemy just long enough for the last stragglers to escape the bloodshed. Before we knew it we were down to two men: myself and a private named Woodcock. There was no point trying to hold out any longer and so we had to find a means of escape. There seemed to be only one way out and that was into the river. I stayed by the gun and fired the last of our ammo, and Woodcock went off to find something, anything, to build a makeshift raft with. He came back five minutes later with a couple of empty petrol cans and some bamboo. He quickly put together a couple of crude 'lifejackets' and we strapped one each to our backs. We jumped into the Sittang and swam for the opposite bank which, being high tide, was now a mile and a half away.

I was a strong swimmer in those days but even I was glad of the assistance of the buoyant petrol can keeping me afloat. The intermittent swirling undercurrent of the river was strong, and there were times that I thought I'd be dragged under. On top of that, and maybe even worse, was the constant barrage of gunfire from the bridge. Bullets whistled and splashed all around us, some so close they almost grazed your ears. I stayed behind Woodcock as he was a weak swimmer and needed the assurance. Unfortunately, just as we were almost out of range, he copped a bullet straight in the back of his nape. His head went limp and around his neck the river turned crimson. I ducked my head under the surface and began to paddle furiously with my arms, and kick wildly with my legs, propelling myself onward to safety. Only when I could no longer hear the splatter of bullets did I dare raise my head again.

Dressed in full combat gear and boots on, it took me almost an hour and a half to reach the far bank. When I got there night had fallen and I unstrapped my floating aid and lay down in the mud. I looked up to the stars in the clear sky and thanked the maker for delivering me from death. Out of the eleven men in my unit I was the only survivor.

I slept in the undergrowth away from the river that night, along with hundreds of others who'd had to swim for it as well. In the morning we all gathered together as best we could and attempted to assemble in our own companies. At first it was chaotic, but gradually everyone sorted themselves out, and we headed northwards in convoy towards Mandalay.

There's not much to tell about that journey except that it was extremely long and arduous. We were almost constantly on the go from dawn to dusk. The tracks we took were dusty and bare and painfully uneven. And when we were off the tracks we were slogging wearily through paddy fields.

The powers that be had somehow managed to get some rations to us, but these were minimal and unappetizing, and mainly consisted of rice. All in all it was a pretty miserable time. Even the usual expletive-ridden banter, which had once kept our spirits up, had disappeared.

We reached Mandalay in mid-April, and we rested there for a couple of days. It was a brief but welcome respite. The soles of my feet were covered in blisters and I was in absolute agony. We ate comparatively well, and for the first time in two months we slept well. Unfortunately the enemy was still advancing north-wards and so we had to keep moving: next stop Kalewa, roughly 200 miles northwest.

We continued in convoy with my company, or what was left of it, towards the rear. My feet were still hurting but had been bandaged in Mandalay, and the sting was becoming less. We steered a path along a tributary of the River Chindwin, which was more or less a direct route to Kalewa. The jungle was becoming increasingly thick on either side. After a week or two, lack of nutrition was beginning to tell. Due to an absence of vitamin C in their diets a lot of the men were starting to break out in jungle sores. These were pink patches that turned a festering pus-ridden red and would not heal.

We were still 80 miles south of Kalewa when it happened. My company had begun to lag behind the main convoy of soldiers and civilians, mainly due to ill health. It was near dusk and we were subjected to a surprise attack by a small unit of Japanese soldiers. There were only twenty of us left, and probably only about ten who were capable of fighting. They ambushed us from both sides of the jungle track, and there was little or no time to react. Before I knew it I had been grabbed from behind and was in a vice-like headlock. My assailant was trying to snap my neck, but even though I was not at full strength I managed to hold firm. My survival instincts kicked in and I flung myself backwards with as much force as I could muster. We fell off the track and tumbled down towards the river.

We crashed into the water and a ferocious fight began. We wrestled and traded blows for what seemed like ages. Eventually I began to tire, and fearing that he would kill me there and then, I reached for the knife that I kept at my right ankle. I drew the blade and thrust at my opponent, but he was too quick and clamped my hand with his and disarmed me. He took the knife and raised it above his head, ready to stab down into my chest. As far as I knew, that was it, I was about to die. I just stood there paralysed with fear. I was so scared that I didn't even hear the shot. The first I knew was when a red hole appeared in the Jap's forehead; his eyes went blank and, as if in slow motion he slumped into the river. I was still in shock and it took a while for the realization to hit me: I was alive; saved by some unknown gunman.

I heard shouting from the riverbank; it seemed distant although it could have only been twenty yards away. I looked round and saw a British soldier holding a rifle. He raised a hand up in greeting, and I reciprocated with relief. I waded slowly to where he stood. "Thank you," I said.

"Don't mention it," said the soldier. He was a lieutenant like me.

I introduced myself. He did likewise. "Charles Mulholland, King's Own Yorkshire Light Infantry," he said. And he shook my hand.

We went back up to the track. There were ten of his men stood where the fight had started. On the ground lay the rest of my company and the Japanese unit. All still. All dead. I was lucky to be alive and I knew it. There was no time to dwell on it though: there were still more Japanese units nearby, we had to move on as fast as we could.

Progress was slow and hard, and it took us another eight days to reach Kalewa. During that march I got to know Charles Mulholland quite well. We walked together, bringing up the rear of his unit. It turned out that we were the same age, twenty five, and had both grown up in the town of Whitby in Yorkshire. We obviously hadn't met before but we did share a few mutual acquaintances, and chatting together came easily. We reminisced about our home town and the characters that resided there, and we talked about the surrounding countryside and the Spartan beauty of Whitby bay. Our fond memories made us quite homesick, and yet at the same time they lifted our spirits and filled us with hope.

We stopped in Kalewa for a whole week, and we took on more rations and more ammunition for the next leg of our journey, which would take us through the Kabbaw Valley to Tamu, and eventually to Imphal in India. We made the most of our seven days rest; I myself spent the majority of it catching up on some much needed sleep; others chatted and laughed and played cards; everyone occupying themselves as best they could, and trying to keep our minds off the next and deadliest stage of our journey.

The Kabbaw valley was a vast stretch of jungle between Kalewa and Tamu. The River Chindwin ran through the basin, fast and treacherous. It was nicknamed 'Death Valley' and was renowned as probably the unhealthiest place in Asia. On the outset it looked fairly innocuous, but the hidden threat of disease was ominous and ever present. Typhus, blackwater fever, malaria and cholera, they all lurked, menacing and unseen, waiting to strike down the weak and malnourished at every turn.

The first two days were uneventful. We marched in near silence, conserving our energy against the brutal and inescapable humidity. We were constantly thirsty but knew we had to conserve our water, as none from that place was drinkable.

Day three saw a turn for the worse, two of Mulholland's men

contracted cholera. First it was leg cramps and then came the vomiting and diarrhoea. We tried to rehydrate them as best we could, but there just wasn't enough spare water. By the end of the day they were dead. Two days later another six of the unit had gone; only four of us remained: myself, Charles Mulholland and two privates called Atkins and Jeremy.

We carried on in fear, knowing that we could be struck down at any time. The water dripped constantly from the huge jungle leaves, and splashed on our faces. Any rogue drop that inadvertently entered our mouths could be carrying bacteria. We guessed that this was how the others had been infected. We upped our pace, desperate to reach our destination and leave the valley far behind.

In the afternoon of the sixth day my worst fears became realized. My legs and stomach were beginning to cramp, and I started to feel an incredible urge to vomit. I began to slow down but nobody noticed as they were slowing too. It seemed as if we had all contracted the bug simultaneously.

Mulholland stopped and looked across at me. "You too?" he said.

I nodded wearily.

We sat ourselves down and sipped some water. Atkins and Jeremy bolted to the side of the track and vomited in the foliage. Mulholland and I followed quickly. Then came the diarrhoea. We tried to move on but it was no use: we couldn't go two yards without one of us being sick or defecating fluid. We just couldn't rehydrate ourselves and we knew our time had come.

The four of us lay there at the side of the jungle path, dehydrated and devoid of strength, and unable to go on.

Too exhausted and weak to talk, we each got lost in our thoughts. My mind started to drift and hallucinations came upon me. In my head I saw my beautiful fiancée Maria standing in front of me, her long blonde hair loose and glimmering in the tropical sun. Her deep blue eyes were filled with life and she smiled her warm comforting smile, the one that made me feel everything was alright. She was bathed in a piercing light that was almost heavenly. Then she and the light began to dissolve into each other, and I felt myself drifting into their combined glow. I knew that I was passing into another world and it felt indescribably beautiful. But just as I started to float I was dragged out of my reverie.

Back in the real world I opened my eyes, and in front of me there stood a thin and elderly Indian man. He was dressed in a white robe and was barefoot, and around his waist was a string belt with a small hessian sack attached to it. His gnarled hands seemed to be writing something in the air over me.

"You better now," he said. It was a statement, not a question.

I still felt weak but I managed to drag myself up into a sitting position. Mulholland and Atkins were already upright and conscious, and the Indian man was now sitting beside a lifeless Jeremy with his hands on Jeremy's head. He bowed his head and mouthed some words to himself, all the time staying in contact with Jeremy. After about thirty seconds Jeremy's eyes started to flicker, and within another ten they were wide open. The man got up and made a sign over Jeremy's body.

"You better now," he said. Again, it wasn't a question.

Jeremy sat up and stretched his arms outwards, like the rest of us he looked slightly bewildered. None of us could really grasp what was happening. Five minutes earlier we had been close to death. And here we were, not in perfect health, but very much alive. Somehow it didn't seem real. Who was this strange old man with the healing hands? How and why had he brought us back from the brink of death? And what was he going to want in return?

"Who are you?" I asked, breaking the silence.

"I am Suri," he said.

"What have you done to us?"

He didn't answer; he just stood there and smiled at us. Then he gathered up our empty canteens and headed for the river. When he returned five minutes later they were full, and he handed them back. We looked at them dubiously.

"Drink," he said.

"But the river is dirty," I said. "Unclean; infected; bad water." Suri just smiled. "I fix it," he said. "Drink."

I looked to the others and saw that they were just as concerned as myself. Nobody wanted to drink the water even though we were all parched beyond belief. We all knew what diseases the Chindwin contained, and there was no way we wanted to expose ourselves to any of them. Not now that we'd had a miracle escape.

"Drink," Suri repeated. He looked at me with reassuring eyes.

There was something about Suri that made me believe that the water was all right. After all he had already done the impossible and saved us once. I took a tentative sip from my canteen; the water was probably bitter and muddy but to me it was nectar. I let it swirl round my mouth eradicating the sticky dryness of my cheeks and gums. After that first sip there was no stopping me, I held the canteen to my mouth and carried on tanking it down until it was half empty. Having seen me drink, the others followed suit, savouring the sensation of liquid hitting the back of their withered throats.

We all thanked Suri for his unbelievable kindness: we couldn't thank him enough. He said nothing; he just grinned and bowed his head to each of us.

It was getting towards night time and we decided to stop where we were for the evening. We built a small fire and boiled a billy can of rice. We insisted that Suri stay and share our meagre rations with us, (he didn't seem to have any of his own, unless it was hidden in the small hessian sack that never left his waist), and he accepted our offer gratefully.

There wasn't much talk around the fire that night. We were all still dazed from the events of the day. It wasn't that we didn't have a million and one questions to ask Suri, we did. It was just that we seemed to have entered a different world from the one that had nearly claimed our lives. We were in the same jungle on the same planet, and yet now we felt almost alien.

Our surroundings had become dreamlike; as if time and space had shifted; like we had entered some sort of parallel universe. But it wasn't the Earth that had changed; it was us and our perception of it.

We slept long and peacefully that night, the first time we had done in ages, and we awoke re-energized and with a fresh hope in our hearts. The haziness of the previous evening had gone and the world around us was sharp and clear. In fact everything around us seemed brighter and more colourful and more defined than it ever had done. And there was now an unspoken bond between us: we had shared an experience that would change our lives.

Suri didn't speak much English, but we discovered through a mixture of signs and broken language, that he too was heading for Tamu. So we all headed off together for the last stage of our journey. We set off at a brisk pace, hopeful that we would reach Tamu before nightfall. Suri had replenished our canteens with his somehow decontaminated water, and we were filled with energy and vigour. We marched on through the morning with purpose and without a care in the world. We had been given a second chance at life and we were determined to take it with thanks and enthusiasm.

In the early afternoon we stopped for lunch. It was rice again, but the previously bland and boring grains had taken on a whole new flavour. Like everything else our taste buds had a whole new clarity about them. We savoured every mouthful as if we were dining on the finest chateaubriand, or the freshest caviar that money could buy. And the portions, although small, seemed to fill our stomachs like never before. We felt like we could march all day on just a handful of rice.

As the afternoon drew on, we began to catch glimpses of the town of Tamu, rising above the deep valley about six miles ahead of us. We felt sure that we would get there by sundown and increased our pace. Our thoughts now turned to the possibility of new rations and perhaps a comfortable bed for the night. But our good fortune was about to take an uncomfortable turn. We were three miles from Tamu, and treading a wide and exposed path by the river, when it happened.

We didn't hear the shot, just a grunt and a thud behind us. We turned around quickly and saw Suri lying on the floor, with an expanding pool of blood tarnishing his robes in the middle of his chest. All four of us went to ground immediately, and locked our eyes on the opposite bank where we believed the shot to have come from.

Jeremy who had the keenest eyes spotted something in the dense brush across the river. "Look over there," he pointed. "Can you see him?"

None of us could see anything except plants and trees.

"I can't see anything," I said.

"It's a sniper," he said. "I can only just make him out, but he's definitely there. I reckon I can pick him off."

Jeremy dragged his rifle up to his head, being careful not to raise his arms into the snipers line of sight. He aimed carefully and breathed out slowly. His shot was straight and true. "Got him," he said.

"Are you sure?" I asked. "I can't see that far."

"Of course I'm sure. Look." He got up and stood in full view to prove his point.

The rest of us waited for a minute to make sure it was safe, and then we got up and turned our attention to Suri. The blood had spread and nearly covered his entire chest. His eyes were open and he was just about breathing, but we could tell from his face that he was not long for the world. He raised his right hand from his chest and beckoned me to come close. I knelt down beside him and he pulled me towards his face.

"Bag," he said weakly. "Take bag."

I reached for the hessian sack that hung from a string on his waist. I undid the string and released the sack. "This...Is this what you mean?" I said.

Suri nodded and pulled me close again. "Keep...Safe." His voice was no louder than a whisper. His eyes closed and he said no more.

No-one spoke for ages. I don't think there was one of us who didn't feel a horrible sense of loss at Suri's passing. Perhaps there was a little bit of guilt mingled in there as well: after all it was probably one of us soldiers who should have been shot, not a gentle, harmless, old man, who only wanted to help people. I didn't take my eyes off him for at least ten minutes. I was half expecting another miracle and that he would just get up and carry on walking with us. But he didn't get up; a bullet to the heart was beyond even his powers.

"We ought to bury him," said Mulholland.

I agreed. "Yes. We can't just leave him here for the vultures, can we?"

We dug a shallow grave with our hands, well away from the path and the river. We lowered Suri gently into it and covered him with earth. Mulholland recited the Lord's Prayer as we bowed our heads over the grave and paid our last respects. We left the grave unmarked so that it wouldn't be disturbed by bandits.

It was gone nightfall by the time we'd laid Suri to rest, and we decided to stay where we were for the night. The last few miles could wait until the morning.

"What's in the bag then?" asked Atkins as we finished off our rice. He echoed what we were all wondering.

I lifted the bag from where I had stowed it, in my rucksack, and put my hand in and carefully removed the contents. We were surprised to find that it only contained one thing: a wooden box, about nine inches by six inches, and three inches deep. It was made of teak and was covered in mysterious symbols, the likes of which we hadn't seen before. Even Jeremy who was a keen archaeologist couldn't place them.

"Open it up," said Atkins.

The hinged lid opened easily, only to reveal an empty box. Disappointment hung in the air. All of us, I suspect, were expecting to find something in the box: perhaps some sacred artefact; an ancient relic; or a long-lost treasure. But there was nothing: just a plain wooden space.

"Is that it?" said Jeremy.

"I think so," I said, and handed it to him.

He examined it closely, running his fingers slowly and methodically around the inside, and then the exterior. "Sometimes these things have hidden compartments," he explained. "But apparently not this one," he added.

I was confused. There had been urgency in Suri's eyes as he lay there dying. There was no doubt about it; the box had been important to him. I took it back from Jeremy and looked at it again, this time more closely. The only striking things about it were the intricately-carved symbols that adorned the lid. Apart from a large one in the centre, they could have only been a quarter inch high. I guessed there must be at least two to three hundred of them, and, as far as I could make out, they were all unique.

"How old do you think it is?" I asked Jeremy.

"Not too sure," he said. "It could be any age. It looks fairly new in historical terms - maybe three to four hundred years old. But it depends on how well it's been looked after and where it's been kept. It could be way, way, older."

"Is there any way of telling?" I asked. "Some scientific way?"

"Nothing particularly accurate. If we knew a bit more about its origin and those symbols it would be a help. We'll have to do some research once we get out of this bloody mess. There's nothing we can do about it now."

Jeremy was right. The most important thing was to concentrate on getting out of Burma. The mystery of the box, however intriguing, would just have to wait.

Chapter 9

Stella stood just outside the back door smoking a cigarette. Stratton had insisted that it was ok to light up indoors, but she wanted some fresh air. The crisp night remained windless, and exhaled smoke hovered above her like a mini mushroom cloud. It was now 2.30am and she'd been up for nearly twenty four hours. Despite having had a couple of Jennings' miracle pills, which, to be fair, had kept her wide awake, she was finding it difficult to concentrate. Sleep deprivation was getting to her, and there was so much to take in.

The day had started strangely with a seemingly impossible murder, and had grown increasingly bizarre by the hour. She badly wanted to keep her train of thought firmly in the reality that she accepted, but it was being slowly dragged into a world of which she knew little to nothing. She wished that, like Jennings, she could dismiss it all out of hand.

The problem was that deep in her bones, she could feel a slow creeping chill developing. There was something in Stratton's voice and manner that disturbed her. She knew him well, and she knew that he was hiding something; and if she wasn't mistaken, it was something dark.

And now to top it all, there was the connection between Mulholland and Stratton. What was the mysterious object they had discovered in Burma all those years ago? Could it really be that important, that people were prepared to kill for it?

Stratton came out of the house and appeared next to her. "You okay?" he said.

"Yes, just a bit tired, that's all. It's been a long day. I'll be glad of some sleep to be honest."

"You can both stay here if you like. Both the spare bedrooms have bedclothes in them. A woman comes once a month to see to the place and air it out."

Stella was relieved at the thought of bed. "Thank you, that'd be great. I'm sure Jennings will appreciate it too."

She looked at him and smiled. She had dreaded it but it was actually good to see him again after all this time. He seemed different now; much less erratic and quick to anger. The booze appeared to have been ditched and the real Stratton, the Stratton she had once loved, was back in command.

And yet on the inside this wasn't the Stratton she had loved, this was an altogether alien version. The exterior was the same and so were his mannerisms, but the man within had changed. Not that anybody else would notice; just her. She had known him almost as well as she knew herself, and now she looked at him with new eyes: something had touched him and changed him; something strange and something deep.

Stratton looked at Stella and held her gaze. "Stella," he said awkwardly.

"Yes." She felt uncomfortable.

"I just wanted to say..." He stopped, as if struggling with emotion. "I just wanted to say, well...I'm sorry...About every-thing that..."

Stella felt herself welling up. "Don't," she said. "Not now Stratton, it's not the time or place for this." She stubbed out her cigarette. "Come on let's go back inside."

When they got back inside Jennings was poring over the transcript, trying to garner more information about Mulholland and the box. Surely there must be something else in this damn thing, he thought. But he had scanned the whole lot and every page had proved fruitless. It was frustrating.

Even though he was dubious about the alleged divine properties of the box, he wanted to know more. He was sure that Stratton was hiding something from them.

"Is this it?" he said.

"I'm afraid so," said Stratton. "But if you look closely you'll notice that there are some pages missing just after the bit about the finding of the box."

Jennings went to the relevant chapter. The pages were numbered at the bottom, and sure enough there was a gap. The numbering ended at 51 and started again at 64: there were twelve pages missing. He was surprised that he hadn't noticed it before. "Do you know where they are or what they say?"

"No I don't," said Stratton honestly. Although he had a vague inkling about their content.

"Great," said Jennings. "That's just great."

"Don't panic," said Stratton. "I'm sure we'll find them somewhere. They could be at my parents' house. It doesn't really matter that much anyway: you know what the killer's after now don't you? And it's pretty obvious that he or she is going to be coming for me at some point, so all you have to do is wait."

"They're not going to come for you while we're about are they," Jennings stated.

"I wouldn't be so sure. They got through the security at Mulholland's house so a detective and an ex-copper isn't going to stop them is it?" said Stella.

Jennings was about to speak again when Stratton interrupted him. "Listen. There's no point talking about this any more this evening. It's been a long day and everybody's tired, so I suggest you guys let me make you up some beds, and we'll sleep on it. You'll think more clearly after a good night's rest."

Stella and Jennings agreed and Stratton made up their beds with the fresh bedclothes that the maid had left. He showed them the bathroom and went back downstairs to check the locks: he wouldn't usually bother, but tonight was different.

After satisfying himself that the cottage was secure, Stratton headed for bed. Stella and Jennings had gone to their respective rooms, no doubt already asleep, and the cottage was almost silent. The only noise was the creaking of the floorboards as he walked into his room. He got into bed and lay there enjoying the quiet.

The clearing of his mind and sleep had been no problem to Stratton for years now. He was usually out for the count as soon as his eyes closed. Tonight though, he couldn't settle. It wasn't the business with Mulholland that was bothering him, he could deal with that. It was the reappearance of Stella Jones in his life. Beautiful, beautiful Stella. His heart had leapt as soon as he had received Oggi's message. And then when she'd turned up at the house, it had leapt again; higher and wilder than he thought imaginable. He had hidden it of course, beneath the calm unflappable exterior that he had cultivated to accompany his inner solidity. Nevertheless she had gotten to him, in a way that no-one else possibly could. She was, and perhaps always would be, his Achilles heel.

He thought back to the way he was in the last months of their relationship, and he winced at the memory. How could he have been so stupid and self-obsessed? She had loved him dearly, and far more than he had deserved. And yet he had still managed to fuck the whole thing up. It would have been easy to blame the alcohol, but that had just been the tip of the iceberg.

The real culprit had been his preoccupation with the secrets of his grandfather's notebook. Had he not been so ensconced with the deciphering of those ancient texts, then he would surely have noticed the steady and inevitable demise of their love. He cursed his grandfather for the inexorable burden that had been placed upon him. Why couldn't he have chosen one of his other grandchildren to harbour his secret? Or better still, why not one of his children? Stratton hadn't wanted the secrets of the universe on his shoulders; he'd just wanted to be happy with his love.

A noise from outside broke into his thoughts. It sounded like the breaking of a thick twig. He went to the window and peeked through the curtains. The porch light was still on and threw a dim glow onto the front garden. There was nothing there. Probably just a fox, he thought, or maybe Titan nosing around.

Although he suspected that Titan would be sleeping off his food in his den in the woods.

He got back into bed and closed his eyes again. Paranoia had begun to creep in; he needed to clear his mind. Lying in the corpse pose, arms at his side and palms facing upwards, he concentrated on his breathing. He began the *pranayama* exercise he had learnt from yoga. He breathed in through his nose for a count of five, held it for a count of fifteen, and then exhaled through his nose for a count of ten. He continued to repeat the process. The practice helped to calm his nerves and promote tranquility. It was simple but highly effective.

Within five minutes his mind was free of its earthly worries and had floated dreamily into the ether; unaware of the man silently picking the lock on the back door.

Chapter 10

Stella woke suddenly and sat bolt upright. She didn't know what the time was, but she knew she hadn't been asleep for long. She turned on the bedside lamp and reached for her mobile phone: the clock indicated that it was 3.15 am. What had woken her so quickly? Something wasn't right. There was no logic behind her worry, there were no nightly noises, and yet she sensed trouble.

Trying not to make a sound, she got out of bed and slipped on her trousers and blouse. The bedroom door opened noiselessly and she slid out onto the landing. Leaving the door slightly ajar for illumination, she tiptoed to the top of the stairs and peeked over the banister. There seemed to be a faint glow coming from the living room. She took a couple of steps down the stairs to get a better view. Sure enough, in the middle of the room, the slender beam of a small flashlight was visible. Her heart started to race with the rush of adrenaline.

Looking back up the stairs she thought about waking Stratton and Jennings, but swiftly rejected the idea. The gung-ho adventurer within her decided to tackle the situation alone. It had been years since she'd seen any real action. Although working for Mulholland had been financially rewarding, she missed the buzz of field work, and now was a perfect opportunity to prove to herself that she still had what it took.

The porch light shone through enough to make the bottom of the staircase and the hallway just about visible. Stella proceeded one cautious step at a time. All was going well until she alighted on the bottom stair, when there was a loud creak of wood. Immediately she looked to the living room and saw the flashlight cut out. Fuck! She thought. She had lost the element of surprise.

"Come out with your hands up," she ordered. "I've got a gun and I'll use it if I have to."

There was no answer. At that point she should have made a

big noise and woken the other two, but she didn't. Instead she decided stubbornly to continue on her own.

She turned on the light in the hallway. "Ok, I'm coming in. You'd better have your hands in the air or you'll get shot."

She approached the living room and put her hand through the door and reached for the light switch. As she groped to find it, a hand grabbed her wrist and pulled her into the darkness. She started to fall to the ground, and as she did, cold, hard metal connected with the back of her head. She was out cold.

Jennings meanwhile had been woken by Stella's voice echoing up the stairs. He had been looking over the landing when she had been dragged in and thudded to the ground. Jennings was no hero: he knew that it would be easier to tackle an intruder with two people, so he went to wake Stratton. But when he opened the door to Stratton's room and looked in, there was nobody there. Where the hell had he gone? Having no other choice, he grabbed his gun and descended the stairs alone. He stood outside the living room and looked for the light switch. He could just make it out, about two feet from the door frame. Acting quickly, he took a breath and lunged for it. Once he had connected he went straight to the ground, rolled head over heels, and turned to face the door on one knee with his gun pointing up.

"Very flash," said a voice coming from the sofa. The voice was American and sounded vaguely familiar.

Jennings looked over to the sofa. Stella was on one side, wrists bound, and next to her was a man holding a gun to her temple. The man was black and was wearing a grey designer suit. It was the man from the service station.

"Ok James Blond, drop the gun and raise your hands," said Grady. His eyes gestured to his own weapon trained at Stella's head.

Jennings could tell from the man's countenance that he meant business. This was not a guy to be fucking with. He dropped his gun to the floor and raised his arms.

Now training his weapon on Jennings, Grady got off the sofa and walked over to his quarry. He picked up Jennings' gun and pocketed it. Then, with a torn T-shirt from Stratton's rucksack, he tied Jennings' wrists behind his back, and ordered him to sit down on the sofa next to Stella.

"Ok, that's two of you," said Grady. "Where's the third little piggy then?"

"What do you mean," said Jennings innocently. "There's only the two of us."

Grady sighed and reached into Jennings' pocket. He pulled out the transmitter that he'd placed there earlier. "Listen dumb ass. This here is a radio microphone. I've heard every word you've said since the service station. I know that your man Stratton owns this place and that he's around here somewhere. So tell me, where the fuck is he?"

"I don't know, he wasn't in his room when I looked just now," said Jennings.

Grady turned to Stella. "What about you Missy, got any ideas?"

Stella could only shake her head. She had just come round and was still groggy.

Grady rolled his eyes. He took another T-shirt out of Stratton's rucksack and ripped it into three. One strip for Stella's feet, one for Jennings' and one to tie them together. He wanted to search the cottage for Stratton, and they weren't going anywhere.

Gun in hand; Grady did a slow and deliberate sweep of the ground floor. When he was satisfied he started up the stairs. He knew that Stratton was somewhere in the cottage, he just had to find out where. The job was starting to piss him off.

All he had wanted to do was search Stratton's rucksack for the rest of the transcript, (he didn't believe that someone else had taken the pages), and now he was in the middle of a pointless game of hide and seek. It was the girl's fault; if she hadn't come snooping, nobody would have been any the wiser. He still couldn't fathom why she'd come down to investigate: he hadn't made a sound. But come down she had, and now things were getting complicated.

At the top of the stairs he took stock. There were four doors on the landing, one behind him to the right, one right front, and two front left. Three bedrooms and a bathroom, he guessed. He decided to start back right and work his way round anticlockwise.

The first door led into a large bedroom with an en-suite shower and toilet; the master bedroom, he thought; Stratton's room. Wary of an attack he checked the built-in cupboards and then under the bed. He then scanned the en-suite but again found nothing. He went to the second door; it was another bedroom that also yielded nothing. The third door was the bathroom; again nothing. The last door; nothing.

Slightly bemused, Grady stood on the landing and tried to be logical. Stratton was definitely not upstairs, that was certain. And he hadn't escaped out of a window because Grady had checked them. There was the possibility that he'd snuck back downstairs whilst Grady was in one of the rooms, but it was only small: Grady had been careful to keep an eye on the landing.

He was starting to get nervy. Stratton's file had indicated time spent in the Orient, and had hinted at some form of martial arts training. Grady himself had spent some time out in Japan learning ninjutsu, and he wondered if Stratton had also studied with the ninjas. If he had then it was going to be dangerous.

At that moment he felt a waft of cold air hit the crown of his head. Of course. How could he have been so fucking stupid? What had he been taught? Always look above; always look above. But by the time he thought this, it was too late: a body had crashed down on him from the loft hatch, and he was tumbling down the stairs with a pair of arms locked around his neck.

Grady held tight to his gun as he fell. At the bottom of the stairs they came to an abrupt halt, and Grady struggled to free himself of Stratton's choke hold. Stratton was no real match for Grady physically, and his arms held firm for a while, but eventually Grady's sheer brute strength won the day. With an almighty effort Grady grabbed Stratton's left arm and wrenched it away from his neck, and the right arm followed soon after. Grady leapt to his feet and Stratton did likewise.

Grady held his gun steady and aimed it at Stratton. "Nice try boy, but that's enough. Get into the living room with the others."

Stratton turned as if to obey, and then, like lightning, his leg came flashing up towards the gun. The weapon shot out from Grady's hand, but not before he'd let off a round in Stratton's direction. Stratton dropped to the floor clutching his left shoulder. Blood oozed out between his fingers. The bullet had gone right through him.

Grady picked up his gun. "Not very clever, was it?"

Stratton said nothing. His breathing was becoming heavy.

"Now, again. Let's join the others," said Grady.

Stratton struggled to his feet and walked into the living room. Still clutching his shoulder he collapsed into his chair. The wound was stinging slightly, but was nowhere near as bad as he'd imagined it would be. Although having never been shot before, he had no reference. Stella gave him a concerned look, so he attempted a reassuring smile.

Grady stood in the middle of the room, holding court. "Ok people, now that we're all here, let's try and get to the bottom of this little mystery." He addressed Stratton. "Now you, Bruce fucking Lee, where are the missing pages from that transcript?"

"I don't know."

"I don't believe you."

"Well, believe me or not, but I really don't know."

Grady looked at him hard and straight in the eye. "Listen buddy, these two might have fallen for your bullshit, but I'm a different box of candy apples. I'm a fucking professional, and I know that you're holding back on me. So stop stalling and tell me the truth." He cocked his gun, and aimed it at Stratton's head.

"I don't know where it is," Stratton insisted.

"Fair enough," said Grady turning the gun in Stella's direction. "Don't say I didn't warn you."

Forgetting about his wound, Stratton leapt out of the chair and flew at Grady. Grady, however, was too quick. He had predicted Stratton's move, and almost effortlessly his fist came out and landed with stinging accuracy on the bullet hole in Stratton's shoulder. Then, howling with pain, Stratton fell to his knees.

"Slow learner are we boy?"

Stratton grimaced and his eyes began to water.

Grady kept his gun on Stella. "Now for the last fucking time. Where is the transcript?"

"I don't know," croaked Stratton.

"Ok then, say bye bye to the girl."

Mustering what strength he had left, Stratton lunged at Grady's legs in a half-hearted attempt at a rugby tackle. Grady did a neat side step and brought his gun crashing down on Stratton's skull. Stratton hit the ground and stayed there, blood running from his temple.

Grady felt Stratton's neck; he still had a pulse; this was good. The last thing he needed was for Stratton to die before he got the information he wanted.

To make sure that there was no more funny business, Grady tied Stratton's hands and legs with yet another of Stratton's own T-shirts.

He was in no mood for any more trouble. The whole evening, in fact the whole day, had gone disastrously wrong; he should have called it a day when he lost Stratton on the subway. Britain had never been his favourite place for assignments; the weather was crap, the people were stuck up, and then there was that shit he'd been caught up in during the mid-nineties. But he didn't want to think about that just now. All he wanted was to get the hell out of the cottage with at least something to show for his troubles.

After placing the still-unconscious Stratton back in his chair, Grady gave him a mild slap to wake him up. Stratton did not move, and neither did he make a sound, so Grady got a glass of water and tipped it over his head.

Still there was no response.

"Wake up sleepy boy," said Grady loudly, as he gave Stratton another, much harder, slap across the face.

Still no response.

Grady laid his fingers on Stratton's neck again; this time there was no pulse. Next he held his hand over Stratton's mouth to check for breath: there was none.

Grady started to panic.

He lay Stratton on the floor and tried to remember his first aid, as it had been a good twenty years since he tried to resuscitate someone. He pumped at Stratton's chest with vigour and blew air into his mouth, but after a couple of minutes he realized that he was onto a loser. Stratton was dead. And so was Grady's only lead.

"Fuck," said Grady. "Fuck it."

Stella, who along with Jennings had been watching the whole episode in silent fear, opened her mouth to speak. She was, however, too shocked to say a word. Her mind told her that this couldn't be happening; that there was no way that Stratton could possibly be dead. Any second now he'll come round, she thought. But his body just lay there, cold and lifeless.

"Well that's fucked you hasn't it?" Jennings piped.

"Thank you Columbo," replied an agitated Grady. "Now just shut the fuck up or you'll be joining him."

Grady thought about his options. With Stratton dead there was no point hanging around any longer. He had searched the rucksack, to no avail, and there were no more obvious places to look. He could spend two days searching the cottage from top to bottom and still not find the transcript, if it was hidden well enough. And maybe Stratton *had* been telling the truth; perhaps it wasn't there at all. Either way he was wasting his time staying here. The only problem now was Stratton's body and the two witnesses. He needed to remove any trace of evidence that he'd ever been there. This left him with only one course of action, and it wasn't a route that he really wanted to go down.

First, he reached into his breast pocket and pulled out a small penknife. He went to the hallway and prised out the bullet that had lodged in the banisters. He couldn't take the risk, however minimal, that the slug would be traced back to him. It was a titanium-coated 9mm casing, only produced in small amounts by a specialist firm in the States. Having removed the evidence he poked his head round the living room door, and told Jennings and Stella that he'd be back and not to try anything.

Jennings and Stella heard the front door open.

"What do you think he's doing?" asked Stella.

"I don't know," said Jennings. "But whatever it is, I'm sure it's not good news for us. Like he said, he's a professional; he's not likely to want to leave any loose ends lying around here. He's either going to take us with him, or…" He paused.

"Or he's going to kill us," finished Stella.

"Exactly," said Jennings. "And I'm pretty sure it's going to be the latter. He's not going to want any extra baggage is he? And he knows that we're as ignorant as he is about the manuscript, so he doesn't need us."

"What are we going to do then?"

"At the moment there's nothing we can do. He could be back at any moment; we'll have to wait and see what his next move is."

Stella looked sadly at the body on the ground. In a curious mark of respect Grady had folded the arms across the torso. The eyes were shut and the face peaceful.

She could have been imagining it, but Stratton's lips almost appeared to be smiling, as if in a state of grace. He'd always believed in life after death, and she wondered if perhaps he was right, and that he was now in a better place. Or maybe his spirit was still in the room, watching over Jennings and herself; just waiting for an opportunity to help them out of their current predicament. This thought was comforting and she held it in her mind. It gave her hope that they might actually escape with their lives.

Jennings meanwhile feared the worst. He didn't know who the guy was or who he was working for, but he was cold and calculating and wouldn't think twice about killing the pair of them if it suited his purpose. Jennings suspected that he was either CIA or NSA. If he had to put money on it he would have probably said the former: this stuff was more in their line of work, and the guy had a pragmatic air about him that pointed towards Langley. Jennings had come across operatives from the Company a couple of times previously, and they too had displayed the same clinical aloofness and disregard for human life that this man was now showing.

The front door closed and seconds later Grady was back in the room. In his right hand he still held his gun. More worrying for Stella and Jennings was the petrol can that he held in his left. Their hearts sank and their stomachs wheeled with foreboding, as it dawned on them that they were not going to get out alive. Grady was going to torch the place with them in it. They were both praying for the same thing: that he was going to kill them first.

Grady saw the look on their faces. "Sorry guys," he said. "But I've got no choice."

He started by pouring the contents of the can over Stratton and the surrounding floor. He then soaked the curtains, and then disappeared to saturate the hallway and kitchen. Lastly he returned to the living room and stared at Jennings and Stella, deciding their fate. The most humane thing to do was to shoot them. Although humanity had never bothered him before, which was why he was so good at his job, recently he had been thinking differently; perhaps it was falling in love, or maybe it was the ageing process; whatever, something alien had entered his brain: it was a conscience. The problem was that he didn't want to leave any bullets. Of course, he could retrieve them, like he had with the one in the banisters, but that would take time; and he had no idea how long it would be before they were missed and someone was sent after them. And perhaps Jennings had already raised the alarm before coming downstairs. No, no bullets, he would have to use another tactic.

"Both of you get on the floor and kneel down," Grady ordered.

Stella and Jennings complied, both terrified yet equally thankful that the inevitable was going to be quick and painless. The situation was such that resistance hadn't crossed their minds. It was like being in the middle of a dream or a film; as if they were watching these events happen to someone else.

They knelt beside each other facing the fireplace and Grady stood behind them, gun in hand. He lifted the gun in the air and brought it down on the back of Stella's neck; again. She fell forward, spark out. He repeated the motion with Jennings, who also lost consciousness.

After dousing their bodies with the small amount of petrol that remained, he drew a smouldering ember from the fire and dropped it on the carpet. It instantly caught and he quickly left the room and the cottage without looking back.

Inside the cottage the flames began to spread.

Chapter 11

David Brennan was restless. He opened one lazy eye to the luminous digits on the bedside alarm: it was 5am, only five minutes since he'd last looked. He had woken earlier that night at 2am and had not been able to sleep properly since. It was becoming an all-too-regular routine for David. Insomnia had taken over his life and he feared that it was now chronic. Of course, he had tried all sorts of different medications of varying strength, yet none of them seemed to work. He didn't like doctors, but soon he was going to have to bite the bullet and actually go and see one. Several Harley Street specialists belonged to his local Lodge; he would ask one of them.

Realizing that he was going to get no more sleep, he eased himself out of the bed quietly, so as not to wake Anna, and grabbed his dressing gown. Anna looked happy in her slumber, carefree and devoid of the pain that plagued her waking hours. After all that she had been through she was still the most beautiful woman in the world, he thought. Her flowing chestnut hair was gone now, replaced by a baby-smooth dome, but even that could never detract from the way he viewed her. She was as lovely now as the day they had met, twenty five years ago. He had been smitten then, as he was smitten now, and as he would be forever. There was no physical blemish or cosmetic deformity that would ever taint the perfection that he saw in this woman. And the ravages of time could never destroy the overpowering love for her that beat at the very heart of his being. She was his everything.

After making himself a strong black coffee, he sat down in his armchair in the living room and turned on the TV. He switched to News24 to catch up on what was happening in the rest of the world. There was the usual fare: soldiers being killed in the Middle East; government ministers taking bribes; rapists and murderers getting lenient sentences; little girls going missing. These were all terrible things, and they were happening right now in a cruel and unforgiving world, yet he watched impassively. Was he alone in his detachment from the horrors of society, or had the rest of the nation, or perhaps the whole world, become desensitized to the moral minefield that passed as Planet Earth?

The murder of Henry Mulholland was still headline news. Brennan suspected that this was the Prime Minister's influence. Mulholland was a well-liked character amongst the sporting fraternity and also the business community, but he was hardly a national hero - although you wouldn't have known it from the disproportionate news coverage that his death was receiving. The report contained interviews with various dignitaries and celebrities, all expressing their shock and dismay. Each one of them saying that it was a tragic loss and that he was a dear friend etc. At the end the reporter stated that the police were still following several leads and that arrests were imminent; but if the public had any further information, however small, then they should contact New Scotland Yard on this number…

'Arrests were imminent' wasn't only optimistic, it was a downright lie, thought Brennan. They weren't even close to figuring out how the murder was executed, let alone who was responsible. His team consisted of the cream of the nation's police forces. The best scene of crime officers, the foremost forensics experts and the shrewdest detectives had all been seconded to the case. They had spent the last 24 hours scanning Addington Hall and the surrounding area in the minutest detail. All this and still they had nothing, not even a fibre of clothing or a footprint; the rain having conspired to wash away any trace of the latter. The only clue they did have was the symbol that had been left on Mulholland's desk, and that was tenuous to say the least as Brennan had found out the previous day; it was used by thousands of people across the UK; and probably tens or hundreds of thousands across the world.

He was beginning to wonder whether he had been too easy on Stella Jones. She was after all, Mulholland's head of security and would have known all the access codes to the alarms. She would also have known the guards' routines and the timing of the canine patrols. And on top of that there was the convenient connection to her ex-boyfriend as well. He was certain that she hadn't done it herself, she had been 70 miles away at the time, but that didn't mean she wasn't involved. She definitely had the means, and yet there was no apparent motive. As far as he knew, she had nothing to gain from Mulholland's death.

Although, perhaps someone had paid her for the information? Money could sway all but the truest of people, and Stella had already shown that she was not immune to its influence when she left Special Branch to work for Mulholland. These thoughts flashed through his mind. For now though he was going to have to rely on his gut instinct which told him to trust her. And in any case he had Jennings watching over her, so she was going nowhere.

Brennan hadn't heard from Jennings since eight o' clock the previous evening, when Jennings had asked permission to follow up on Stella's lead. With a few misgivings Brennan had assented; he didn't really see the point of travelling halfway across the country on a hunch. Stella's ex-boyfriend might know about the symbol, but that was no great help; and there was no obvious connection between him and Mulholland. His disappearance however, was interesting; and that, along with Stella's excellent track record, and the fact that there was nothing else to go on, had swayed him to permit what was effectively a wild goose chase.

Brennan reached for his home phone and dialled the number for Operation Control. The young female constable at the other end of the line informed him that Jennings had reported in at 2.30 am. She said that Jennings had found the man they were looking for and stated his intention to stay overnight in the cottage in the West Country. He would call Brennan in the morning to update him on their progress. Brennan asked her if that was all. She said it was.

Brennan put the phone back in its cradle. He was pleased that Jennings' trip had not been fruitless. Jennings was a good man; one of Brennan's best. He was a bit excitable, some might have said highly strung, but he was nevertheless a brilliant detective. Brennan didn't know anyone else who could read people as well as Jennings could. He could sniff out a lie at a thousand paces; if a suspect's story didn't add up then Jennings would sit there and manipulate them until it did. It was almost as if he was inside the person's head. If Brennan had believed in such a thing then he would have said that Jennings had telepathic powers.

On top of this, and the main reason for Brennan's fondness of him, was Jennings' unstinting honesty. Incorruptible was not a word that Brennan bandied about. He had dealt with the fallout of bribery and corruption for most of his working life, and he knew from experience that nearly everyone was susceptible; from the highest judge to the lowest nonce. But just occasionally, amidst the swirling stream of seedy silt and sludge, he came across a golden nugget of truth and probity; and Jennings was one of those very rare nuggets.

The clock on the TV screen indicated that it was 6.15am; it was time for Brennan to get ready for work. His driver was picking him up from the house at seven. This was earlier than normal, but it was not an average day. He had an eight o' clock meeting with the Prime Minister, who wanted briefing on all that had happened and how the case was coming along. Brennan wasn't looking forward to informing his head of government of the decidedly limp progress that was being made in the investigation. He hoped that Jennings would phone with positive news before he arrived at Downing Street.

He showered quickly and, for the Prime Minister's benefit, put on his best suit: a made-to-measure dark blue Armani that his wife had forced him to buy. He thought it was far too flash and expensive, but Anna had been most insistent, telling him not to be such an old fart and to get with the times. He then went back downstairs and had another coffee and a bowl of muesli (for his health; Anna's influence again). And then he went back upstairs to say goodbye to Anna, who was now awake and lay there smiling as Brennan entered the room. He sat himself down next to her on the edge of the bed and smiled back.

"How's you?" he said.

"I'm good," she said. "I think it's a good day today." She looked at him, concerned. "More to the point, what about you? You're still not sleeping properly are you? You look awful."

Brennan laughed. "Thanks for that. I'm meeting the Prime Minister in just under an hour. What I really need is my wife telling me that I look awful."

"Sorry," she said. "But I worry about you. I don't want you fretting yourself into an early grave along with me."

Brennan frowned. "Don't say things like that. You are not heading for an early grave. You can beat this thing."

"Maybe. But maybe I won't. Either way I want you to live." She lifted her hand and caressed his cheek. "I want you to start looking after yourself David. I need your support, and you can't give me that if you fall to pieces as well."

"You're right. As you always are. Don't worry I'm going to make an appointment to see someone about my insomnia. It's just a difficult time right now with this Mulholland case landing on my lap. I'll sort it out soon; I promise."

A horn sounded from the driveway, telling Brennan that his driver had arrived.

"That'll be Jerry," he said. "I'd better go. I don't want to keep the PM waiting now, do I?"

He kissed her softly on the lips and said goodbye.

Jerry was revving the Mercedes' engine impatiently as Brennan opened the front door of the house. He needed to get a new driver, he thought; one who actually realized that he was the boss. Jerry treated the job as beneath him and a massive inconvenience. Perhaps Jerry should have thought about that before he started taking backhanders from dodgy MP's, mused Brennan. It was his own fault that he'd ended up as a glorified chauffeur; he was lucky to have a job at all. It was only through Brennan's good nature that he did.

Brennan got into the back of the car.

"Morning sir," said Jerry chirpily. Disguising his tetchiness. Badly.

"Morning Jerry," he said. "Sorry to keep you waiting. I know you're a busy man," he added with more than a hint of sarcasm.

Jerry's face turned almost as red as his hair. "Sorry sir, there's just a lot of traffic about this morning and I wouldn't want you to be late."

"Well let's get going then," said Brennan.

Jerry eased the Mercedes down the gravel drive and out into the leafy lane. He flicked a remote control and the electric gates shut behind them. A minute later they were leaving the private road with its set-back houses and heading out into the morning rush hour. The traffic was indeed bad, as Jerry had said it would be. On a good day the journey to Downing Street from SW19 would take 25 minutes. Today it was going to be nearly double that. Brennan settled himself on the back seat and tried to relax. He turned on Classic FM: they were playing Sull'aria from The Marriage of Figaro. It was a nice piece; he remembered it from the film The Shawshank Redemption. He enjoyed classical music, although he was no expert, and listened to it in the car whenever he needed to de-stress.

Now, as he waited for Jennings to call, was one of those times. He checked his mobile phone to make sure that it was turned on: it was. Seven thirty, along with Vauxhall Bridge, came and went. They were now only a mile away from their destination, but the traffic showed no sign of abating; if anything it was getting worse. The Congestion Charge had had seemingly no effect whatsoever on the amount of traffic flowing through central London. Brennan looked at his watch edgily.

They hit Parliament Square just after seven forty five, and, as they turned left out of it, the road began to clear. Brennan checked his phone again, like a man with OCD. He knew that there had been no phone call, but he kept looking anyway; as if by sheer willpower he was going to make the damn thing ring.

As they passed through the gates of Downing Street, Brennan's watch showed seven fifty. Still his phone hadn't rung. Where the hell was Jennings? What was he up to? Didn't he realize how important this case was?

The black door of number ten shut behind him. Anthony Bliss, the Prime Minister's private secretary, was waiting for him. They exchanged pleasantries and Bliss led him up the stairs to the PM's office. Bliss knocked on the thick oak door and a voice from inside beckoned them to come in.

Brennan's phone started to ring.

Chapter 12

Professor Sharlo Miles enjoyed good wine and good company. Which was why he was especially pleased to have spent the evening at Grant Romano's. Grant Romano possessed one of the best cellars in California, and once a month, on the eighth, he would hold a lavish dinner party. There would always be seven guests, no more, no less, and of course Romano himself, making eight. Romano liked the number eight for various reasons; his birthday was on the eighth of August; it was supposed to be lucky in Chinese superstition; and it was also an expression of infinity. On top of that it was an ideal number of people to invite to dinner; it was neither too intimate nor too crowded. It also rhymed with the word 'plate'.

The guest list for a 'Romano Eight', as it had come to be known, was, like the host's tastes, an eclectic mix. He enjoyed nothing more than putting together a group of people who would never usually encounter each other in a social situation. He would invite High Court Judges and seat them next to career criminals; and he would invite members of the clergy and seat them next to pimps or hookers. Romano believed that there was too much snobbery in the world, and it was his mission in life to be a great leveller of class divides. This task was made easier by the fact that he was Hollywood A-list; if not Hollywood royalty. To bridge the gap between the highest and the lowest, first you had to be at the top.

Sharlo Miles had been to quite a few 'Romano Eights' over the last couple of years. He had met the host through a mutual acquaintance: a medium called Bettina Bartram, who was a darling of the Beverly Hills jet set, and had also done some tests with Miles up at NIPS. He looked forward to Romano's dinners as they were always entertaining and the food and wine were faultless. He also had a soft spot for Romano whom he found to be one of the most genuine and charming characters that he had met; a long way from the starry egotistical stereotype that he would have imagined. Romano was also very intelligent and knowledgeable on a whole range of subjects, but not so much that anybody thought he was a smart ass or a know all; just enough for the respect of his peers.

That particular evening had been one of the best that Sharlo Miles had attended. In addition to Miles and Romano, Bettina Bartram had been there. .Also present had been Jim Davis - a lawyer; Carl Finstrom - a stunt man; Tony Pelloni - a drug dealer; Sister Mary McKee - a nun; and Sherry Downing - an upmarket hooker.

The food had been exquisite and had even surpassed its customary high standard. And the wine, as usual, had been of the finest quality and plentiful. The conversation had been stimulating and unceasing, and an air of good humour had enveloped the room. Whatever problems the respective guests may or may not have had, they had been left at the door of this magical mansion high up on Beverly Hills.

It was now midnight and Miles and Romano were standing outside by the pool, each smoking a Montecristo and holding a balloon of Hennessey XO. The remainder of the party didn't smoke, and Romano being a gracious host had taken himself and Miles outside. It was no hardship though; the night was mild and the sky was clear, and the bright lights of LA stretched out below them in a refulgent neon panorama.

Romano swilled his brandy under his nose and breathed in the sweet sharp vapours. He took a sip and then puffed on his cigar, all the time staring happily across at the iconic Hollywood sign, lit up in the Hills a mile away. "I don't think I could ever tire of this you know Sharlo," he said. "It's what I always dreamed of when I was a kid. And it's why I got into acting in the first place. I know it sounds shallow, but that's just the way it is." He took another swig of Brandy. "What do you think Sharlo? Do you think I'm shallow?"

"If I thought you were shallow I wouldn't be here," Miles replied honestly. "Enjoying the fruits of your labour is not shallow - it's what you're supposed to do. You worked hard to get where you are Grant, and now that you're there you don't use it as a weapon like most stars do. You don't court publicity and you don't make an ostentatious display of your wealth. You help the less well off without any fanfare or thanks and you treat people as you like to be treated. You are probably the biggest name in this city full of names, and yet you are the most unshowbizzy person I've met here; and believe me I've met most of them. If there was a blueprint for how someone in your position should act, then you have followed it, down to the last detail." He puffed on his cigar. "So, no Grant, in answer to your question, I don't think you are shallow at all."

Romano smiled, half pleased, half embarrassed. He wasn't very good at taking compliments - well not genuine ones anyway. "Thank you Sharlo, I appreciate that coming from you. I wasn't fishing; I just sometimes question myself, that's all."

"It's good that you do question yourself," said Miles. "The only way to stay true to oneself is to constantly question ones own actions."

"You do come out with some good stuff you know Sharlo. It's no wonder you're a professor."

Miles laughed. "Being a professor only means that you have knowledge; it doesn't mean that you are particularly wise. I for one am no wiser than you or anyone else."

Romano liked Sharlo Miles a great deal. Although he'd only known him for a little over two years, he looked on Miles as a trusted old friend. In fact, it was more than that; he was almost a father figure.

Romano was never short of 'friends' in his line of work; he made new friends all the time; they popped up ten to the dozen; it was rare for a day to go by without someone new wanting to be his friend. But unlike these people, Miles' friendship was not due to expedience. He was not in the 'business', and so didn't need any favours in that respect; and he had plenty of money, so he wasn't after financial backing. Also Miles had a wife, so Romano assumed he wasn't after anything of a fruity nature. They were just two people who got on and had a mutual respect for each other's abilities. Miles was the one person he could rely on to give him an honest opinion without having to worry that he was being a 'suck up'. And because Miles was older and had been around the block a bit, it meant that Romano could trust him to give sage advice.

Tony Pelloni came out of the house and joined them by the pool. "Hey Guys, whass up," he said. Pelloni was in his late twenties and of Sicilian descent. He was tanned and dark and handsome, and he came from a well-connected family.

"Hi Tony," said Romano. "We're just enjoying some night air. Join us if you like."

"Thanks Grant, but I've just come out to settle an argument that me and Sherry are having about your career."

"Oh, okay. What do you want to know?"

"Well Sherry reckons that your first film appearance was in 'Tomorrow's Baby' in 1985. But I reckon it was in 'Hell for Leather' in 1984."

"Well, I did have minor roles in both those films. But my first ever appearance was in 1982 in a film called 'Tom's Holiday', where I played a barman. I had one line, which was, 'Don't you think you've had enough buddy', if I remember rightly. So I'm afraid you're both wrong."

"Oh well," said Pelloni. "I'll go let Sherry know. I'll see you guys in a bit."

Pelloni left and Romano and Miles chatted about Romano's latest project, which as well as starring in, was also going to be his first try at directing. The film was a thriller about the kidnap of a young girl on holiday with her parents. He had got the idea from a real-life event that had happened in Europe, where a girl had vanished from her family's apartment. He was going to call it 'The Loss of Innocence'. He had managed to get Benicio Del Toro on board to play the detective, and Julia Roberts to play the mother alongside himself as the father. The movie had been shot already and was now in the editing suite. Romano was very excited about it.

"A long overdue Oscar in the offing then maybe?" said Miles.

Romano laughed. "Not for me I don't think, but Benicio is awesome and I wouldn't bet against him getting one."

The sound of laughter resonated from inside the house.

"I suppose we ought to go back in," said Romano. "I'm neglecting my guests."

"I'm sure they'll forgive you, it's been a great evening so far and you've been a perfect host as usual," said Miles. "Before we go back I just wanted to ask you if you'd had any more of those dreams."

Romano thought for a moment. "I've had a few, but nothing really clear. They've mainly been about people I haven't seen for years, and then suddenly the next day I've bumped into them in the street or in a bar."

"So no more sports results or disasters."

"Not since I spoke to you last."

"Well, be sure to call me if you do. And remember to log the dates when they occur. Even if they're minor premonitions, like the ones you've just described, it will be helpful. I'm trying to establish a link between prescience and the position of the stars and geographical location. Also if you could note if you're under any particular stress at the time, it would be helpful as well. A person's emotional state seems so have an effect on their psychic abilities too."

"That's a lot of information," said Romano. "Tell you what Sharlo; I'll get myself a new diary specifically to log all the details you want. I'll keep a daily record even if I don't dream anything;

then you can look for correlations in the dormant periods as well."

"Thank you Grant. I only wish that everyone I dealt with was as helpful as you. Unfortunately most people with any form of ESP are quite scatterbrained or just not interested in the science of it. They seem to be under the impression that their gift is given by some divine being and so ignore the idea that it could have a rational explanation, and may not be as random as they think."

Romano was only too happy to help. He'd been fascinated by the paranormal since his childhood. He remembered his father telling him stories about people with magical powers. Men from the mysterious East who could read people's minds and see into the future; and men and women who could heal people with a touch of their hand. These were real people mind, his father had said, not comic book heroes like Superman or Batman; real live people with amazing gifts. His father had travelled all over the world, so the young Grant had seen him as an authority on such matters.

As time went on and Romano had entered his teens, he started to have odd dreams of the future. He would dream football results and baseball results, days before the games were played. He told his father about these and the old man began to fleece the bookies with his 'inside information'.

After a while Romano stopped telling his father about his dreams because he was getting greedy. The dreams were becoming increasingly sporadic anyway, and by his early twenties they had all but dried up. This had coincided with his rise as an actor. Over the last few years the dreams had made a gradual reappearance; although now, as well as the sports results, he would dream of car crashes and disasters before they occurred. He was pleased to have Miles around to discuss it with; anyone else would think he was wrong in the head.

Romano headed back inside and Miles followed just behind.

"Have you had any luck tracing that box I told you about?"

Romano asked.

Miles hesitated and looked awkward, but Romano didn't see. "No Grant I haven't. It's probably just a myth that your father heard; or maybe he just made it up. He wouldn't have been the first parent to have made up a story to impress his kid."

"I agree," said Romano. "But he seemed very certain, and said he had first-hand knowledge of it."

"Well if you're sure I'll keep on it. I'm not holding out too much hope though; it all sounds a bit fantastical - even to me."

They walked back into the dining room and rejoined the rest of the company.

Romano was feeling slightly guilty; he had omitted to tell Miles about one of his dreams. It had been an unpleasant vision and it had involved Miles himself. He hoped that it wouldn't come to be.

Chapter 13

The living room was thick with smoke. Stella drifted back into consciousness. She opened her eyes briefly and then closed them again. She could see nothing and they stung like hell. The last thing she remembered was kneeling down next to Jennings, waiting to be executed. She was alive, that was clear, at least, if nothing else.

She started to choke, suddenly aware of the acrid vapours that were slowly filling her lungs. At the same time she felt a burning sensation on her legs; they felt like they were on fire; and they were. Instinctively she began to thrash wildly on the floor, trying to quell the flames. Jennings' body lay next to her, and as she writhed, her arms and legs lashed into him. He didn't make a sound, and she guessed that he was already dead.

She needed to get out of the house, but she was weakening by the second and the smoke had left her disorientated. She gathered all her strength and tried to pull herself to her feet. It was no use; her body just wouldn't obey. The flames began to penetrate her clothing. She screamed loudly and then screamed again. She was burning in hell.

Part of a beam fell from the ceiling and thudded to the floor next to her head. She screamed for a third time; a piercing keen that would have been heard a mile away, should anyone have lived in that radius.

Her wailing was stopped abruptly halfway through; muffled by wet and heavy fabric dropping onto her face and body. Before she had time to think, a strong pair of arms had swept her off the ground and manoeuvred her into a fireman's lift. The ride was uncomfortable but quick. Her rescuer's shoulders dug into her stomach and she nearly retched; he was swift on his feet though, and in no time she found herself lying face upwards at the back of the cottage, gazing at the stars. Still dizzy and confused she coughed and spluttered, thankfully she could now get some oxygen into her lungs. The cold and frosty air was a blessed relief from the inferno that she had been rescued from. And where was her rescuer? He had laid her on the ground and shot off without a word. She hadn't even got a look at his face.

Her question was answered almost immediately. She raised her head slightly to look towards the cottage, and as she did so a dark figure came rushing out with Jennings slung over his shoulder. He laid Jennings on the floor next to her and then collapsed on the ground catching his breath. Stella couldn't believe her eyes - it was Stratton.

She wanted to ask him what had happened and how the hell he'd managed to get them out. She was still too fragile to speak properly though. Her mouth opened but only hoarse whisper came out of her sandpaper throat. She gave up, and instead she lay there with her head turned towards him; staring in wonder at the man, who but half an hour before, she thought dead.

Stratton saw the look in Stella's eyes. "Don't worry, I'll explain it later," he said. "Best you just lay there a while and enjoy the air."

Stella looked across at Jennings lifeless body.

"He'll be all right, leave it to me," said Stratton.

Stratton laid his hands on Jennings' chest. He kept them there for almost a minute. Jennings began to cough himself back to life. He opened his eyes and saw Stratton staring down at him. The events of the evening came flooding back and he eyed Stratton with a bemused curiosity. Wasn't this guy supposed to be dead?

Jennings carried on coughing uncontrollably, his throat burning and his lungs bursting. He had no idea what was going on. The last memory he had was of Stella crashing to the ground next to him; and then nothing. The only thing he knew was that he was, quite painfully, alive. He lifted his head and saw the orange glow from the living room window and realized that the cottage was on fire.

He also realized that Stratton had saved him from certain death.

Stratton looked on forlornly. His lovely cottage was going to burn to the ground and there was nothing he could do about it. "Have either of you got your phones?" he asked. Both prostrate bodies shook their heads. His own phone was now probably a black splodge on the living room floor. There was no chance of getting the fire service; and more importantly there was no chance of getting an ambulance out to get the three of them. His bullet wound stung, but he would survive. He had no idea about Stella and Jennings though; his first aid was sketchy to say the least and they were in pretty bad shape.

Stella was now breathing easier and her coughing had reduced to the occasional tickle. Her lungs were clearing and her head was swimming less. What she really needed was a drink of water to soothe her arid throat. She sat up straight and turned to Stratton. "I need some water," she croaked softly.

"Sorry Stella, I can't go back in there," said Stratton.

"There's some," she stopped to gulp, "...some in the car."

Jennings, hearing the conversation, reached down to his trouser pocket and produced the car keys. Stratton got to his feet and raced round the side of the cottage.

Stella watched the cottage burn; it was faintly mesmeric. The fire had now engulfed the kitchen as well and was probably working its way up the stairs. The heat from the blaze was keeping them from freezing, but they were far enough away for it to be bearable; and the orange flames danced and flickered lightly, belying their true menace. She could almost be back in the Girl Guides sitting by a camp fire if the situation wasn't so dire.

Now that her breathing was less erratic, Stella's attention turned to her burns. She was still covered with the wet blanket that Stratton had dropped on her, and was loath to look underneath. Her legs weren't in any pain, but she didn't know if that was due to the soothing effect of the blanket, or because the wounds were superficial. She had witnessed the horrible sight of burns victims first hand, and she hoped that fortune had been kind, and that she had escaped before serious damage had been done.

She slowly lifted the blanket off her shoulders and looked down at her body. What was left of her blouse was a mixture of brown and black, with only a hint of the original white left at the sides. At first inspection her torso appeared to be unscarred, and for that she was grateful. She then peeled the blanket from her lower half, ripped off the remnants of her trousers, and scanned for damage on her legs. It was difficult to tell with only the light of the fire to go by, but apart from a few patches here and there, they appeared relatively unscathed. She had been lucky.

Jennings' breathing was still laboured. He too was covered with a wet blanket. He had been exposed to the flames for longer than Stella and she wondered how much damage he had sustained. She felt guilty that Stratton had rescued her first, even though it would have been natural for him to do so. On top of that, Jennings had stayed unconscious throughout, and wouldn't have had a chance to beat off the flames.

"How are you feeling?" said Stella. She knew it was a dumb question to be asking, but she thought it would be helpful to engage him and keep him conscious.

"I've been better," he whispered. His head stayed focused on the sky.

"Well, look on the bright side. By rights we should be dead now." She tried to be cheerful.

"Yes. It feels great to be alive. If we had some marshmallows we could toast them on a stick and sing campfire songs."

"There's no need to be sarcastic," said Stella. "I'm only trying to lighten the mood. I don't feel so great myself you know."

"Sorry," he said. "I'm just in a lot of pain at the moment."

Stella got to her feet and walked about. She was feeling stiff and needed to stretch her legs. She caught Jennings ogling her out of the corner of his eye, and became suddenly aware of her near nakedness. All that she had on was a singed blouse and a pair of knickers. "Never seen a pair of legs before?" she said.

"Not like those," said Jennings.

Stella took the compliment but swiftly changed the subject. "Before you woke up Stratton had his hands on your chest. I don't know what he was doing but it seemed to bring you round. Did you feel anything or don't you remember?"

"I don't remember a lot; just that when I came to it was like a bolt of lightning had hit me. It was sudden, and quite frightening to be honest. I still feel a bit freaked now. That man is strange."

"Isn't he just," agreed Stella.

It was then that Stratton reappeared in the back garden, holding two bottles of mineral water. He gave one to Stella and took the other to Jennings. He knelt beside Jennings, lifted his head slightly off the ground, and gently poured water into his mouth. Jennings sipped the water gladly, and although he found it difficult to swallow, it relieved the soreness in his throat wonderfully.

"If you two are ok for the moment, I'm going to take the car and get to a phone and call for help," said Stratton.

Both Stella and Jennings said they would be alright.

Stratton hurried round the side of the blazing building and ran to the car. It had been years since he had driven, and he was slightly worried about his capability to do so, particularly with his injured shoulder. But there was no time to dwell on the negatives; he had to get a move on.

He reversed the Lexus through the gate without trouble, and then backed it onto the grass verge and swung forwards onto the dirt track. He depressed the accelerator to the floor and sped off.

After a hundred yards he hit the brakes and skidded to an abrupt halt. At the side of the road there was another car, a green Ford Focus. The driver's door was open and next to it a man lay on the floor; the man was Scott Grady. On top of him, pinning him to the ground, was a large animal.

Stratton killed the engine and got out of the car. Titan was growling in the face of his quarry, who lay there motionless with fearful eyes.

Stratton chuckled to himself. "Having trouble are we?" he said.

Grady gave Stratton a pleading look. "Listen man, you've got to help me. This thing's going to eat me alive if you don't do something. Have you got a gun?"

"No I haven't," said Stratton. "But you have. Why haven't you used it? You were quick enough to shoot me."

"My gun's in its holster, I can't get to it. This fucking overgrown moggy is right on top of it."

Stratton moved closer to the supine Grady. "So you shoot me; set fire to my cottage; and leave me and my friends for dead; and now you expect me to help you. Is that right?"

"Well it doesn't sound good I know," said Grady. "But you know what it says in the Bible about turning the other cheek and forgiveness and all that other shit. Be the bigger man and help me out here brother."

Stratton shrugged his shoulders and opened his palms. "I don't know what you expect me to do. You've got a full-grown black panther on top of you. Who do you think I am? Doctor Dolittle?"

"Look, I don't know what you should do. Just do something quickly or I'm breakfast for Tiddles here."

Stratton walked over and put his hand on Titan's head and stroked him. The panther stopped growling and purred loudly. Stratton reached beneath Titan's paws and pulled the gun from Grady's holster.

"Okay, I'm going to call him off now," said Stratton. "Don't try anything or I'll shoot you."

"Don't worry, I know when the odds are against me," said

Grady.

At a word from Stratton the panther removed himself from Grady's torso and padded up to Stratton's side. He whispered something in Titan's ear, which Grady didn't catch, and the panther sloped off into the darkness.

"Nice pet," said Grady. "Where can I get myself one of those then?"

"Listen; cut the wisecracks for a minute will you mate. Have you got a mobile phone with you?"

"You mean a cell phone?"

"Yes. Mobile phone, cell phone, whatever. Have you got one?"

Grady said that he had and that it was in his jacket pocket. Stratton made him produce it slowly, all the time covering him with the gun. Grady complied and handed the phone to Stratton, who immediately called the emergency services.

With help now on its way Stratton returned to the back garden, taking Grady with him. Stella and Jennings were where he had left them, although Jennings was now sitting up. They stared in disbelief as Stratton walked up to them, holding a gun to the subdued Grady's back.

"Look what I found out front," said Stratton.

"Unbelievable," said Jennings. "How the hell did you catch him?"

"Never mind, it doesn't matter," said Stratton. "What's important is that the emergency services are on their way now. So hopefully we're all going to live."

At Stratton's instruction, Stella removed Grady's neck tie and used it to secure his wrists behind his back. She made sure she repaid the favour to Grady and made the binding extra tight. He pretended not to notice, but the tie bit into his wrists and hurt like hell.

It was now six am and dawn was breaking. To the left of the blazing cottage the horizon glowed salmon pink underneath a mackerel sky. Stella gazed out across the desolate frosty grassland; everything looked so peaceful. She wished that circumstances were different, and that she could go wandering off to enjoy the sweet solitude of the moors. Her mind had been crammed with so much information in the last twenty seven hours that she couldn't think any more. One thought after another collided in her brain; her head felt like a nuclear reactor. And with the added emotional stress of seeing Stratton, she was cracking up. She felt so tired that she could cry, and the only thing stopping her was pride. It wasn't fear of looking weak in front of the men though - it was more than that to Stella; she needed to prove to herself that she could handle the toughest of situations. Life was a constant challenge to her; once one obstacle had been overcome, there was another to conquer. The harder the test the more tenaciously she conditioned herself to beat it. There was no room for tears in Stella's world; tears were akin to defeat.

"Are you going to tell us how you got us out of there?" Jennings asked Stratton. "I mean, we thought you were dead, then suddenly you're up and about saving people."

"Yeah man," said Grady. "You were definitely dead. I've been around corpses long enough to know when someone's copped it."

"Okay, I'll tell you," said Stratton, who was secretly pleased with himself and his ingenuity. "After I got hit on the head I was out cold but only for a while. When I came to I realized that the only way I was going to save Stella was by taking myself out of the equation. I've practised yogic breathing techniques for years now, and I'm a bit of an expert. I can slow my breathing and heart rate down so that my pulse is virtually undetectable. Given the situation it was difficult, but I managed to switch myself off enough to get away with it. After you thought I was dead, I just lay there listening and deciding my next move. I smelled the petrol and realized that the cottage was going to go up in flames. I waited until the man here had gone," he pointed to Grady, "and then I got up. By this time the flames had spread all round the living room. I grabbed a couple of blankets from the hall cupboard, doused them in water and flung one over each of you. Then, as you know, I took you out one at a time. That's about it really."

"Wow," said Grady. "I'd heard stories of people slowing their pulse down to nothing; I never thought it was possible though. I'll have to learn that trick for myself. It'll be handy in the field."

Jennings looked curiously across at Grady. The man had been caught and tied up, and yet here he was chatting away without a care in the world, like they were all old friends. "You seem to be very calm and chatty for someone who's about to be charged with arson and three attempted murders."

Grady laughed. "Well there's no point worrying is there. And besides, I don't think I'll be in custody for long - you never heard of diplomatic immunity?"

"I don't think it'll count in this case," said Jennings defiantly.

"Well, whatever," said Grady. "But I don't think that my paymasters are going to want me locked up for too long. I know too much."

Jennings let it go. He could tell from his casual air that Grady fully expected to get away scot-free. And it would be no surprise to Jennings if he did. The US intelligence services got away with pretty much what they liked nowadays. Nobody ever wanted to jeopardize the 'special relationship' that existed between Britain and their transatlantic cousins. The faceless Whitehall suits would only too happily sweep something like this under the carpet, if it meant appeasing their precious Yankee masters; best keep it quiet, don't rock the boat. Carry on being the subservient poodle that the nation had become. Grady was right, justice would not be served this time.

In the distance the sound of sirens began to pierce the air.

"They're probably only a couple of miles away," said Stratton.

"Good," said Jennings. "I need to get somewhere

comfortable, and I don't care if it is a hospital bed. At least I'll get some food and some rest."

Stratton and Stella were thinking along the same lines. Stella wanted a bed and Stratton wanted his wound seen to. Grady was just thinking about how quickly he could get out of custody and onto a plane back to the States. There didn't seem much point hanging around now. There was also the cute blonde waitress that he'd been dating back home, he'd fallen for her big time and couldn't wait to see her again.

As the sirens approached Stratton handed the gun to Stella and went round to greet them. Stella kept the gun trained on Grady; he wasn't going anywhere but she still didn't trust him. Jennings saw the paramedics running into the back garden and lay down and closed his eyes; he cleared his mind and relaxed; someone else could do the worrying for a while.

Chapter 14

Jonathan Ayres had made the Prime Minister's office his own. One of his first actions when he came to power was to give his workplace a makeover. If he was going to spend the majority of his waking hours in one room, then that room had to be as he liked it. He had kept the grand mahogany desk and sumptuous leather chair left by his predecessor, but nearly everything else had gone. The once magnolia walls were now a warm turf green; and gone was the threadbare red carpet, replaced by a thick, close weave, cream material that you could lose your feet in. Pictures of his favourite racehorses were hung above and opposite the desk. And centre stage, across from his chair, was a brand new, state-of-the-art, multi media station; with a 52 inch plasma TV, hi-fi, PC, and various games consoles built in.

David Brennan had sat in this office before, with both Jonathan Ayres and the previous incumbent. He much preferred the new décor; it felt warmer and less like it was haunted by the ghosts of Prime Ministers past. It was now a room that you could speak your mind in; a room where an opinion would be listened to and taken on board, rather than dismissed out of hand as the ramblings of a child. This was the appeal of Jonathan Ayres. It was why people voted for him. His landslide victory had been based on his open easiness, and his 'man of the people' accessibility. He was a man that made you feel comfortable.

This morning however was not comfortable, for either Brennan or Ayres. Brennan had received a phone call from Stella Jones just before he went into the Prime Minister's office. She had brought him up to speed with a brief overview of the events of the previous night. Brennan had just relayed the information to Ayres and the Prime Minister sat opposite taking it in.

"So we don't know who this American is then?" said Ayres.

"No sir," replied Brennan. "But the suspicion is that he's

American intelligence; probably CIA. Whatever he is, he's given the impression that he'll get diplomatic immunity. Wasn't fazed by his arrest at all apparently."

Jonathan Ayres became visibly angry. "If he's got anything to do with Henry's murder then he's not going anywhere. I don't care how much of a stink the bloody Yanks make about it. I've had enough of them riding roughshod over this country; they're not infallible like they seem to think."

Brennan didn't know what to say, he'd never seen the Prime Minister lose his temper before. In the circumstances it was understandable, but it was still a shock to witness your head of government lose his cool nevertheless.

Jonathan Ayres picked up the phone and instructed the switchboard to get him Alan Weedon the head of MI5. There followed a brief conversation where Ayres told Weedon to find out exactly who the American was and for whom he was working. Weedon said he'd get straight onto it.

Ayres reached into his desk drawer and got out an ashtray. "Do you mind if I smoke David?" he asked. "I know I'm not supposed to in the workplace but I'm the Prime Minister for Christ's sake. I've got to have some privileges. Do you want one?"

"No thank you sir. I stopped a couple of years ago. But you go ahead," said Brennan.

Ayres lit a cigarette and took a deep drag. He exhaled slowly savouring the taste in his mouth and throat. He looked across at Brennan sitting obediently opposite, and sensed a slight discomfort in the man from Special Branch. His mind suddenly registered his faux pas and he stubbed out the cigarette. "Sorry David. That was really insensitive of me. I completely forgot."

"It's all right sir, you didn't have to put it out," said Brennan.

"Nonsense David, I should have thought before I even lit it up," Ayres said genuinely. "How is Anna by the way? Is the chemotherapy working?"

"She's not too bad thank you sir. She has good days and bad

days. She's got another scan tomorrow so we should know more then. I hope she'll have improved but you just don't know."

Jonathan Ayres eyed Brennan with admiration. "You do know that you can have compassionate leave whenever you want David? I can clear anything for you. You can have as long you like off: your job's always going to be there for you."

"Thank you sir, I appreciate it," said Brennan. "The thing is, I'd rather keep myself busy and not think about things at the moment. My job keeps me occupied, and it also keeps me sane. I'd go mad if I sat around at home all day. And more to the point, I'd drive Anna mad as well; she's told me as much. She wants to be independent for as long as is possible. She has a nurse pop in every day to see her and that's all she wants. She doesn't want to be treated like an invalid. She's a proud and brave woman: that's why I love her so much."

"Okay David, I appreciate the situation. Just remember: anytime."

The Prime Minister's phone rang loudly. It was Alan Weedon. After another brief exchange Ayres replaced the handset. "Well that's interesting," he said. "Weedon can't find anything out about this American bloke. But the Bitch Queen's on her way. Should be here in less than five minutes."

Both Brennan and Ayres rolled their eyes.

The Bitch Queen's real name was Helen Johnson and she was head of MI6, the British Secret Service. Brennan, Ayres, and just about anyone that knew her, shared a dislike for Ms Johnson. She was what Ayres described as an Uber Feminist. Women were revered and men were treated as a major inconvenience; she believed the world should be a matriarchy. And yet even her female colleagues secretly despised her. She was a manipulative, calculating, objectionably obdurate old witch. Her unfortunate appearance didn't help her cause either. Her slightly greasy black hair was always tied tightly back like an old schoolmarm, and her sharp features resembled those of the child catcher from

Chitty Chitty Bang Bang. She was 45 but her fashion sense, or lack of it, made her look about 65. She was the archetypical spinster, destined to grow old and bitter and lonely. As a consequence of this she was married to her job and, as nearly everyone agreed, was exceptionally good at it.

Helen Johnson knocked on the door and entered the Prime Minister's office simultaneously; a habit that constantly annoyed Ayres. It showed a blatant lack of respect for his position as head of government, and it was also downright rude.

"I don't know why you bother knocking Helen, just come straight in," said Ayres, half jovially.

Johnson said nothing, but gave the Prime Minister daggers and sat down on a chair next to Brennan.

"So Helen, what can I do for you this morning?" said Ayres.

"It's more what I can do for you Prime Minister," she replied curtly. "I've got the information you wanted about the American they're holding down in Exeter. I'm afraid you're not going to like it very much."

Ayres sighed; he never liked any information provided by Johnson very much. "Well go on then Helen. Who is he? And who does he work for?"

"His name is Scott Grady and he doesn't officially work for anybody," said Johnson. "He's a computer salesman from Ohio according to his papers. Unofficially though, I suspect that he's one of these floaters the Yanks use from time to time. UFA's I believe they're called: unaffiliated field agents. Very professional and very dangerous."

Ayres interrupted. "What do you mean you suspect? Don't you know for sure?"

Helen Johnson looked agitated but kept her composure. "There's no way of knowing for sure - he has no file; not anywhere. All I know is that I've had a call from Bob Tobin at the CIA this morning, and this Grady chap is to be released without charge."

Jonathan Ayres banged his hand on the desk. "I will not kowtow to those bloody Yanks anymore. This man's shot someone and tried to murder three people that we know of. He may have murdered Henry Mulholland as well, for all that we know. We're going to keep him in custody and get the truth from him."

"With all due respect Prime Minister, I don't think you understand the situation fully," said Johnson.

"I understand that yet again we're expected to roll over and have our tummy tickled like a good dog. I've told you before Helen, this has got to stop." Ayres gave her a look that even she couldn't stare down.

"Believe me Prime Minister, if it could be any other way then it would be. But in the intelligence community it has to be give and take, and the Americans do help us out an awful lot. We can't afford to jeopardize our relationship with them. The best I can do is to try and get the Americans to cooperate with us. With a little sweet talking they might let us question Grady in an unofficial capacity."

"Well that's better than nothing I suppose," said Ayres, resigned to it. "He obviously knows something about this business. Do you think they'll help us out?"

"There's only one way to find out," said Johnson, and picked up her phone and stepped outside the office.

When Johnson was out of earshot Ayres turned to Brennan. "Listen David, if she does get them to agree, I want you to speak to this guy. I want to be kept in the loop on this one. M16 will do things their own way and Johnson will feed me bullshit just to pacify me. I trust you and I know you'll play it straight with me."

"Of course sir, whatever you think is best," said Brennan. "If he knows something then we'll get it out of him. I'll keep you informed of all developments. I know how important this is to you. I'd feel the same if it were my best friend."

"Thank you David. I know you won't let me down."

Two minutes later Helen Johnson returned to the room. She

informed Ayres and Brennan that, under orders from the CIA, Scott Grady would be cooperating with the investigation.

"Excellent," said Ayres. "Thank you Helen."

"No problem," she replied. "We'll get someone down there to pick him up straight away."

Ayres shifted awkwardly. "Actually Helen, the thing is, I'd prefer it if we left this one to David here and Special Branch. It is their investigation after all, and bringing too many departments in is just going to confuse matters. Too many cooks spoil the broth and all that."

Helen Johnson's lips thinned and her nostrils flared, but she kept her composure. "Well, if that's the way you want it Prime Minister. Although technically this has become an intelligence matter now and therefore falls under my jurisdiction."

"I'm aware of that Helen and it's no disrespect to you but I'd really like to keep this in David's hands. I'm sure he's quite capable of dealing with it, and I'm sure if he has any problems with the Americans he'll come straight to you," he turned to Brennan. "Won't you David?"

"Of course sir," Brennan agreed.

With that, Helen Johnson mumbled a couple of goodbyes and exited the room with a face that would have made Medusa envious.

Both men, who had been sitting stiffly, relaxed in their chairs again.

"Thank God for that," said Ayres. "I thought she was going to be really difficult about this."

"I wouldn't be too certain that she's going to leave us to it, sir. I'm sure she's going to monitor the situation and stick her huge proboscis in at some point. She's not the type to let anything go, she's a control freak."

"Maybe so," said Ayres. "But for now it's in your hands David. So I suggest you get onto this Grady character straight away and see what he knows."

Chapter 15

Jennings sat up in his hospital bed and pushed some nondescript food around his plate. He was feeling much better now and needed to eat. As unappetising as it was, the meal in front of him was the only thing available. There were mashed potatoes and there were peas and carrots. The remainder of the plate was filled with a layer of pastry that covered some gravy, and a few sorry-looking bits of grey meat of dubious origin. In the absence of anyone willing to go down to Burger King he began to tuck in.

Stella walked into G bay where Jennings was situated and sat down next to the bed. "Mmm, that looks nice," she said. "Makes me want some myself."

Jennings raised an eyebrow to her. "Don't be funny. I'm starving, and this is all there is. Did you call Brennan on the number I gave you?"

"Yes, I did," replied Stella. "I let him know what happened last night and about Stratton and the American. I didn't go into lots of detail, he was just on his way in to see the Prime Minister, but I gave him the facts. He didn't seem that happy with the situation, and he was concerned about you when I told him you were being treated and couldn't come to the phone."

"What does he want us to do now?" asked Jennings between mouthfuls.

"Nothing really. He's not going to tell me a lot is he? Remember I'm not part of Special Branch any more. He did say that he'd call me back after he'd finished with the Prime Minister to see how you were."

As if on cue, the mobile in her pocket (which they'd confiscated from Grady) began to ring. She rushed out of the ward, with the nurse giving her a dirty look for having a phone switched on, and took the call in the corridor.

Jennings carried on eating his food thoughtfully. Everything had happened so quickly that he was only just starting to take in the events of the previous evening. He had been close to death, he knew that, and the enigmatic Stratton had saved him. He was glad to be alive but he felt hugely indebted to Stratton.

As a general rule Jennings didn't like to owe anybody anything, he was careful with his money, and if someone did him a favour he would return it as soon as he could. Self-sufficiency was his way of life and he firmly believed in the old adage 'neither a borrower nor a lender be'. Now he owed somebody his life, and although he was filled with gratitude he couldn't help feeling there would be a price to pay.

What scared him the most was that this debt couldn't be repaid by material means; he felt that Stratton now owned part of his soul and that it would take a colossal act of self-sacrifice to reclaim it.

"How are you feeling?" said a voice beside him, waking him from his thoughts. It was Stratton.

"I'm good thanks," said Jennings. "Thanks to you, that is."

"Don't mention it. I'm sure you would have done the same thing."

"Would I? I suppose so," said Jennings, not convinced that he was either that strong or that brave. "Either way, I owe you one."

"Don't be silly," said Stratton, his eyes beaming. "I did what anybody would have done. If you're in a position to help somebody, then you do it. Right?"

Jennings eyed Stratton carefully. There was something warm and kindly about him today. He still had an air of peculiarity, but in the light of day it was welcoming, not like the unsettling presence Jennings had felt the night before. He didn't know whether it was due to having become used to Stratton's manner, or whether Stratton's mood had lightened. Either way his worries about owing Stratton his life had dissipated; the man beside him definitely wanted nothing in return for his courageous actions; the deed itself appeared reward enough.

"Anyway, more to the point, how are you?" Jennings asked. "You're the one who got shot."

"I'll survive," said Stratton smiling. "I've had an X-ray and all my bones are still intact; the bullet went straight through my flesh. Clean entry and clean exit wound. The nurse has put a dressing on it and we'll just have to see how it heals. There could be some muscle damage but to be honest it feels ok. I've got away pretty lightly considering."

"Did she give you any painkillers?"

"Yes, but I haven't taken any yet. I'll save them; just in case it really starts to hurt. Like I said, at the moment I'm fine."

Jennings was amazed by Stratton's resilience. He'd been with gunshot victims before and none of them had been as nonchalant as this about their wounds. There was always some sign of pain, be it an intake of breath, or a contortion of the features, or both. But not so much as a wince had crossed Stratton's face, even when using his arm to gesticulate. It was totally unnatural, yet completely in keeping with Stratton's anomalous character. He was the sort of person that would always surprise you even after a lifetime of friendship, thought Jennings; a man of unplumbable depths.

Stella arrived back and grabbed a chair next to Stratton. "Well do you want the bad news or the worse news?" She said.

"Either will do," said Jennings.

"Well, first of all, Brennan's on his way down here."

"Oh, ok," said Jennings. "Why's that?"

"Well that's the worse news," said Stella. "They're letting that American agent go without charge."

Jennings choked and spat out the mouthful of pie that he'd just forked into his mouth. "What!?"

"Turns out that he's got diplomatic immunity. Brennan didn't say as much or go into detail, but it seems pretty clear that the Yanks have put the pressure on us to release him," said Stella. "There is some good news though: he's got to assist Brennan with the investigation and tell us all he knows."

"Well that'll be helpful," said Jennings. "If he knew that much he wouldn't have followed us all the way down here, would he?"

Stella and Stratton chatted to each other as Jennings finished his food. He was annoyed about the American and there was little point talking to him. The conversation was light and trivial but not stilted as it can be with ex-lovers. There were underlying depths of feeling that both were aware of, but for the moment they had hit upon a comfortable, unspoken understanding. An onlooker would have put them down as old friends, catching up with each other after a couple of years.

Jennings pushed his plate away and took a drink of water. "What time does Brennan expect to be here?" He asked.

"Well, it's ten now and he was just leaving when I spoke to him, so traffic permitting, and with some fast driving, he should be here between one and half past."

"Okay then, good. That'll give me a chance for a couple of hours' sleep, and then I can discharge myself," said Jennings, who was feeling more than optimistic about his state of health.

Stella and Stratton were both extremely tired as well. They left Jennings to doze and got a taxi to the local Travelodge, where they booked a twin room and settled down for their first sleep in over twenty four hours. They were out cold as soon as they hit their beds.

Chapter 16

David Brennan didn't arrive in Exeter until four o'clock in the afternoon. There had been a major accident where the M4 met the M5. By the time Jerry pulled the car up outside the Royal Devon and Exeter hospital he was grouchy and hungry.

After hastily finding a toilet, he followed the signs to reception so as to enquire after Jennings. To his surprise Jennings was waiting patiently on a blue plastic chair next to the reception desk.

"You're not that bad then," he said grumpily.

"Depends what you consider bad sir," Jennings replied. "I was bad enough for them to admit me this morning, and I'm still bad enough for them to want to keep me in overnight. I've grabbed four hours' sleep but I'm still dog tired, and the only reason I've signed myself out is because you were coming down and I want to help you with the investigation. So no sir, I'm not *that* bad."

"Sorry Jennings," said Brennan. "I've had a long journey and I've been stuck in a traffic jam for over two hours."

"That's ok sir, I understand."

"Nice outfit by the way, very retro," said Brennan, remarking on the brown corduroy trousers and light blue Hawaiian shirt that he was dressed in.

"Yes, isn't it? My clothes were burnt in the fire and I had to get one of the nurses to find me something to wear. I don't know where she found these; probably lost property or else they're some dead person's. Either way I'm not going to be wowing them down at China White's am I?"

Brennan laughed. "Not unless they're holding a seventies night."

They walked out of the hospital and went to the car where Jerry was waiting for them. Brennan instructed him to take them to Exeter Central police station, where Grady was still in custody. Jerry typed the destination into his SatNav and they set off.

When they arrived at Exeter Central the desk sergeant was unusually pleased to see them. "Thank God you're here," he said. "That Yank's been doing our heads in all day. Keeps ringing his bell wanting to go to the toilet, wanting to have a cigarette, wanting to have a MacDonald's, wanting to make phone calls...the list goes on and on. The only reason we're putting up with it is because of orders from above to treat him well. If it wasn't for that then...." The sergeant stopped before incriminating himself. "Anyway, we'll be glad to see the back of him."

Two minutes later a young constable appeared at the desk, with a handcuffed and sour-looking Grady in tow.

"Can we take these off?" asked the constable, addressing Brennan and pointing to the cuffs.

"Yes you can. I don't think he's going anywhere," said Brennan. "Are you Mr Grady?"

Grady grunted. "No, I'm all yours."

The handcuffs were removed and Grady followed Brennan and Jennings out to the car. Brennan and Jennings were both hungry and so it was decided that they should find somewhere to eat, and at the same time get some answers from Grady. Jennings nipped back into the police station to get the name of somewhere good to eat, and returned to the car with the suggestion of an excellent curry house called Vinda Roo, which was just down the road. The restaurant was run by an Indian man and his Australian wife, and they were on friendly terms with the local police who were regular customers. The desk sergeant suggested that they would get a discount if they mentioned his name.

"Do they serve steak?" asked Grady.

"I don't know," said Jennings, "they might do. Why? Don't you like Indian food?"

"No idea, never had the stuff," replied Grady. "Don't they cook dogs and cats and shit like that? Give me a good old New

Yorker steak any day."

Jennings laughed. "No they don't cook cats and dogs. I think that happens in Korea. Indian food is great, a staple of the British diet; you have to try it."

"Well whatever," said Grady. He remained unconvinced.

It was just gone six o'clock when they entered Vinda Roo. They were the first customers and received a friendly welcome from the proprietor; an attractive blonde lady in her thirties with a mild antipodean accent. The restaurant had room for 60 diners; to the back there were six cubicles that seated four each; these niches were separated by rows of tropical plants and gave a high level of comfort and privacy. In keeping with the foliage the walls were decorated with a warm green paper with an exotic gold print.

After being seated at the back in the secluded area they ordered some drinks. Grady wasn't happy at the lack of Budweiser and, on the recommendation of Jennings, had to settle for a bottle of Cobra. Marie, the proprietor, assured him that it was good and wasn't made of real cobras.

Grady stared blankly at the menu. "What is all this shit?" he said. "What's a pakora? Sounds like you should be wearing it, not eating it."

Jennings shook his head. "I'll tell you what, just let me order for you, I'll make sure you get something you'll enjoy. How hot do you like your food?"

"Well, I like it to be cooked through," replied Grady.

"No. How spicy do you like it?"

"Hey, the hotter the better for me. I've got an iron stomach and an asbestos mouth."

"Oh ok," said Jennings, only too happy to test out Grady's bravado.

For appearances sake, Jennings was being sociable to Grady, but underneath there was a part of him that was seething at the lack of justice. To him it seemed grossly unfair that a man who had left him for dead was now being fed and pampered at the expense of the taxpayer; and all in the name of international relations.

He knew that this sort of thing went on all the time in the world of secret service politics, and it was something that happened to a lesser extent at his own level, but it didn't make it any easier to take when it was yourself on the receiving end, and it didn't make it right.

The drinks arrived along with some poppadums and relishes. Grady nibbled tentatively at first, but once he'd had a taste his misgivings soon began to disappear, and he found the beer was good too. Brennan, Jennings and Jerry dived in hungrily as well.

"So Mr Grady," said Brennan between mouthfuls, "what is the purpose of your visit to the UK? And why did you try to kill my man Jennings here?"

Grady took a swig of beer. "I'm here because I was sent here to locate some sort of antique box. I don't know what it's for or what it's worth, I was just told to find it." He dipped a poppadum into some raita and took a bite. "The only reason I tried to kill Jennings here, is because he'd witnessed me shooting that Stratton guy, who I thought was dead. I'm not paid to leave witnesses; I'm paid to be invisible and to be in and out of places like a ghost. Of course, all that's fucked now. Your lot at M15 and M16 will have me on their computer, and that means I'm virtually worthless: I rely on my anonymity. Does that answer your questions?"

"To a certain extent," said Brennan. "I'm more interested about what you know about Henry Mulholland."

"That's the rich guy who got whacked the other night right?"

"Yes. What do you know about it?"

"Only what I heard on the radio," said Grady. "Why? What should I know about it?"

"Well, it appears that there is a connection between his murder and this box you're trying to find," said Brennan.

Grady finished his poppadum and wiped his mouth with a serviette. "I know there's a connection. I heard Jennings and the other two talking about it last night. But I didn't know of any connection until then. Are you suggesting I had something to do with Mulholland's murder? Because if you are then you're barking up the wrong tree. You're not even in the right wood."

"Do you have an alibi?" asked Brennan. "Where were you between the hours of one o'clock and three thirty early Thursday morning?"

"On a Boeing 747 heading for Heathrow airport," Grady said confidently. "I believe we landed at four thirteen am GMT. You can check the flight records if you like. I've got nothing to do with it."

"Ok then, but I will check you were on the flight," said Brennan.

Marie arrived with the main course and they ate in semi silence. Jennings had ordered the hottest dish on the menu for Grady, a chicken phaal. He took great pleasure in watching Grady's face strain as he chewed on the first mouthful.

"Ok, is it?" Jennings asked.

"Yeah, real tasty," said Grady reaching for the water jug and pouring himself a large glass.

After the meal was finished Brennan continued to question Grady. "So Mr Grady, can you tell us who you actually work for, or is that off limits?"

Grady, still suffering from toxic shock, wiped the sweat from his brow and mopped his moistened eyes. "No it's not off limits. I've been told to cooperate fully with you, so that's what I'm going to do." He filled his glass with water again and took a sip.

"I don't work for anybody in particular, I'm a freelance. I'm over here at the request of a Professor Miles from the National Institute of Paranormal Studies in California. He gave me Stratton's name and where to locate him, don't ask me how he knew, and he also gave me a description of the box. Like I said before, I don't know anything more than you do about Mulholland or the whereabouts of the box. And quite frankly I'm past caring, I just want to get on home and get back to a normal life. As of now I'm retired."

"We'll get you home as soon as possible Mr Grady, but for the moment I'd like to keep you over here. And I'd also like to speak with this Professor Miles if I could. Will that be possible?"

"I guess so," said Grady. "And you can just call me Grady if you like; I don't like all this 'Mr' shit. Makes me feel like I'm being questioned by the IRS."

Brennan called for the bill.

"What do we do now sir?" asked Jennings.

"We carry on searching for Mulholland's killer," said Brennan.

Jennings shuffled tentatively in his seat. "With your permission sir, I'd quite like to keep on the trail of this box. It appears to hold the key to everything. If we find it then maybe we'll find the killer as well. We could draw him out."

"I think you've been watching too many movies Jennings. Murderers don't just show themselves on a whim because of some antique. If he's clever enough to elude the security at Addington House then he's not going to turn up right in front of us to get this box."

"I understand what you're saying sir," said Jennings deferentially. "But it really is the only lead we have. And I think that with Stratton's help we can find it. And also, if someone's willing to kill to get hold of this thing then they're not going to give up the chase lightly. Are they?"

The bill arrived and Brennan handed over his credit card. He had mentioned the desk sergeant's name; and did indeed receive a discount.

"I suppose you have a point there," Brennan conceded. "The trouble is, I'm not sure if I can justify you going off on some wild goose chase when I need you working with the rest of the team. There is a more conventional investigation going on you know;

involving forensics and a lot of officers door knocking in the local area. I know it's boring work but it does pay dividends in the long run."

Jennings didn't want to appear insubordinate, but neither did he want to give up. "Again sir, I see your point. But I really think this is the way forward; if I thought it was a waste of time I wouldn't have suggested it. Just give me a few days to come up with some more information. If it comes to nothing then I'll join the rest of the team and work extra hours to make up the time."

Brennan recognized the determined look on his face and knew that Jennings was going to keep on until he relented. "Ok then, if you're that certain about it I'll give you this weekend to find the box. I'll put you down as on sick leave; recovering from the trauma of last night. You probably deserve a few days off anyway. But come Monday morning I want you back on the case with the rest of us. Ok."

Jennings tried not to look too pleased with himself. "Yes sir, thank you very much," he said.

It was seven thirty by the time they left the restaurant, and Brennan was in a hurry to start the journey back to London. After phoning Stella and finding out where she and Stratton were, Jennings was dropped off at the Travelodge, and Brennan headed back for home with Grady in tow.

Jennings booked himself a room and headed to the bar to meet up with Stratton and Stella. They were sitting at a table in the corner of a typically sterile and lifeless lounge area. He ordered himself a double scotch with ice and went to join them.

"Nice threads," said Stratton as Jennings approached. "How are the rest of the Brady Bunch?"

Jennings ignored the comment and sat down. "Right then, I've got 'til Monday morning before Brennan wants me back. So where do we go from here?"

"We've just been discussing that," said Stella, "and Stratton thinks we should head up to his parents' house. He thinks that the missing pages of the transcript are probably up there with the rest of his grandfather's things."

"Ok, we'll go first thing in the morning," said Jennings.

"Is there no chance of going tonight?" asked Stratton. "I really don't think we should waste any time on this."

Jennings sipped his whisky. "I appreciate that, but I'm tired and I need a good night's sleep. And besides, I've just paid for a room and we won't be able to get the car back until the morning. We'll all think a lot better after a rest." He downed the rest of his drink and bade them a good night.

Stratton looked unhappy but accepted the situation. Maybe Jennings was right, he thought, perhaps a good night's sleep was what they all needed. His brain saw the logic in it, and yet there was an underlying doubt eating away at him. A voice inside was telling him that delaying their departure was a mistake. He felt his sixth sense trying to warn him of something but he didn't know what.

"Are you all right?" asked Stella.

"Yes I'm fine," he said. "Just a bit overtired: I'm thinking too much. Paranoia's kicking in. I'm sure I'll be ok in the morning." He finished his mineral water. "Come on, let's get some sleep."

They went to their room and went to bed. Stratton's sleep was fitful. However hard he tried to silence his mind, the voice kept coming back. Something was terribly wrong.

Chapter 17

Behind the row of shops that sit beneath the maisonettes on the Chobham Road, Sunningdale, lies a private road called Broomfield Park. It is a quiet and leafy estate populated by wealthy stockbrokers, CEOs, and the occasional famous person. The houses are all set back from the road, and the majority have driveways barred by large, ornately wrought gates, and there is a twenty four hour security patrol funded by the residents. Both Sunningdale and Wentworth lie within close proximity for the avid golfer.

Kitty and Howard had lived on Broomfield since the early seventies. It was there that they had brought up their two boys. Howard had been a highly successful broker in the city, and Kitty had been a stay-at-home wife; as was the way in the days before women's lib had truly captured the female imagination. She had doted on her two sons, and had watched them grow from mischievous young scamps into fine young men, both of whom had graduated from Oxford with firsts. Of course there had been ups and downs, as there were in any family, but all in all life had treated them very kindly. Some might have said that the house was too big for them, now that the boys were long gone. But it was filled with so many warm memories that neither could envisage themselves living anywhere else. This was their home and would be until they passed on.

It was ten to midnight when Howard stepped through the front door. He had been having a late dinner at Wentworth with a couple of friends. Kitty was sitting in a chair by the fire engrossed in the latest Michael Crichton. She barely looked up as she asked if he'd had a good evening. Howard poured himself a large Lafraoig and sat down in his own chair on the opposite side of the inglenook. He took a delicious sip and felt the honeyed liquid warm his throat as he reflected in the glow of the flames.

He'd been retired for five years now and was still enjoying every minute of it. Many of his peers had found retirement boring and had gone back to work, if only part time, to keep themselves occupied. Howard, however, didn't miss working at all; he'd done his stint, thirty five years in the city to provide for his brood, and now he was reaping the benefits. He played golf four days a week and bridge three nights a week. The rest of his time was devoted to his garden and his beloved Kitty.

Howard finished his whisky and said goodnight to Kitty, who said that she'd be up in a while, after she'd finished the next chapter of her book. Fifteen minutes later Kitty put down her novel and got ready to go upstairs. As always, she went to the kitchen to make sure that all the appliances were switched off. Then, as usual, she poured herself a glass of water to take to bed. She turned off the strip light in the kitchen and made her way to the bottom of the stairs, where, as was the norm, Howard's loafers were strewn haphazardly: having been kicked off in a carefree stupor. She picked up the offending items and placed them neatly on the shoe rack. She was about to turn off the hall light when she noticed something odd: the landing light was switched off.

Howard, for all his faults, like Kitty, was very much a creature of habit. However drunk he got of an evening, he would always leave the landing light on for her. Perhaps he really was out of it this evening, she thought. She flicked the switch at the bottom of the stairs and realized that Howard hadn't forgotten at all: the light bulb had gone. Leaving the hall light on to guide her, she made her way up the stairs slowly, watching every step carefully. At the top she noticed that, thankfully, Howard had had the sense to leave the bedroom light on.

Kitty turned into the bedroom expecting to find Howard snoring away on the far side of the bed. He wasn't there. Before she had time to really register this fact a gloved hand had reached from behind and covered her mouth; her glass of water went flying. Instinctively she bit hard into one of the fingers, but the hand didn't budge. She was forced forward onto the bed and she felt a sharp pain on the back of her head.

When she came to, she found herself still in the bedroom, sitting upright in her make up chair. Across from her on the other side of the bed was Howard, sitting stiff as a board in a chair acquired from his office. Behind him was a Japanese man, dressed in black, holding a knife to his throat.

Kitty tried to scream but found herself unable to make a sound.

"Don't bother Madam Kitty, you cannot speak unless I release you," said the man. "And in any case it would be pointless, and very harmful to your husband here. If you refuse to cooperate with me then I will slit his throat right across. I believe that they call it a 'Chelsea smile': such a cheerful phrase for such a bloody deed - don't you think?...Anyway, let us get to the business in hand. I'm looking for a small wooden box..."

He described the box to Kitty and showed her a picture of the Cho Ku Rei symbol. She had seen the symbol before - her youngest son was into Oriental therapy - but she knew nothing of any box. She had no way of conveying this information though, because she was paralysed and her voice box was frozen.

Yoshima made a sign in the air and released Kitty from her temporary paralysis. "Anything to tell me?" he asked.

Kitty found herself shaking. "I...I recognize the symbol," she stammered, "B...b...but I don't know anything about a box."

"How do you recognize the symbol?" Yoshima pressed.

Kitty took a deep breath and calmed herself. "My son. I recognize it from some of his writings. I think it has something to do with Oriental medicine."

Yoshima briefly held Kitty's eyes with a look that bored through her skull; then his gaze slackened and he took in her whole face. She was very beautiful. He could tell from her eyes and cheekbones that she was of Oriental descent: Burmese if he wasn't mistaken. It was a pity that it had come to this, he thought; having to torture an Easterner; one of his own as he saw her. His fight was with the West; the greedy self-serving West. It saddened him that the rapacious appetite of the Occident had forced this situation. But ultimately, he told himself, she had chosen her own fate and she was one of them now. She had slept with the enemy and now she was the enemy.

"Are you sure that you know nothing of a box?" he asked again.

"I'm sure. I promise you," she said.

Yoshima looked into her eyes again, and deemed that she was telling the truth. But there was no harm in double checking, he thought. With a wave of his hand he paralysed her again and went back to the conscious but motionless Howard. He drew his sharp knife and in one swift movement he brought it down on the little finger of Howard's left hand, and sliced it clean off. He then made a sign and released Howard, who felt a sudden surge of pain coming from where his smallest digit had been. He let out a cry and his eyes started to water.

"Quiet!" ordered Yoshima. "Or your wife will receive the same treatment."

Howard whimpered softly but kept his mouth closed.

"Now Madam Kitty," said Yoshima releasing her. "I ask you again. Are you sure you know nothing about a box?"

"No, I don't," said Kitty despairingly. "Please don't hurt him any more."

Realizing that he would get nothing else from her, he paralysed her again and turned his inquisition to Howard.

"Now Howard," he said, as if speaking to an old friend. "Let us resolve this without any more unpleasantness. All I want is to find the box that I have spoken of. Do you know where I might find such an item?"

"I don't know what you're talking about. Just go away and leave my wife and I in peace," said Howard bravely, trying to hide his fear.

"Well Howard, I would gladly go away, but I don't believe you. I believe that your wife knows nothing - it is in her eyes. But your eyes are telling me a very different story. Your eyes are hiding something. Years of experience tell me so."

"Well your experience must be wrong then," said Howard, "because I don't know anything."

"Ok, we'll play it your way," said Yoshima, walking back towards Kitty, knife in hand.

Howard, realizing that Yoshima had forgotten to restrain him, leaped out of his chair and dived for Yoshima's legs. Yoshima was caught unawares and crashed to the ground. Howard forced himself on top of the Japanese and tried to wrestle the knife from his hand. But although Howard was himself a strong man, and larger and heavier than his opponent, he was no match for Yoshima's disproportionate power and superior technique. As quickly as it had started, it was over, and Yoshima had Howard pinned to the ground unable to move.

"That was silly of me," said Yoshima. "Forgetting to keep you disabled. I shall have to be more careful."

He picked Howard up off the floor and marched him back to the chair. After disabling him he moved back to Kitty. Without a word he sliced off her ring finger, wedding band and all.

"You have yourself to thank for that Howard," said Yoshima coldly. "Now, tell me about the box."

He released Howard and waited.

"Ok, ok. Just don't hurt her again," Howard pleaded. "I know that there is a box like the one you described, but I have no idea where it is. I remember seeing it as a child, it was my father's. I never got a good look at it because he was always very secretive about it. But I knew it was obviously important because of the way he acted."

"Ok, well done Howard," said Yoshima. "Now we are getting somewhere. So what happened to it?"

"I told you before, I have no idea. I never saw it after about the age of ten. Whenever I mentioned it after that my father would only say 'what box?' and tell me that I was imagining things. Whatever happened to it, only he knew."

Yoshima sighed. "What happened to your father's belongings when he died?"

"We auctioned a lot of it off, but we kept the important family stuff. There was definitely no box."

"What about letters and diaries? Did he leave anything like that?"

Howard wanted to clam up, but found himself unable to do so under Yoshima's icy glare. "Yes, there were some, he loved to write and keep a diary."

There was a silence.

"Well, what happened to them?" growled Yoshima, becoming impatient.

Howard thought for a moment. If he told the truth then his children would be in danger. If he lied Yoshima would know, then it would be Kitty. He would have to tell the truth and hope that he could get word to the boys when Yoshima left. "They were passed on. Kept in the family," he admitted.

Yoshima saw the truth in Howard's eyes and was satisfied. "Thank you Howard. You have been most helpful."

Before Howard could make another sound, Yoshima had thrust the knife directly into his heart. He turned round, walked over to Kitty, and repeated the action. There could be no witnesses.

He looked at his watch; it was one twenty five am. He had five minutes before the security patrol did its half-hourly lap of the estate. He took his balaclava out of his pocket and pulled it over his head. Then, with athletic grace, he climbed out of the window and disappeared into the dark.

Chapter 18

Stratton woke up again. He was drifting in and out of sleep; such as he hadn't done in a long, long while. The last time he had slept so badly was years before, in the times when his daily diet consisted of two bottles of vodka and three grams of charley. Nowadays he didn't touch the stuff, but tonight the paranoid nightmares had returned to haunt him nevertheless. He felt cold and clammy, just like he used to, and his head was filled with terrifying images; bloody and violent and yet non-specific. The 'drunken horrors' had come back, but this time they were unaided, this time they were just 'horrors'.

He looked at the clock on the bedside table: it was four am. In the old days he would have rolled a strong joint to knock himself out for the rest of the night. Now he didn't know what to do. He'd tried all his breathing exercises, and they had worked, but only briefly. Within half an hour he was waking up again.

As quietly as he could, so as not to disturb Stella, he fumbled around for his clothes and got dressed. It was no use trying to sleep any more so he decided to go for a walk. He slipped out of the room with a minimum of fuss and gently clicked the door shut behind him. He walked down the long and sterile corridor and turned into the main reception area. There was no-one about except the night watchman, who gave him no more than a cursory glance, and went back to reading his book. Stratton breezed past and wandered out of the double doors into the cold.

The air was fresh but not unpleasant, and he took a few deep breaths to empty his lungs of the stuffiness of the motel. The heating had been up way too high and had probably contributed to his inability to sleep. Now he was outside he felt his acute claustrophobia lift and his head began to clear. He strode through the car park and up to the main road. Then he took a left turn and started down the grass verge adjacent to the highway.

He had no idea where he was going, he just needed to keep on the move. He would have preferred to go for a run, but as his trainers were now toast along with the rest of his belongings, he would have to settle for a lesser pace.

The road was quiet, but not unnervingly so. There was a constant trickle of traffic heading towards the city centre: mainly vans and lorries bearing supplies for stores and restaurants. Though Stratton hardly noticed these as he strolled along, suffused in the bright orange glow of the street lights. His mind was elsewhere: his mind was with his parents.

It had been years since he had visited the family home. The last time he had been there was back in his mid-twenties, when he was still with Stella. It was a time when his drinking and drug taking had been at their height. His parents had thrown a New Year's Eve party, and invited nearly all of their relatives and most of the neighbourhood. The evening had been going well, and everyone was having a great time, until just gone midnight. This was when Stratton's father had caught him snorting cocaine in the bathroom. Stratton had stupidly forgotten to lock the door, and his father had walked in just as he bent down; nose to note and note to mirror. Harsh words had been exchanged. The argument had snowballed and turned into a blazing row that covered nearly everything that had ever happened between them, culminating in Stratton blaming his dad for his grandfather's death. This had stung and Stratton had been told to leave and not come back.

Relations had thawed somewhat in the intervening years, but there was still an atmosphere hanging over them. They had met up at various family functions, and gotten along as best they could, but Stratton had not been back to the house since. He knew that his father had forgiven him, he just wasn't sure that he'd forgiven himself. What he'd said had cut deep, and he could blame the drink and coke all he wanted, but the words had been uttered and there was no way of taking them back.

The argument with his father wasn't the only thing bothering him though. There was something else, something he couldn't quite explain. When he had phoned his mother the previous evening to tell her that he was coming up, he had felt a strange knotting in his stomach. There had been a sudden, frantic urge to get there as soon as possible. Although there had not been even a hint of worry in her voice, something was telling him that he was needed back home. He had put it down to the anxiety of the day's events, but he had not been able to shake it off. And although his bloody dreams had been faceless, he had woken up thinking about his parents.

After he had walked what felt like a couple of miles he decided to turn around and go back to the motel. His head was feeling much clearer and he wanted to get back into the warm. He also wanted to talk to Stella, not for any particular reason, but just because chatting to her and being around her was comforting. Over the years he had forgotten how good a friend she had been. When he got back to the room the light was on and Stella was sitting on the edge of her bed.

"Where've you been?" she asked. "I was starting to worry."

"I've been out for a walk. I couldn't sleep. Don't know why, I was just feeling restless," he said. "And you don't need to worry about me. I'm a big boy, I can look after myself."

"Can you?" she said. "I don't remember you ever doing that."

Stratton laughed. "I suppose you're right, but times have changed; I've changed."

She smiled. "Yes you have."

They held each other's eyes affectionately for a brief moment and then, each feeling a little awkward, they both looked away. Stella became suddenly aware that she was dressed in only a T-shirt and pulled it a little further down her legs.

"What time do they start serving breakfast here?" asked Stratton. "I'm starving."

"Seven o'clock I think," said Stella. "That gives us half an hour. I'm going to have a shower, unless you want to use it first?"

"No, you go ahead. I'll grab one later on."

Stella locked herself in the bathroom and Stratton lay on the bed and closed his eyes. He wondered how his life would have turned out had Stella not left him all those years ago. If he had stopped drinking sooner would they have stayed together? Perhaps they would have got married and by now they might have had children. Would this have been better than his current situation?

He had learnt so much in the years they had been apart, and not just acquired knowledge; he had learnt about himself. He doubted very much if he would have attained so much spiritual growth if he had been married with kids. And yet however happy he was within, and however much of a wall he built around himself, there had always been a part of him that missed Stella. The feeling of being at one with yourself could never match the feeling of being at one with someone else, especially if that someone was Stella. Still, what was done was done. They were where they were, and the clock couldn't be turned back to change it.

They were joined at breakfast by Jennings, who, unlike Stratton, had managed to get a good night's sleep, and was in high spirits compared to the day before. Even the shameful plasticky food was eaten without criticism. He told them that the car was being picked up by the local force and would be at the motel by nine o'clock.

"That's good," said Stratton. "We need to get on. We've stayed here too long already."

"What does it matter to you?" asked Jennings. "It's not your job to find the killer is it?"

"No, you're right, it isn't. But I'm just as keen to get to the bottom of this as you are. For me it's not so much about catching the killer as finding the box. We need to find it before anyone else gets their hands on it."

"Well, I agree with you there," said Jennings.

The car arrived just before nine and they set off straight away. Jennings wanted to stop off in Exeter to get some new clothes, but Stella persuaded him to wait until a more convenient time: clothes were the last thing he should be worrying about.

When they were well on their way and had hit the M5, Stratton borrowed the phone from Stella and called his parents' house to let them know that they were on their way. First he tried the landline, which rang three times and went to answer phone. He then tried his mother's mobile and then his father's mobile in turn: again, both went to answer phone. He left messages on all three.

"No joy then?" said Stella, craning her head back from the passenger seat.

"No. Not yet," said Stratton, looking agitated. "Mum's probably in the middle of a book or something, and Dad's probably out on the golf course with the local dignitaries. They know we're coming up, I spoke to Mum yesterday."

"How are things with your dad nowadays?" she asked.

"They're ok I suppose," he said. "We've come to an understanding. I haven't been back to the house though. Not since that New Year's Eve debacle."

"Is it going to be awkward then?"

"No, not really. I've seen him at family gatherings, and we speak on the phone occasionally. I just haven't been home for a while, for one reason or another…" He thought for a moment. "I'm looking forward to seeing the place again."

"Do they know I'm coming?" she asked.

"Yes, they do. They're looking forward to seeing you again. They always liked you. They were really upset when…well, when we split up."

The Saturday morning traffic was quiet and they made good time. As they drew nearer to their destination, Stratton started to get butterflies. He had been away too long, he thought. The nervous excitement became greater the closer they got; and by the time they reached Ascot High Street, and he saw the racecourse on his left, he knew he was back. Then it was on and out of Ascot and past the Victory Fields, where he had played football in his youth; the memories hit him thick and hard. Sunninghill was next: he remembered this particularly for their New Year pantomimes. And then a mile down the road was Sunningdale.

As they drove past the park Stratton smiled and almost laughed out loud. He could feel the emotion welling up inside. Memories of his grandfather came rushing through his mind like floodwater. His earliest recollections in life were of the park and his grandfather. He remembered carefree Sunday mornings, when his grandfather would turn up to the house early and walk him and his brother down there. In those days it seemed like the longest trek in the world, but it was never boring with grandad telling them funny stories on the way, and giving them piggy backs if they tired. And the park itself was a wonderland to Stratton. There were tunnels, slides, swings, roundabouts, climbing frames, and a big horizontal wooden barrel that you got in and worked like a hamster's wheel. Children played together regardless of whether they knew each other or not; and adults relaxed on the benches, chatting or reading the Sunday paper, or just enjoying the morning air, grateful that the kids had something to do. These days parks were just a place for teenage gangs to hang out and get pissed in, Stratton reflected ruefully.

Jennings stopped the car at the metal gates that barred the drive to the house, and pressed the intercom button. They waited for at least a minute but there was no answer. He buzzed again. Still there was no reply.

"Maybe they're both out," suggested Stella.

"Maybe," said Stratton, not convinced. "I'd be surprised if mum was out though, she knows I'm coming up and she'd make sure she didn't miss me."

Stratton got out of the car and approached the intercom. Beneath the 'speak' button was a numbered keypad. He typed in the code 270913, his grandmother's birthday, and was relieved when the gates slowly creaked open. He walked up the short drive and Jennings and Stella followed in the car.

Stratton walked round to the alleyway that separated the house from the garage. He opened the side door to the garage and entered it. Both his parents' cars were parked inside: his father's Mercedes and his mother's Clio. His stomach tightened: if they were out, at least one of the cars would be gone. He opened the drawer of the old workbench and pulled out the spare house key that was always kept there, hidden beneath the false bottom.

Jennings and Stella were waiting by the front door.

"Have you got a key then?" asked Jennings.

"Yes," replied Stratton. "I'm worried though: both cars are in the garage, mum and dad should be in."

Stratton opened the door and hurried over to the alarm to disable it, but as he approached he realized that it wasn't switched on. They had to be in.

"Mum!" he shouted. "Dad!"

There was no answer, just an eerie silence.

He shouted again. "Mum! Dad! It's me!"

This time the silence was so loud he could almost hear it. His stomach tightened even more; he felt sick. Stella said something to him but he didn't hear it, his head was elsewhere.

Instinctively he slowly climbed the stairs; an invisible force was drawing him towards the landing. At the top he made the left turn towards his parents' bedroom, again being led by an unseen energy. His heart began to beat faster and louder; he could hear it pounding in his ears.

Stella and Jennings had followed him up but he was oblivious to them. It was just him now; the world was only himself and whatever lay behind his parents' bedroom door. Nothing else existed.

He stopped at the door, terrified and fearful of what he might see; of what he knew he was going to see. Then he carefully and cautiously pushed it open; and in that instant both he and the world he inhabited were savagely ripped apart.

Chapter 19

"Do you think he can hear us?" asked Jennings.

"I don't know," replied Stella. "He's gone catatonic. He's still in shock."

Stratton was sitting in his father's armchair in the living room, his eyes glued to the TV screen. He hadn't said a word since the discovery of his parents' bodies an hour before.

His immediate reaction had been to vomit, vigorously and uncontrollably, over the bedroom floor. Then he had pulled himself upright and ambled downstairs. And that was where he'd been since, aimlessly watching daytime TV; losing himself in the light-hearted ramblings of Philip and Fern. From what Stella and Jennings could make out, he was more interested in the intricacies of making the perfect soufflé, than having anything to do with the circus of police officers who were now searching the house for evidence.

"How long do people stay like this?" asked Jennings. "Do you know?"

"No idea really. I suppose it's only temporary, although I guess it affects different people in different ways," said Stella.

At that moment Stratton lifted himself out of the armchair, and went to the mahogany cabinet at the side of the room. "I need a drink," he said, and took out a bottle of Smirnoff Blue Label.

"Are you sure about this?" said Stella.

Stratton looked at her coldly. "Listen Stella, I don't want to get into an argument with you about this. In case you hadn't noticed, my parents are dead upstairs. Murdered. I need a drink, and I'm going to have a drink." He undid the top and took a swig from the bottle.

"Ok whatever, but you'll only make yourself more miserable. You know it, and I know it," she said.

Stratton shrugged his shoulders. "Just because my mother's dead doesn't mean there's a vacancy," he snapped.

Stella let the subject drop. The atmosphere was terrible enough as it was, without adding to it with an argument about drink. She just hoped that he wouldn't go overboard and make matters worse for himself.

Five minutes later David Brennan arrived at the scene. Jennings had phoned him as soon as they had discovered the bodies. "So it looks like our man has struck again then," he said.

"Yes sir," replied Jennings. "The wounds are in the same place, and it looks like the same type of knife was used. We'll know for certain after we get the results from pathology."

"Found anything else?"

"No sir, nothing as yet. But SOCO are still searching upstairs. To be honest though I don't think we're going to find anything. This guy, whoever he is, is ultra professional, he's just too careful to leave any trace."

"What about our man here?" said Brennan, pointing to Stratton, who was mid-swig. "Haven't we got a psychologist to help him out?"

"I don't need a psychologist," said Stratton. "I'll be fine. I just want to be left alone."

Brennan shrugged and took himself upstairs, closely followed by Jennings. Stella stayed with Stratton, even though he was making her feel extremely uncomfortable. There was nothing she could say to comfort him: what could you say in a situation like this? All the training she'd had in the police counted for nothing now that it came down to it. It was all very easy to dish out advice and help in hypothetical situations, but no amount of instruction could prepare you for the awkward reality of loss. The fact that she knew Stratton was making it more difficult. Perhaps if he had been a stranger then she could have been more objective, and able to put her limited experience into practice. But he wasn't a stranger, he was Stratton, and her longing to help him was clouding her judgement.

"I need to get out of here," said Stratton.

"Ok," said Stella. "Where do you want to go?"

"Down the pub. Are you coming?"

"Yeah, ok," she said. She didn't particularly want to go but at the same time she didn't want to leave Stratton drowning his sorrows alone. He was a loose cannon at the moment, and left to his own devices she knew there would be trouble.

She let Jennings know where they were going and they headed for the pub. As soon as they left the house she could feel the tension lift, and the bright winter sun lifted her sense of gloom. They walked the short distance to the pub in comfortable silence. It took her back to years before when they had taken the same route while visiting his parents. She almost felt like holding his hand, but quickly put the thought out of her head: it was a road that would inevitably lead to trouble and a distraction that neither of them needed right now.

The Chequers was situated on the main road and had been Stratton's local as a teenager, back in the days when a few years here or there didn't matter to landlords. In a village pub, if you said you were eighteen, then you were eighteen. Of course, times had changed since then and the Chequers had gone through more than one revolution. Stratton hadn't drunk in there for over six years now, not since his self-imposed exile from Sunningdale, and he didn't know what to expect from the place; he didn't even know if it was still there.

The pub was in fact still there and, apart from being brighter and cleaner, and changing its name to Chatt's, it had changed very little since his last visit. It was two o'clock when they walked in and the place was still fairly busy with people enjoying a relaxing lunch. Stratton found a table in the corner for them and went to the bar to order some drinks. Stella, who had asked for an orange juice, was annoyed when he returned with a bottle of red wine and two glasses.

"I told you I wanted an orange juice," she said. "I don't want any wine. One of us needs to keep a clear head, and from experience I know it won't be you."

"Come on Stella," he said, his mood having lifted slightly. "I need to relax, and sharing one bottle of wine with me isn't going to hurt, is it? I thought we'd get some food as well, that'll take the edge off the alcohol."

Stella relented, knowing that he wouldn't stop pestering until she did. Stratton went back to the bar to order them some food.

"How long is it since you've had a drink?" she asked him when he returned.

"About twenty minutes, I had some vodka at the house, remember?"

"You know what I mean Stratton."

He grinned. "Oh I see. Well, probably last Saturday I would think. Why? You didn't think that I was teetotal did you?"

"Well yes, I did actually," she admitted. "I just thought with all this yoga and Reiki and other mystic stuff you seem to be into that you'd stopped drinking. The other night you were drinking fennel tea, and then last night at the motel you just had a mineral water when Jennings and I both had a drink."

"You're right, and I don't drink like I used to; not even near. But I do like to have the odd pint here and there and some wine if I go out for a meal. I enjoy having a drink when I'm in the mood; I've just learnt to control it."

"And what about today? Should you really be drinking today?" she said her voice full of concern.

"No, probably not," he admitted. "But I'm going to anyway. Don't worry about me, I'll be fine. And besides, I hardly touched that vodka and I'm not going to have any more after this wine."

The food arrived and was excellent. Stratton had a rare fillet steak with pepper sauce and Stella had a homemade cheeseburger. Stella only picked at her food, the day's events having soured her appetite, but Stratton devoured his meal with fervour.

In the circumstances she was surprised at this: an hour before he had been a lifeless zombie. The change of mood didn't seem right. But then he always had been a bit of an anomaly, she thought; his unpredictability was one of the reasons that she had loved him so much.

Stratton had just finished his meal when a hand grabbed his shoulder. "Stratton!" said a cheery voice from behind. Stratton looked round and up and found himself facing a man in his early thirties with mousy, side-parted hair. He was wearing an England rugby shirt and jeans and trainers. He was tall, at least six two; and from his chin and belly, it looked like he lived well. Stratton knew the face but was having trouble placing it

"You don't recognize me do you mate," said the man. He was well-spoken.

Stratton stared for a moment, and then it hit him. "Tim?" he said. "Tim Braithwaite?"

"Yes mate. I haven't seen you for ages. What are you doing back here? I thought you were abroad. Well, that's the last I heard anyway."

"I was abroad for a while, but I'm living in London at the moment. Just haven't had the time to come back," said Stratton. "Listen. Why don't you come and join us? We can catch up," he added.

Stratton and Tim had been childhood friends. They hadn't been to school together, Tim had gone to Eton, but they had lived down the road from each other and had hung out together during school holidays. The first time Stratton had got properly drunk was with Tim; they were fourteen and had stolen a bottle of Johnny Walker from Tim's parents' drinks cabinet. They had drunk half each and were both incredibly sick; Stratton hadn't touched scotch since. They had also shared their first joint, which they rolled with grass that Stratton had stolen from his older brother. Again they were both sick; not from the dope, but from the stupid amount of chocolate that they had eaten as a result of the 'munchies'. Stratton chuckled to himself as he remembered.

"It's good to see you Tim," he said. "Sorry I didn't recognize you, but you're…well, you look different."

Tim laughed. "You mean this?" he said patting his belly. "Don't worry about it. I know I'm not the skinny rake I used to be. Too much good living."

Stratton introduced Stella, who was becoming anxious at the turn of events, and they drank and chatted. They hadn't seen each other since both left for university: Stratton to Oxford and Tim to St Andrews. After graduating, it turned out, Tim had taken a year off to travel and had then bagged a job in the city, courtesy of the old school network. Now he was an extremely successful broker with a leading bank, and had moved back to the area. He was married to a girl ten years his junior, and they had a two-year-old boy and another child on the way.

"What about you mate?" said Tim. "I feel like I've been going on. What's your story?"

Stratton, who had been quite happy listening to Tim, felt uncomfortable. The last thing he wanted to be doing was to talk about himself. "There's not much to tell really mate. I got my degree and I've been dossing about ever since."

Tim took the hint and didn't press the point. "Oh well, I'm sure there's more to it than that. What about your parents? How are they?"

"Oh, they're fine. You know," said Stratton casually.

"That's good," said Tim. "I've seen your dad up at the golf club a few times, just not had a chance to have a good chat. I ought to arrange to have a game with him at some point, apparently he's quite good. Plays off two I believe."

"Yes he does," said Stratton, and quickly changed the subject. "Anyway, how about another drink; or have you got to get home soon?"

"No, I've got a pass out for the whole day. She's away at her parents' this weekend; I can do what I like. We can have an old school all-dayer if you want."

Stella gave Stratton a fierce look.

"We'll see," said Stratton. "I've got nothing better to do though."

Stratton got another bottle of wine and they spent the rest of the afternoon drinking and reminiscing. Stella had no more alcohol and, after Stratton and Tim had polished off three bottles between them, she felt like she was gate crashing an exclusive party. At any other time she would have left, but she knew that if she did then she would only be worrying about Stratton even more.

By seven o'clock they had stopped drinking wine and had moved on to champagne. Stella knew that there would be no stopping them now. Tim suggested that they order a taxi and head into Windsor for something to eat. Then, he said, he would take them to a club that he knew, where the owner was a friend of his. Stratton accepted the offer without reservation, and Stella reluctantly agreed, although she was half inclined to say 'fuck it' and let Stratton get into trouble on his own.

Stella's mood lightened a bit after Tim treated them both to a meal in a superb Chinese restaurant. But her levity was short-lived as she watched Stratton become progressively drunker and louder. Tim was buying champagne like there was no tomorrow, and Stratton was drinking it just as quickly. By the time they left the restaurant neither of them could walk in a straight line, and they were staggering down the road propping each other up and singing, in a hearty show of male camaraderie. There was no way that they were going to get into a club, thought Stella. But she was wrong.

At first Stella thought she was in luck; when they arrived at the door of the club owned by Tim's friend, it was shut. In fact the club had gone out of business six months previously.

"Oh well," said Stella. "Never mind. We'll just have to call it a night."

"No," slurred Tim, looking at his watch. "I don't think so. It's only eleven thirty. We'll go to another place I know. It's just down the road near the train station."

Before Stella could protest, the skid row chorus were making their way down the street towards their next drink. She followed them, keeping a safe distance so as to disassociate herself from the ongoing shambles. She had relented in the restaurant and allowed herself a couple of glasses of champagne, but she was still sober enough to be embarrassed by their highly vocal inebriation.

The queue for Bar Indigo was fairly small and, much to Stella's disgust, Stratton and Tim had miraculously regained their lucidity: the way that professional drinkers do when attempting to circumnavigate door staff. After standing in line for five minutes they were let in without any problem.

Tim headed straight for the bar and ordered a bottle of champagne, waving his platinum card in the face of the attractive barmaid. Stella decided to stick to mineral water, her female intuition telling her that one person at least should keep their wits about them. She could feel trouble brewing.

"Come on Stella, have a drink," pleaded Tim.

"No thanks," said Stella politely. "I've got an early start in the morning and I need to keep my head straight."

"Pah!" he sneered drunkenly, and then turned back to the bar and instantly forgot what he was sneering for.

Stratton was nowhere to be seen. He had disappeared in the direction of the dance floor as soon as they had entered the club. Stella got on her toes and craned her neck to see if she could make him out; but it was impossible to pinpoint anybody amongst the sea of sweating, heaving, bottle-waving bodies. The intermittent lights were no aid and the fact that he was wearing black didn't help her cause either.

"Did you see where Stratton went?" she asked Tim.

"No idea," he slurred.

They grabbed a table in the corner, away from the incessant, gut-pounding noise of the speakers. Tim attempted to make conversation with Stella, and Stella attempted to listen. But whatever he was trying to get across was getting lost in translation. In his head he may well have been saying something profound and interesting, or even have discovered the meaning of life; unfortunately, in reality, he was spouting nonsensical rubbish. In the end she gave up trying and left him blabbering away to himself.

Fifteen minutes later Stratton still hadn't appeared. Stella found herself eyeing her watch obsessively, and trying to avoid half-assed advances from the piss artist formerly known as Tim. She was bored and she wanted leave as soon as possible.

Her concern for Stratton's welfare was wearing thin, and the only reason she was hanging around was because she needed him. He was the key to the murders, and the only person who could make sense of what was happening. She was sure of it.

After another ten minutes Stratton finally showed his face again. He seemed to have sobered up and was grinning mischievously.

"Where have you been?" asked Stella. "I was starting to get worried."

"Oh, just about, you know," he said. "I went to have a dance - wanted to let off some steam."

Stratton never danced, thought Stella. He had been up to something.

"Oh, champagne - excellent!" said Stratton, and poured himself a glass and sat down.

"Listen Stratton, I'm tired and I want to go soon. We need to find somewhere to stay," said Stella.

"Tim said we could stay at his. He's got plenty of room. His house is almost a mansion. Isn't that right Tim?" he said, slapping his comatose friend on the back. "And anyway the night's still young. It's only half twelve, there's plenty of party time left. Don't be such an old spinster."

The facetious delivery of the last remark pushed Stella over the edge. "Listen to me you fucking bastard!" she shouted. "What the fuck do you think you're playing at?! I know that you've taken something; what is it? Speed? Ecstasy? Crystal meth? Or is it your old friend charley? This isn't the time or the place to be going back to your old ways. I thought you'd changed. Get a fucking grip on yourself!"

Stratton looked straight ahead and ignored her. He downed half his glass of Krug and carried on grinning to himself.

Stella became more frustrated. "You can't carry on like this, just blocking things out. Your parents are dead Stratton. They've been murdered. They're not coming back. I know everyone has their own way of dealing with loss, but this isn't helping anyone, least of all yourself. We need to find out who killed them and Henry, and we need to find that box. Me and Jennings are clueless, and so is everybody else. You're the only person who can make sense of all this, you're the only one who understands it. Do it for your parents."

Stratton continued to avoid eye contact but the smile had gone.

"Oh for fuck's sake man. Do you think your parents would be proud of you?" she said cuttingly. "Do you think your grand-father would be proud?"

Stratton's face soured. He smashed the champagne flute on the table in fury; breaking the stem and sending liquid flying through the air. He got up and pushed his face right in Stella's own. He was so close she could almost taste the alcohol on his breath. "Leave me the fuck alone!" he growled, and stormed off towards the dance floor.

Stella got up and followed him. Before Stratton could reach the dance floor, a hand came out and barred his way. The hand belonged to a keen-eyed doorman who had been watching events between Stella and Stratton unfold.

"Sorry sir, but I'm afraid you're going to have to leave," said the doorman, firmly and politely.

For a moment Stratton looked mystified, and then he clicked. "Oh, the glass, sorry. Listen, I'll pay for it if you like."

"Sorry sir," repeated the doorman, "but you really have to leave."

"Look, just let me go to the toilet ok," said Stratton, becoming more agitated.

"Just leave please sir," said the doorman. His face remained impassive.

Stratton flicked the doorman's hand away dismissively and turned in the direction of the toilets. The doorman grabbed him roughly by the shoulders with both hands. Stratton turned back round to face him, his eyes blazing with anger. The doorman made a move to get him into a restraining hold, but even the alcohol hadn't dented Stratton's speed. Before the doorman knew what was happening he was doubled up on the floor; having received a vicious blow to the solar plexus, followed by a sweeping kick that had taken his legs away. Stratton saw three more door staff approaching and decided to leave. He made his way to the door quickly; unimpeded by the other bouncers, who seemed wary of tackling him.

Outside, the queue had grown longer. Stratton barged his way through the line of drunken revellers, unaware of their existence. A group of beered-up lads at the back were making lewd suggestions to a couple of young girls in front. Stratton bumped shoulders with them on the way past.

"Oi mate!" shouted one of them. "What's your fucking problem?!"

Stratton carried on, paying no attention.

He walked to the end of the street and turned right. He had no idea where he was headed; he just needed to keep on going. His head had completely gone. The excessive alcohol had charged him up, and the two huge lines of coke he'd secured in the club, had pushed him over the edge. Differing emotions poured through his mind one after the other. Anger, sadness, bitterness, regret and hatred all came and disappeared; and then reappeared in a vicious circle of self-loathing.

He felt the familiar but long-forgotten rush of his world spinning out of control. His preoccupation was total, and rendered him oblivious to the sound of footsteps approaching from behind.

He reached the end of another street and this time he turned left. After a hundred yards he realized that he'd wandered into a dead end. He turned about face; and that's when he saw them.

The group of lads from the Bar Indigo queue had followed him. They were now advancing with ominous intent. There were six of them, and they were fanned out along the narrow street, cutting off any chance of escape. They were only young, most in their late teens, and they didn't say a word; but Stratton could feel their menace in the air. He had no choice, he had to try and fight his way out; and he was in no mood for taking prisoners.

He made straight for the largest of the gang who was ahead of the others in the centre of the line. Before the unfortunate youth had a chance to raise his fists, Stratton had landed a combination of punches to his face. He fell to the ground and Stratton turned his attention to the rest of the group who, although taken aback, were still closing in. Stratton's eyes had become an inferno of rage and he lashed out, punching and kicking haphazardly, forgetting the discipline he'd taken years to achieve.

One by one his assailants gave up and backed away. The wild animal they had cornered was just too much to handle. Soon only one remained: the largest lad, who Stratton had gone for initially. Reaching into his pocket the lad drew out a switchblade. He advanced on Stratton waving the knife in his face. Stratton backed away.

"Not so hard now, are you mate?" gloated the youth.

Stratton's ire was reawoken and, like lightning, he grabbed the youth's wrist and twisted it round. The knife fell to the floor. The events of the day had reached a head and Stratton welled up with an uncontrollable fury. With incredible force he wrenched the youth's wrist further and flipped him to the ground. He stood over the cowering body and brought his boot up above the youth's head.

"Stratton!" shouted a voice. "Stratton! No!"

Stratton's boot continued to hover. He looked down on the youth's face and his anger began to fade. He no longer saw a vicious thug: he was looking at a frightened kid; a boy not even out of his teens; a boy with terror in his startled, watery eyes.

A hand gently grabbed his arm. It was Stella. "Leave him Stratton," she said, softly. "Let's get out of here."

He removed his boot from its position of attack and turned to Stella. She caressed his cheek. Reality hit him swiftly and brutally. He wrapped his arms round her and started to cry.

Chapter 20

The bar at the Heathrow Hilton was quiet. It was one thirty in the morning, and the majority of guests had gone to bed ready for early-morning flights. There were a few couples scattered around the lounge, and a few lone businessmen, but the atmosphere was sedate with an air of sterility. A man sat at the bar on his own, sipping a large whiskey on the rocks and chewing the occasional cashew nut. That man was Scott Grady.

Grady's flight wasn't until two o' clock in the afternoon, and after flicking through the television channels in his room, he had decided that a drink was the best option.

The day had gone well for Grady. Owing to the new murders he was no longer a suspect in the Mulholland case, and he was free to leave the country and get back to the States. Earlier in the day he'd phoned Brooke, the heavenly waitress with whom he was smitten, and told her he was on his way home. She had taken his flight details and was going to pick him up from JFK. They were going to spend a few romantic days and nights in New York and then head back to Columbus.

Grady couldn't wait to see Brooke again; she was so unlike any other girl. She buzzed with an endless flow of energy, and she made him feel alive like he'd never felt. Everything she said, and every move she made, was filled with positivity. And she was kind, kinder than anyone Grady had ever met. Nothing was ever too much trouble for her; she would go out of her way to help anybody, even strangers. And she was beautiful, man was she beautiful. Her eyes were the brightest blue he'd ever seen and they shimmered like rippling water in the sun. Her pronounced cheekbones coupled with her creamy complexion gave her face an almost elfin quality, and her lips were soft and full. She had natural blonde hair cut to shoulder length, and she was tall and athletic. Grady smiled to himself as he thought of her.

He finished his drink and waved to the barman for another. A man came and sat on the bar stool next to him. He was in his mid-forties and was smartly dressed. He wore a blazer, dark grey slacks, a red patterned silk tie, and snappy black Gucci loafers. Grady tried to ignore him. He hated small talk, particularly late at night in a bar.

After Grady's drink arrived, the man ordered a large gin and tonic for himself. He was American and softly spoken; his accent pointed to New England.

"Slow night in here, isn't it," said the man, trying to engage Grady in conversation.

"Yeah, it sure is," said Grady bluntly.

Despite Grady's offhand manner the man persevered.

"Alan Douglas," he said, extending a hand.

Grady shook his hand but said nothing.

"And you are?" pressed the man called Douglas.

"Very tired," replied Grady.

"Hey sorry. I'm just trying to be friendly," said Douglas, and took a sip of his drink.

Grady thought about Brooke again and his mood softened. If she were in this situation she would be sociable with this lonely guy. After all, being friendly wouldn't hurt.

"Sorry man," said Grady. "I'm being really rude. My name's Scott Grady."

Alan Douglas smiled. "Pleased to meet you Scott. What kind of business are you in?"

"Computers. I sell hardware. It's pretty boring actually."

"I'm in computers too," said Douglas. "I'm a sales rep for a company called International Micro."

At the words 'International Micro', Grady's heart sank. Alan Douglas was CIA. International Micro was a dummy company used as a cover for agents.

Grady looked around to see if anyone was listening to their conversation. Nobody was. "All right Douglas, what the hell do you want?" he said quietly. "I'm catching a plane at two o' clock this afternoon, and I'm going to spend some time with my girl. I'm leaving all this shit behind me."

"Hey, calm down Scott," said Douglas raising his hands. "I'm only a messenger. As far as I'm concerned you can get on the plane and do what the hell you like."

Grady calmed himself. "Ok. What's the message?"

Douglas checked that no-one was watching them and reached into his pocket. He got out a slim cell phone and palmed it into Grady's left pocket. "There's a number programmed into the phone. You have to ring it before you go to bed. It's a secure line. I don't know whose number it is or what it's about."

"And what if I don't want to ring this number?" said Grady.

"Then I've been told that you will be stopped at passport control and detained in this country. But like I said, it's nothing to do with me, I'm only the messenger."

He got up to leave. "Well it's been good meeting you," he said loudly. "Have a good journey home."

Grady remained at the bar and stared at his drink in contemplation. He felt like taking the phone, flushing it down the toilet, and taking his chances at passport control. Or alternatively he could try and get a plane now, before they had a chance to stop him. Neither of these ideas was feasible. There was no escape once they had their claws in you. He only had one option: and that was to play along.

He finished his drink and left the barman a ten pound tip. It was the last of his English money but he wouldn't be needing it any more. He walked towards the bank of elevators but then changed his mind and made for the toilets: MI6 knew where he was staying and may have bugged his room.

Inside the toilets there was a man at the urinals. Grady locked himself in a cubicle and waited for the man to leave. After he heard the main door open, he came out of the cubicle. He made sure there was no-one else hanging around and dialled the number programmed into the phone. It rang three times and then someone picked up.

"Hello," said a vaguely familiar voice. "Is that you Grady?"

"Yes, it's me," Grady answered. "Who's this?"

"It's Professor Miles. I need to talk to you. I need you to stay in England for a while longer."

Grady's face soured. "Listen Miles. I am not staying in this country a minute longer than I have to. I'm booked to fly out at two o'clock, and that's what I intend to do. My cover is blown now. I'm no use to you any more. I'm no use to anyone. I just want to retire gracefully and try and lead a normal life."

"Listen Grady," said Miles. "I know things haven't been going that well over there but I still need to get hold of that box. The British are obviously trying their best to find it, from what I can make out, but I want us to locate it first. I don't want anyone else getting their hands on it; it's just too important."

"For Christ's sake Miles, are you not listening to me? There is no way I could get to the box, even if I wanted to. I'm up to my neck in shit over here. If I don't get on that plane tomorrow the authorities are going to be all over me. I'll have every fucking agency in the country watching my ass. I won't be able to shit without them knowing."

"It's worth a lot of money to you," said Miles. "Enough for you to enjoy a lavish retirement." He paused for a moment. "What shall we say? Two million dollars. Is that enough?"

Grady sighed. "You're still not hearing me man. I can't do it; I don't want to do it. It doesn't matter how much money you offer me. Money's not going to be any use to me if I'm stuck in jail. You'll be better off finding someone else."

"I don't want someone else, I want you. Apparently you're the best; so they tell me."

"Listen Miles," Grady insisted. "In five seconds I'm going to put this phone down. I don't care whether you get me detained or not. I'm out of the espionage business…Five, four, three, two…"

Miles interrupted. "I wouldn't do that if I were you Grady. It could be very hazardous. I know how much you're looking forward to seeing the delightful Brooke."

Grady's stomach knotted. "How the hell do you know about her?"

"It doesn't matter, does it? All that matters is the fact that at the moment she is safe and unharmed. She's going about her business without a care in the world. You wouldn't want that to change, would you?"

Grady was silent for a moment. "No," he replied.

"Well then," said Miles. "I suggest you cancel your flight and get searching for that box again. Remember, you've got two million and one reasons to find it."

With that Miles hung up.

Grady cursed and threw the phone across the toilet. It smashed against the far wall. He couldn't believe that Miles had found out about Brooke, but then nothing in the game surprised him these days; there was no such thing as a private life any more; not that there ever had been.

He resigned himself to staying. There was no point feeling sorry for himself; he had to get hold of that box.

Chapter 21

When Stratton woke up he was still buzzing with alcohol. He was in an unfamiliar bed in an unfamiliar room. Bright sunlight was peeking through the gap in the dark blue curtains. His clothes were in a heap on the floor next to the bed, but he had no memory of getting undressed. He did however remember most of the night before and his mind began to sting with remorse. How could he have been so stupid?

He knew that drinking to forget, or 'traubibulation' as he called it, was the worst, most self-destructive activity you could engage in. Yet with all his knowledge and experience of it, he'd still succumbed; and he'd nearly put some kid in hospital - or worse.

There was a knock on the door. It opened and in walked Stella carrying a large glass of water.

"How are you feeling?" she asked. "Terrible, I hope."

"Thanks for your concern," replied Stratton. "My head's not too bad at the moment, to be honest. I think I'm still half-cut. I expect the real pain will hit me later on."

Stella sat on the side of the bed, and Stratton dragged himself up and leaned against the headboard. He took a sip of water, and then a huge gulp.

"What time is it?" he asked. "And more to the point - where the hell are we?"

"The time is just gone eleven, and we're at Tim's house," she answered. "I went back into the club and got him while you waited in the taxi, remember?"

"No I don't," said Stratton. "To be honest everything's a bit hazy in my mind at the moment."

"I'm not surprised. You two drank enough wine and champagne to floor a rhinoceros," she said. "And God knows what else you were up to in that club," she added with an accusing stare.

Stratton looked sheepish but didn't comment. There was no need to get into an argument about drugs at the moment. He knew well enough that he'd been stupid, he didn't need anyone else to tell him so.

"You really scared me last night you know," she said. "I really thought you were going to kill that poor kid."

"To be fair, he was waving a knife in my face."

"I know, but you scared me all the same," said Stella. "You were like a wild animal. It wasn't you in your body; it was like you'd been taken over by some malignant spirit. Your eyes had completely gone. I didn't think I'd be able to get through to you."

"I'm glad you did," said Stratton. "If you hadn't shouted me, I don't like to think what would have happened. All I wanted to do was defend myself, but with the alcohol and my state of mind, I just lost it. I wasn't angry with him or his gang, I was angry at myself. I wasn't fighting them, I was fighting my own demons. And you're right, I was like a wild animal...I unleashed The Beast."

"The Beast?" said Stella.

"Yes, The Beast," Stratton repeated. "It's what I call the mass of energy that runs through my body; it runs through everyone's body."

"What? Like the life force energy you talked about when you were describing Reiki?"

"Yes. That's the one," said Stratton. "Anyway, we're all part of this energy - a rampant sweeping energy that knows neither good nor bad: it just is. It can create and it can destroy." He slapped his hand down for effect.

"All the old Masters, Jesus and Buddha, amongst others, knew how to use this energy, and although they became frustrated at the way the world was, just like we do, unlike us, they saw the futility of hatred and stood for peace. We all have the capacity to destroy others, but by doing this we really only destroy ourselves. It's all about the way we harness the unstoppable power within us. It's all about controlling The Beast."

Stella thought for a moment. "I can sort of see where you're coming from. It's just a bit heavy for a Sunday morning."

Stratton laughed. "Yeah, I suppose it is. I was just trying to explain why I frightened you so much last night. The thing is, I learnt to tap into this power through Reiki, and it changes the way you feel, and the way you view the world and the universe. It causes you to vibrate at a much higher level. You can literally draw energy into yourself at will." He took a sip of water.

"This is all well and good when you're calm and at peace with yourself, but when you become upset or angry, the power can manifest itself in extremely ugly ways. It's particularly uncontrollable when artificial stimulants like drink or drugs are involved. I made a massive mistake yesterday, and the worst thing is I couldn't stop myself. I really thought I'd reached a stage where I could cope with just about everything. I was obviously wrong."

"Don't be so hard on yourself. You'd just found your parents murdered. I don't think anyone could deal with that rationally."

"I suppose not," Stratton conceded. "But I could have dealt with it better, that's all I'm saying. Still, I'll learn from it."

Stella got up off the bed. "I'm going downstairs now, Tim's going to cook us breakfast. Do you want some?"

"Yeah, sure. I think I'll manage some. It'll probably soak up some of this excess alcohol that seems to be floating around in me."

When Stella had gone, he lay back down for a while and tried to clear his head. In the bad old days he would have got out of bed and found himself some more alcohol, before a hangover set in. He was tempted by the thought, but he knew where it would end up. So even though his body was screaming for more booze, he had to override the physical craving.

As Stella had pointed out the night before: people were

relying on him; he was the only one who could make sense of it all. It was a burden he could do without, but a burden that he would just have to bear.

After finding the bathroom and having a long hot shower, he made his way downstairs. Stella and Tim were in the kitchen. Tim was standing at a central island with a large extractor above it, making breakfast. Stella was seated at a rustic-looking oak table, sipping a cup of tea. The smell of sausages and bacon filled the room. Stratton's mouth started to water.

"Morning mate," said Tim. "Hope you slept well. How do you feel?"

"I'm ok, maybe a bit fragile," he replied. "The food smells great."

"Well, you can't beat a good old fry up when you're feeling a bit delicate," Tim said cheerily. "We'll soon be on the road to recovery."

Stratton poured himself another glass of water and sat down opposite Stella. "What's the plan for the day then?" he asked. "Have you spoken to Jennings yet?"

"Yes, he phoned me at about eight thirty this morning. He wanted to make sure we were all right. I left a message on his phone last night," she said. "And as for plans, that depends on you doesn't it? We need to find that missing transcript."

"We're going to have to get into my parents' house then," said Stratton. "Have the police finished up there yet?"

"I don't know. But it doesn't matter anyway, we'll be allowed in to search around."

"Ok then, we'll go after breakfast. I just hope my parents didn't throw my stuff out from the loft."

The food tasted as good as it looked and smelt. Stratton ate hungrily, feeling his body grow stronger with every mouthful. When he had finished, he pushed his empty plate forward with a contented sigh. His head was still slightly mashed but the rest of him was ready for the day ahead. "Cheers Tim, that was great," he said.

"No problem mate, it's a pleasure."

After Stella had finished her breakfast, they got ready to leave. Tim offered to drive them up to the house. Stratton declined the offer for two reasons: the first being that it was a beautiful morning for a walk, and the second being that he imagined Tim was still well over the limit for driving.

It was only a half mile walk from Tim's house up to Broomfield Park. On the way Stratton took deep breaths of the crisp air, to clear his head. The low sun was unusually bright and he had to walk with his head down to avoid its stinging glare. Stella wandered along happily by his side, secretly smug that she had refrained from joining the previous night's drinking binge.

When they arrived at the house Jennings was already there. "What time do you call this?" he said, looking at his watch and smiling.

"Sorry," said Stella. "But I had to wait for Robert Downey Jr here to get out of bed."

"Rough night then?" said Jennings, observing Stratton's still-bloodshot eyes.

"Something like that," he replied.

The front door was still barred by crime scene tape, but there were no police in the house. Forensics had done a clean sweep. Any evidence that was going to be found would have been picked up already.

Inside the house it was eerily silent. Stratton was hit by a wave of nostalgia. Scenes from his childhood played themselves out in his head. He could see himself and his brother running around the house playing soldiers, wreaking havoc wherever they went. He could see his mother and father sitting quietly trying to ignore them. He could see his mother in the kitchen preparing the Sunday roast, while his father and grandfather played games with the children. The years flashed through his head on fast forward. For a brief moment the place came alive with the ghosts of the past. And then, just as quickly, they faded and the silence hit him again.

"Where do we start then?" asked Jennings.

"The loft," said Stratton.

No-one had been in the upstairs loft for years. A cloud of dust dropped down on Stratton as he opened the hatch. He choked and rubbed his eyes. With one hand on either side of the opening he pushed his feet off the step ladder and pulled himself into the dark space. He reached up for the string switch and, after finding it easily, he turned the light on. A sea of boxes and piles of old papers covered the entire attic. Some of the boxes were marked, and some not. Being careful to stay on the beams, Stratton made his way to the far side of the loft. He moved a couple of boxes marked 'old toys', and reached down for an unmarked box that had previously been hidden. It was fairly heavy but he had no trouble lifting it out. He made his way back across the beams to the hatch.

"Take this will you," he said to Jennings, who was standing at the bottom of the ladder.

Jennings reached up and grabbed the box.

Stratton turned off the light and manoeuvred himself back onto the ladder. He replaced the hatch and eased himself down to the landing. He took the box downstairs to the living room. Stella and Jennings followed.

"How come you haven't bothered to find the missing pages before?" asked Jennings.

"For a start, my father only sent the transcript to me earlier this year. And secondly, I didn't know where to look. I still don't to be honest. My only guess is that my grandfather hid the pages inside something else; something unconnected. If he'd gone to the lengths of ripping out the pages then he would have made sure they were well hidden. He wouldn't have wanted anybody else to find them but me."

"But if he wanted you to have them, why didn't he just give

you the whole thing when he was alive?" asked Jennings.

"It's complicated," said Stratton. "He made the tapes when he knew he didn't have long to live. My father typed up the content for him. He asked my father to get me to come and see him because he wanted me to have the transcript. He told my father that I was the only one who could make any use of it.

"My father tried to get me to visit my grandfather, but at the time I was going through one of my heavy-drinking phases and didn't bother. I didn't realize how close to death he was. After he died, me and my father fell out. Out of guilt, I wrongly blamed him for granddad's death and we didn't speak for years, which is why it took me so long to get hold of the transcript."

"Fair enough," said Jennings. "But what if it was your father who ripped out the pages?"

"It wasn't his style. Whatever our differences he wouldn't have held anything back from me, he was too honest."

"What about the tapes?" asked Stella.

"Erased at my grandfather's request," said Stratton wearily. "Is that everything? Because I really want to get on and find these pages."

The brown cardboard box was two feet square and three feet high. It contained old books and newspapers, and bits of bric-a-brac that his grandfather had decided to leave to him. He worked his way down through the box, placing its contents in neat lines on the floor so as not to miss anything. When he'd got everything out he started to check each item one by one. Stella and Jennings sat down with him and helped.

"Where do you think he would have hidden them?" asked Jennings. "In one of the books?"

"Maybe," said Stratton. "Or maybe the newspapers. But they could be in anything, just go through everything that could possibly hold loose leaves of paper."

Jennings took a pile of books and searched through each one methodically. Meanwhile Stella was filing through the yellowing newspapers, some of which dated back to the 1930s. She had to focus hard as her mind kept getting distracted by the interesting stories of yesteryear.

Stratton had ignored the books and newspapers and gone straight to searching through the rest of the stuff. There were old spectacle cases, small boxes, old electrical gadgets from the 1960s, and toys that looked like they were made in the 1920s. The pages could have been hidden inside any of them.

For over an hour they carefully combed through each item, but without success. Stratton had even taken apart the electrical gadgets in case the pages had been secreted inside.

"Well that's it then," said Jennings. "They're obviously not here - we've gone through the whole lot."

Stratton looked perplexed. "There's got to be something here," he said. "I'm absolutely sure of it. I can't think of anywhere else."

He scanned the items again. Everything that could be stripped had been taken apart and looked inside.

"You're sure that you went through those newspapers and books thoroughly, are you?" he asked.

Stella and Jennings both said yes.

Stratton's eyes fell upon the bits of the small travel iron he'd taken apart. Part of the old material flex had worn out and, in true granddad style, had been covered with insulating tape. It was a bodged job but typical of his grandfather's DIY. Then a thought occurred to him. He took the flex and slowly began to peel away the tape. As the tape unravelled, it revealed not wires, but paper. A grin spread across his face, but he continued with caution. When he had completely unravelled the tape he reached into the flex and removed the paper with care.

"Is that them?" asked Jennings excitedly.

Stratton unrolled the pieces of paper. There were six A5-sized pages with writing on both sides. They were numbered 52 through to 63. "It looks like it," he said. He began to read.

"Well, does it tell you where the box is?" said Jennings after a couple of minutes.

"I haven't read it all yet," said Stratton testily. "Give me a chance."

He scanned through the rest of the pages quickly. His face remained impassive throughout.

"Well?" said Stella, when he'd finished.

Stratton put the pages down. "I don't know," he said. "It mentions the box but it doesn't say where it is. It just says that my grandfather took it and hid it out of harm's way."

"But why did your grandfather need to hide it?" asked Jennings.

Stratton handed him the pages. "Read it and you'll find out."

Chapter 22

Transcript of Stratton's grandfather's tape recording:

I returned to England in 1945. The first thing I did was to marry Maria. It was a fairly small affair, with just close friends and family in attendance. I did of course invite my three comrades from my jungle adventures. They too had survived the war and I was eager to see them again. We had parted company after we had escaped Burma and it had been three years since I'd seen them. The day after the wedding, before I left for my honeymoon, Jeremy called us all together for dinner at his hotel. We ate and chatted about our respective experiences during the latter part of the war. After we'd had our pudding and were enjoying port with cheese and biscuits, the subject of Suri and the box finally came up. It had been on my mind, but it had been such an experience that I didn't feel comfortable bringing it up. It was almost as if I were scared that the others had not been quite so dramatically affected by the episode.

As soon as the subject was broached Jeremy's eyes lit up with a boyish excitement. It was he who had kept hold of the box after I had left them in Imphal. He, Mulholland and Atkins had spent the rest of the war in India, and with Mulholland's permission, he had disappeared every so often to do some research into the origin of the box. His sorties had taken him to many out of the way villages and temples.

Most of the people he encountered looked blankly when he produced the box. But one day, on a trip to Simla in the Himalayas, he came across an old swami who appeared to recognize some of the symbols. Through an interpreter, he found out that the few symbols the swami recognized dated back thousands of years. They were used by spiritual leaders, who believed that they were a way of communicating directly with the gods. As Jeremy talked, a shiver of exhilaration ran up and down my spine. For three years I had been thinking about Suri and the box. Deep down inside I knew that something divine had touched me that day in Burma, and Jeremy's talk of communicating with the gods fitted in perfectly with the way I was feeling. My stomach knotted with giddy anticipation. The four of us, by accident, or maybe design, had stumbled across a hot line to the spirit world. If we could tap into it, I thought, who knows what we could achieve.

Of course, at that time it was all hypothetical. Although Jeremy had discovered a possible link with the spirit world, we still had no proof that the symbols worked, and no idea how to activate or utilize them. At the end of the evening we agreed that we would dedicate all our spare time to finding out the secrets of the box.

When I returned from honeymoon all I could think about was finding out more about the symbols. I got a job working for a merchant bank in the city, but my mind was hardly ever there. The four of us arranged to meet once a month to discuss any progress that we'd made. Jeremy kept hold of the box, but each of us had a sheet of paper with the symbols drawn on it to work from.

Over the period of a couple of years we experimented with the symbols. We drew them in different sequences; we drew them on our bodies; we drew them in the air around us; we went to churches and spiritual sites and tried to use them; yet nothing worked. We became frustrated, and the idea that we were being stupid, and that the symbols had no significance whatsoever, went through each of our minds. By 1949 our monthly meetings had been replaced by half yearly get togethers. I was losing interest rapidly and, if it hadn't been for a chance meeting in the August of that year, I would probably have given up on the whole thing.

Maria and I had decided to take our three-year-old son on his first seaside holiday. I booked some time off work and we went down to Littlehampton for the week. During our stay we went to various shows on the pier. One evening there was a martial arts demonstration. At the end of the demonstration, an old Japanese man, probably in his sixties, invited members of the audience to try and get him to the ground. There was a ten pound prize for anyone that could do it. Lots of men had a go, the odd riler, some of them huge burly beasts, but he was so quick with his hands that no-one could get near him. Everyone that tried to floor him ended up on the ground themselves. I was fascinated by the skill of the man, and after the show I dragged Maria backstage so that I could speak with him.

The man's name was Shonigi and he spoke English fairly well, if a little broken. I expressed my admiration for his expertise and asked him where one could learn these skills. He gave me the name of a Judo club in South Kingston called Budokwai, run by a man called Gunji Kazumi. He explained that he himself had learnt his skills in Japan, and that he was over here because he was unable to go back. He had refused to join the Japanese army during the war as he did not believe in killing people. He now made a living travelling Europe and America with his demonstrations.

I was just about to take my leave, when it came into my head to show him the symbols. Even though I had almost given up on them, I still carried them around in my pocket through habit. As soon as I produced the piece of paper his eyes lit up with recognition.

"Reiki," he said, and pointed to one of the symbols. "This is Reiki symbol."

The symbol he was pointing to was the largest one that was positioned in the centre of Suri's box.

"What does it mean?" I asked.

Dominic C. James

"It mean, 'put power of universe here'," he said.

I asked him if he recognized any of the other symbols. He looked through and he picked out three more, but the rest he couldn't place.

I asked him what Reiki was and he explained to me that it was a healing system that had originated in Japan at the end of the last century. The symbols were used to connect the healer with the energy of the universe. He said that literally translated Reiki meant 'universal life force energy'. I asked him how I could get the symbols to work. He replied that I couldn't, unless I had a Reiki Master attune me to them. The process took years he said. A Master would only attune you when you fully understood what the attunement meant.

Undaunted, I asked him where I might find a Master. He said there were very few in the world, but he himself was one. I left him my address and he said that he would contact me when he returned to England after his tour of America.

Six months later he turned up at my house unannounced. I welcomed him and asked him to stay with us for a while. I would give him food and board in return for him teaching myself and my friends about Reiki and the symbols. He agreed to teach us the basics.

Shonigi's instruction was based on us clearing ourselves of mental debris, and any hang ups we might have, or grudges we might bear. He said that we had to heal ourselves before we could attempt to heal others. He explained that the bitterness and anger that humans harboured in their mind manifested itself in the form of physical illness. We needed to look deep inside ourselves and our respective histories before we could progress. He said that the process was painful but necessary. Our lives would appear to turn for the worse, but would then get better.

Jeremy and Atkins were highly dubious about Shonigi and his methods, but what he said made sense to Mulholland and I, so they went along with us.

As part of the cleansing process Shonigi gave us Reiki sessions once a week. My first session was the most amazing experience of my life. Shonigi laid me on a reed mat on the floor and told me to close my eyes and relax. He placed his hands gently over my face and began. At first I felt nothing, but as I became less self-conscious and more relaxed a subtle wave of energy crept over me. After a while I felt like I was floating in mid-air. Colours swirled around my head, vivid and bright. I felt like I was flying across the universe, travelling through space and time, leaving a trail of flaming stars in my wake. It was exhilarating yet at the same time, slightly frightening. I was being swept away by a force over which I had absolutely no control. Lurking beneath the electric surge of well being was an underlying sense of helplessness. It was almost as if at any moment my spirit would leave my body, and my very being would dissolve into the cosmos, in one beautiful, seamless motion.

The session lasted an hour but in my mind I had only closed my eyes for five minutes. When I opened them again, Shonigi was sitting in a chair next to me holding a glass of water. He told me to sit up very slowly and handed me the drink. I couldn't believe how thirsty I was. I drank the water down quickly and he went to get me another glass. When he came back a minute later my head was gradually returning to earth, although I still felt dizzy and light. I also found that I couldn't stop smiling. I was grinning like a madman.

"You enjoy, yes?" said Shonigi.

I just beamed at him and nodded, feeling it unnecessary to speak. I had been touched by something that no words could ever do justice to.

The other three had similar experiences, but over the next three days we became quite sick. Shonigi explained that this was our bodies purging ill-feeling and bad experiences. After the brief sickness I felt better than I ever had done. I was filled with an energy and vigour that a few days before would have been incomprehensible to me. The others felt it too and we knew that our journey into Reiki had begun.

Shonigi stayed with me for almost six months and during this time he taught us about the seven chakras in the human body, and how each one influenced different parts of our emotional and physical lives. By the time he left all four of us had been attuned to the second level of Reiki and were able to heal ourselves and others.

We paid Shonigi well for his services as we felt that it was fair and just to do so.

Whereas Jeremy, Atkins and I were happy with the enlightening knowledge that we had come across, Mulholland wanted more. As second-level practitioners we could use only three symbols - even Shonigi could only use four, and there were over three hundred on the box. Mulholland wanted to know what purpose the other symbols had. He was convinced that they were the source of a much deeper and greater power. He was also convinced that the box itself contained other secrets.

Mulholland gradually drifted away from the group and communicated with us less and less. He removed the box from Jeremy's keeping and took its guardianship upon himself, claiming that as the senior officer it should be his responsibility. We were no longer in the army, but old habits die hard and we didn't question his authority.

Over the next few years Mulholland began to make money; a lot of money. He would buy troubled companies for a pittance, and then, as if by magic, he would turn them around and they would be turning a profit again. He would buy seemingly worthless bits of land from farmers, and suddenly find that the land was wanted by the government for a new road or bypass; or by the Ministry of Defence for a testing site or an airstrip. Everything he touched was turning to rock solid twenty four carat gold. He had been fairly successful before, but now his luck was bordering on outrageous.

By 1955 he was one of the wealthiest men in Britain, if not the world. He had long since distanced himself from our little group and we had ceased to have any contact with him. I became convinced that he had somehow tapped into the power of the box and was greedily taking what he could from an unsuspecting world.

During our instruction Shonigi had told us that as our spiritual power grew, so the universe would provide us with more of what we needed. But he cautioned us of the perils; "Take what you need from life," he had said. "But never be greedy or take too much because everything has a price." I believed that Mulholland was taking way too much and needed to be confronted.

After a lot of fobbing off from his minions I eventually managed to organize an audience with him. He invited me round to Addington Hall, the stately home he'd bought, for dinner and drinks. It was the first time I'd seen him in four years. At first glance he appeared to be the same person that I knew and admired. He greeted me warmly and we sat in his drawing room having a sherry. But after a while I sensed that he had changed. His eyes, once bright and welcoming, had turned cold and sour; and the way he gruffly called and dismissed his butler, was in no way redolent of the kindly manner with which he had previously treated his staff. He did his best to hide this new cruelness under a façade of amiable banter, but I had seen through him and I started to worry.

Over dinner I questioned him about the box. He became defensive as soon as I mentioned it. He said that it was all a load of bunkum and he didn't think about it any more. When I asked him where it was he waved his hands in the air and said that he didn't know. He said that it must have got lost in the move to his new home. I didn't believe him for one minute and so I kept pressing him on it. Eventually he lost his temper and demanded that I leave the house. As I left I saw his wife and teenage son sitting in one of the reception rooms, they had heard Mulholland's voice raised and they both looked absolutely terrified. The fear in their eyes convinced me that my friend had become a power-mad monster.

After that visit I knew that something had to be done. Somehow or other we were going to have to get the box away from Mulholland. The problem was that we had no way of getting into his house, or any way of knowing where he kept it. A break-in was out of the question and the chances of any of us being invited again were non existent. In desperation I suggested to Jeremy and Atkins that we try to get Mulholland's wife on board. They thought the idea to be ludicrous, but I persuaded them of the fearful look that she had given me at the house, and after much debating they agreed to give it a shot.

The major flaw in my plan was getting into contact with Mrs Mulholland. I couldn't go back to Addington Hall and there would be no way of ringing her without her husband finding out. In the end I decided to turn private detective and tail her whenever she left the house.

Luckily Mrs Mulholland was a woman of routine and after three weeks of on-and-off spying on her I had worked out the best time to approach her. Every Wednesday she would take a trip into the local town to have her hair done. It was the only time she didn't use her chauffeur. She would leave her vehicle around the corner in the car park of the local pub, and walk the two hundred yards to the hairdressers. So, one Wednesday afternoon I happened to stroll down the street and bump into her.

"Hello," I said, stopping her in the street. "Daphne Mulholland isn't it?"

"Yes," she said cautiously.

"I'm David. I'm a friend of your husband's. You came to my wedding about ten years ago," I said. "And I was up at the house last month," I added with a knowing look.

At first she was slightly flustered and uncomfortable, but as I chatted she became more cordial and receptive, although, whenever I mentioned her husband she changed the subject quickly. I could tell she was scared of him and that her gilt-edged lifestyle was heaped with an underlying sadness. I just needed a way to get her on side. Not wanting to push her too far too soon I made my excuses and left her to get to the hairdressers.

A couple of weeks later I happened to bump into her again. I made the excuse that I had business in the town every Wednesday. Again we talked briefly and went our separate ways. This happened another three or four times over the next few months, until I felt sure that I had gained her trust.

One Wednesday afternoon I just came straight out and asked her about the box. I gave her a brief rundown of all that had happened and explained that I was worried about her husband. I said that I thought he'd changed and that he was becoming dangerous. She said nothing, but the look she gave confirmed what I already guessed. I gave her my card and told her to contact me if she could be any help. She gave me a look of disgust, but took the card anyway.

It was almost six months before she contacted me. By that time I'd given up hope of ever getting the box back. I didn't know what had happened to her, but when she rang me she was in a highly emotional state. I suggested that we meet and she agreed to come to my house.

When she arrived she was in a mess. I took her through to the living room and Maria made her a cup of tea. She had been crying and mascara ran down her cheeks. I let her sit quietly for a while and then, after she'd had some tea, I asked her what had happened.

She said that Charles had gone crazy and hit her. She had heard him shouting at Travis the butler in the study and as it had sounded particularly animated, she had gone to investigate and try to calm things down. When she arrived in the room she saw

Charles strike Travis violently in the head. She tried to intervene to stop any further violence, but as she did, Charles flung his arm back and smashed her in the cheek. Far from apologizing, he just shouted at her, and told her to mind her own business. It was then that something clicked inside her and she had phoned me.

She went on to tell me that over the years Charles had become increasingly irrational and brutal. He was prone to unprovoked fits of rage. She and her son and his staff were all scared witless by him. She said it hadn't always been like that, only since he had become successful in business. For years now she had lived in fear of his ferocious temper. She had only stayed with him because that was what wives did. She hoped that one day he would see the light and return to his old self: the man she had fallen in love with. The more she talked to me, the more she relaxed. After years of quiet torture and frustration she was finally unburdening herself.

When I felt the time was right, I broached the subject of the box. She said that she had only seen it once; years ago when Charles had come home with it tucked under his arm. She had asked what it was and he had dismissed it as nothing. He had taken it straight to his study and she had not seen it since. She said that he probably kept it in his personal safe.

It was then that I confided in her and gave her a detailed explanation of my friendship with Mulholland, Jeremy and Atkins, the miracle in the jungle, and how important I believed the box to be. She found it all a bit fantastical and bewildering. But when she saw the gravity in my eyes she realized that this may be serious and she had to help me find it. I told her that we had to retrieve the box; and she had to get me into the house and up to Mulholland's safe.

She knew that Charles would be out of the house the following evening as he always played bridge at his London club, Blades, on a Tuesday, and he stayed in the city overnight. I arranged to call at the house at around eight o'clock. She didn't think there would be a problem with the servants as they all hated Mulholland with a passion.

The major stumbling block in my plan was getting into the safe. Daphne had no idea what the combination was, and I was no Raffles. I had to find somebody who could get it open for us. I called Atkins and explained the situation to him. I knew that he bought a lot of stuff on the black market; and I hoped that one of his connections might know the name of a good safe-cracker. Atkins called me back the next day and told me that he'd found someone.

At six o'clock on Tuesday evening the doorbell rang. Standing on the step was an oldish man, probably in his sixties, wearing a grey overcoat and a black cap. He introduced himself by his first name, Brian, and said that he'd been sent by Atkins to help me. He didn't look like much of a criminal to me, but I didn't have time to get anyone else, so he had to suffice. His fee was to be forty pounds, a large sum in those days, and it was payable up front.

We arrived at Addington Hall just before eight. The butler answered the door and led us to Daphne Mulholland who was reading in the drawing room. She looked at Brian quizzically. When Travis the butler had gone I explained who he was.

She led us up the sweeping staircase to the first floor, and then on to the study. The safe was positioned behind a painting by Renoir. Brian carefully removed the work and took off his coat. The puzzled look he gave the safe was not inspiring. He explained that it was a fairly new design and he wasn't that familiar with it. He could open it, but it would take a while. I assured him that time wasn't a problem as we had all night.

Despite his conservativeness Brian had the safe open in what seemed to be no time at all. I looked inside but all I could see were stacks of papers. I reached inside and one by one removed all the contents. There was no sign of the box.

"It's not here," I said despondently. "Is there anywhere else he would keep it?"

"I can't think of anywhere," replied Daphne. "This study is his stronghold."

"Don't worry sir," said Brian pushing me aside. "I've got an idea."

He stuck his hand into the safe and began to feel about. His face was tight with concentration. After about ten seconds I heard a click. From the safe he withdrew a rectangular metal plate. "False bottom," he said. He reached back in and when his hand came out again it was holding the box. "This what you're after?" he said.

I thanked him and took the box.

At that moment I heard shouting from downstairs. Daphne gave me a look of horror. Mulholland wasn't in London; he was back in the house. I felt my stomach go real tight. My first thought was to make a break for it. But that would leave Daphne to face him alone, and my conscience wouldn't let me do it. I had to stay with her.

I opened the study door ever so slightly and peeked out. Mulholland had climbed the stairs and was storming down the landing towards us, his face contorted and red with anger. There was no escape.

Mulholland burst into the study. "What the hell do you think you're doing David!" he shouted at me. "Give me that box back immediately! This is theft!"

"I'm only taking back what you stole," I said defiantly. "I know what you've been up to Charles. This is a sacred object; you can't be using its power on a whim, just to make yourself a bit of money."

"It's mine and I can do what I like with it, so do yourself a favour and give it back to me." He held out his hand in a demanding fashion.

"No," I said, standing firm. "This box and these symbols are meant for the benefit of everyone. It's not some rich man's play thing. You know that. You were there in the Kabbaw Valley. You know what can be done if the energy's harnessed properly."

He gave a sardonic laugh. "Yes I do know what can be done. Look at all this," he gestured around. "You're just too narrow-minded David. All that business with Shonigi and the Reiki; it's just kids' stuff. I've only just started to realize the potential of the other symbols. There are infinite possibilities."

"Maybe so," I said. "But it has to be gone into responsibly. Look what it's done to you already. You're not the Charles Mulholland I know. You've turned into a tyrant with a God complex."

"Whatever," he said with a sneer. "Just give me the box back and nobody will get hurt."

I stood my ground and refused.

"Very well," he said and produced a gun from his jacket pocket. "Now give me the box," he demanded.

Still I didn't move. Our eyes locked. He knew he would have to shoot me to get the box back. As we stared each other down Daphne made her move. She raised her arm up high, and with all her strength, brought it swinging down onto Mulholland's hand. The gun fell to the floor. Mulholland cursed and instinctively turned to strike his wife. With the box held tightly in my left hand I darted over and picked up the gun with my right. "Don't!" I said to Mulholland. He'd slapped his wife once and was getting ready to do so again. His hands dropped to his sides.

"I don't think you've got the balls to use that thing, have you David?"

"Don't try me," I said, attempting to hide my shakiness. "I'm going to leave now and I'm going to take the box and Daphne with me." I turned to her. "What about your son?" I asked.

"He's at boarding school," she replied.

"You won't get very far," said Mulholland. "As soon as you leave I'll call the police. You'll be arrested for theft and kidnapping. Just give me the box back and we'll forget all about it."

"No," I said and made for the door.

Mulholland sprang at me and before I could react we were wrestling on the floor. He was a big man, much bigger than myself, and he grabbed my right hand and tried to wrench the gun away from me. I held on as tightly as I could, but he was just too strong. I could feel the gun slipping out of my hand and made one last attempt to keep hold of it. My groping fingers must have hit the trigger, because the next thing I knew an almighty bang had pierced my ear. Mulholland's body went limp on top of me.

I extricated myself from my awkward position and stood up. I looked down on Mulholland. He was dead. Blood oozed from his temple, staining the cream carpet.

Daphne was trembling. "What are we going to do?" she stammered.

"I don't know," I said. "I just don't know."

Luckily for us Brian was there. "Listen," he said. "It's simple. Just tell the truth. You had an argument with the bloke; he pulled a gun on you; you wrestled with him; the gun went off. It was an accident, end of story."

"But what do I say we were arguing about?" I asked.

"His wife. Say that he thought you two were having an affair. They'll go for something like that: crime of passion and all."

So that's what we did. Brian put everything, apart from the box, back in the safe just the way it had been and Daphne called the police. Over the next few weeks we were both questioned intensely by them, but in the end they believed us and the coroner recorded it as an accidental death.

Although it had been an accident I still felt guilty about Mulholland's death. The man had saved my life out in Burma, and whatever he had become in the meantime, it didn't make it any more justifiable in my head. Part of me wished that we'd never found the box, it would almost have been better to have died out there in the jungle.

I decided that the box, even though it was obviously a source of spiritual power, was also a source of discontent, and that I had to hide it away until I could figure out its exact origins. I told Atkins and Jeremy that the police had confiscated the box and later given it back to Mrs Mulholland. I told them that she had no idea as to its provenance, and that she just wanted to keep it as an heirloom for her son. They seemed dubious and pressed me to retrieve it from her. I suggested that it was best left alone and that only trouble would come of pursuing it further. I said that we should be grateful for the knowledge that Shonigi had given us and to leave it at that. Daphne Mulholland later told me that both Atkins and Jeremy had called at the house trying to get hold of the box. She had backed up my story and told them that she was keeping it for her son.

With the scent well and truly away from me, I had to find a place to hide the box. Somewhere that it would be safe until I could make up my mind what to do with it...

Chapter 23

Jennings threw the pages down in disgust. "Well that's a lot of good isn't it?" he said. "He's gone through all that and still not let on where the bloody thing is. What was the point of hiding the transcript?"

"I don't know," said Stratton. "But my grandfather never did anything for no reason. The answer's got to be hidden in these pages somewhere. By keeping this part separate he's automatically telling me that the clues are in there. He was an intelligent man, and we understood each other."

"So what are we looking for then?" asked Jennings.

"Probably something subtle in the text. Any anomaly, no matter how small. It could be a turn of phrase, a factual inaccuracy, a spelling mistake; anything really. But I'm certain that the answer's in there somewhere."

Whilst Jennings read through the transcript again, Stratton went outside to the back garden to clear his head some more. He was feeling less than one hundred percent. The excesses of the previous evening were still weighing him down. Physically he wasn't too bad, but his brain was in no fit state to be tackling his grandfather's riddles. What he really needed was a day of rest; a day of lounging on the sofa watching old movies.

At the bottom of the garden there was an old bench. It had been there ever since Stratton could remember. He sat down on it and enjoyed the afternoon sun. He closed his eyes and relaxed his breathing. Drawing the crisp air deep into his lungs he held it there momentarily, letting it run through his body, cleansing and invigorating. He exhaled slowly, releasing the stale air and expelling the disorder from his mind. Memories of his parents still dominated his thoughts, and he knew that he had to temporarily efface them.

After five minutes of this he was interrupted by Stella. She sat down beside him on the bench. "Jennings thinks he might have found something," she said. "It's not much, just a strange word in the text, but you did say to look for the smallest thing."

"Yes I did," said Stratton. "Hopefully he's onto something. I'll come back in. I just needed a few minutes to get my head straight. I'd forgotten how bad the after-effects of a night out were."

"Well, it's probably good to remind yourself every now and then. It'll keep you from doing it again any time soon."

Jennings was still poring over the transcript when they got back inside. His face was a picture of concentration as he went through every sentence looking for the slightest quirk.

"What have you got for me then?" asked Stratton.

"Just a word really," said Jennings. "It's when he's talking about the martial arts demonstration on the pier. He uses the word 'riler'. It just seems strange. You'd think he'd use heckler. Is 'riler' even a word? I mean, 'one who riles'?!"

"I don't know," said Stratton. "It could be an ancient noun, but I doubt it. Let me have a look at it in context."

Jennings handed the sheet of paper to Stratton who looked at it closely. He smiled to himself. "I think you're right Jennings. The way it's worded - 'the odd riler' is just the sort of thing he'd do. It's like a crossword clue."

"How do you mean?" said Jennings.

"Well, it's not actually the whole word that's the clue. We're just meant to take three letters from it: the two r's and the l," said Stratton.

Jennings stared blankly.

"The word 'odd' means that we're meant to take the odd letters from the word 'riler'. The first, the third and the fifth letter."

"Well, when you say it like that, it makes perfect sense," said Jennings sarcastically.

"It's a trick that crossword compilers use all the time," said Stratton. "My grandfather was a great fan. He used to do The

Times crossword every day."

"Fair enough," said Jennings. "But it's just three letters, surely they don't mean anything on their own."

"Of course not. They're just a part of it, I'm sure. He's probably spread letters about the transcript. I suspect our challenge is to pick up on the clues and then rearrange the letters into something that makes sense."

Jennings' face fell. "That means we could be here all day then. It's an almost impossible task. How are we supposed to know when we've got enough letters if we don't know what they're supposed to spell out. We could get ten letters, make some sense out of them, and still be wrong because we've missed out another five that change the message completely. How do we know when to stop? And on top of that we may be collecting needless letters. How do we know that he definitely meant us to pick up on the phrase 'odd riler'. It could be a red herring. If you think about it, we're clutching at straws."

"I can see your point," Stratton admitted. "And you're right to a certain extent, but I don't think he'll have made it ridiculously difficult. It'll be hard enough so as to confuse unwelcome eyes, but it should be easy enough for me to figure out. He knew my mind better than anyone." He paused in reflection. "The problem is that my mind isn't at its best today, so, as you said, we could well be here for some time."

Stratton filed through the transcript again. He read slowly, trying to take in every word and phrase and looking for the slightest anomaly. Hard as he tried though, he just couldn't concentrate. Every time he tried to focus for more than ten seconds, his eyes would glaze over and his brain would reduce to a spongy fuzz. He was frustrated, and cursed himself for being so weak-willed the day before.

"I'll have another look through if you like," said Stella, seeing that Stratton was struggling.

"Good idea," said Stratton as he handed her the transcript. "I just can't seem to concentrate at the moment."

While Stella studied the transcript once more, Stratton went to the kitchen to make coffee. He thought that maybe some caffeine would help him focus. He smiled to himself as the water boiled. The coffee, tea and sugar jars were placed neatly in a row by the kettle, as they had been for the last thirty years. Next to these was the old mug tree that had been there for just as long, only the mugs had changed. Further along was the spice rack, with all the containers arranged in alphabetical order. His mother may have gone, but her systematic organization was still well and truly alive.

"Did you know all this stuff about your grandfather beforehand?" asked Jennings, walking into the kitchen and breaking Stratton from his thoughts.

"Some of it," he replied. "But a lot of gaps have been filled in as well. Why do you ask?"

"Because you never seem surprised by anything new that we discover," said Jennings. "To me all this stuff is like something you'd see in a film or read in a book. It borders on the realms of fantasy. But you take it in your stride and treat everything like it's normal. What if your grandfather was right and this box is a connection to the spirit world? What if it can change people's fortunes and make them powerful? What if it does contain the secrets of healing? Doesn't it do your head in just thinking about the possibilities? I know it does mine."

Stratton looked at Jennings curiously. "It almost sounds like you're starting to believe," he said.

"Maybe," said Jennings with ambivalence. "But you still haven't answered my question. Doesn't it freak you out?"

"Not any more," said Stratton. "You get used to it. I've known that not everything in this world is as it seems for a long time now. My grandfather was always telling me what seemed like outlandish stories, right from when I was a child. Of course I soon learnt at school that those tales were based in myth and legend. The real world is based on science and hard facts, and that's what we grow up believing; miracles are just coincidences, the Bible is full of old wives' tales etc. Circumstance and brain-washing close your mind to any possibilities that can't be explained scientifically. The modern world beats spirituality out of your system.

"The thing with me was: I couldn't shake my gut feeling that things weren't as black and white as science had made them. There's always been a little voice inside me, telling me that there's something else. When I was at university, my grandfather started to confide in me about his experience in the war and about Reiki. I was sceptical at first, but somehow what he said had a ring of truth about it. I was studying theology at the time and things just started to fall into place. I began to research the historical facts behind the biblical myths and started to make connections. During my research I came across information that indirectly corresponded with my grandfather's stories. Ancient texts came into my possession that threatened to blow apart a whole system of belief, and yet validate that belief at the same time. The more I got drawn into the strange world of my grand-father, the more it fucked with my head. I was discovering stuff that I just wasn't ready for...I turned to drink to stop me thinking about it. Since then, my head's gradually caught up and I've accepted these wild ideas as normal. I'm a Reiki Master and I understand things a lot better now. There's a big difference between thinking something's possible and actually knowing it. Do you see what I mean?"

"Sort of," said Jennings.

"Ok. Look at it like this: millions, if not billions, of people believe in Jesus and his miracles right?"

Jennings nodded.

"Well then," Stratton continued. "Imagine if these people actually saw Jesus walking on water; or turning the water into wine; or healing lepers with the wave of his hand. They would be astounded; it would totally fuck their heads up. However much they believed in his divinity, seeing it with their own eyes would be too much. Two thousand years ago people would have been amazed, but they would have had an easier time accepting it. These days people would be looking for hidden mirrors and wine up the guy's sleeve. Once they realized there was no trick and that he actually was the son of God, it would blow them away. In one fell swoop the physical world that they know would be turned on its head. Everything they'd learnt would be rendered obsolete.

"Anyway, the point I'm making is that the reason you're freaked and I'm not is that I've had time to adjust. Once you get used to all this esoteric stuff it just becomes second nature."

"Well, you've certainly made your point," said Jennings. "You've got me curious though. What are those ancient texts that you found? What's in them?"

"I'll let you know what's in them in good time. Let's just concentrate on the task at hand for now - finding that box."

When they returned to the living room Stella's head was still deep in the transcript. "I think I've found something," she said.

"Ok then," said Stratton, handing her a mug of black coffee, "what is it?"

"It's in that bit where he talks about the judo club," said Stella.

"What, the Budokwai?"

"Yes, that's the one," she said. "Anyway he says that it's in South Kingston. Why would you say something was in South Kingston. Surely you'd just say Kingston...Wouldn't you?"

Stratton slapped his palm on his forehead. "South Kingston, of course, what an idiot."

"So it is something then?" said Stella hopefully.

"Yes it is," said Stratton. "My head's so mashed I've been reading it as South Kensington, which is where the Budokwai is situated. I've just been reading what I expected to see, not what was actually written on the paper."

"So what does it mean then? Does it mean that he's hidden it somewhere in Kingston? Or does it mean that he's hidden it somewhere in Kensington?" asked Jennings.

"I don't know. It could be either," said Stratton. "Or it might be neither. We've still got those three letters as well remember. Let's keep looking for something else; we can't stop until it makes sense."

Stella read through the whole thing again, and then Jennings did the same. Stratton drank his coffee deep in thought. The caffeine was perking him up.

"What about this?" said Jennings.

"What's that?" asked Stratton.

"It's his use of words. He says 'I felt my stomach go real tight'. It sounds a bit American to me. Your grandfather seemed quite old school in most of his phrasing; it doesn't seem to fit somehow."

"You're right," said Stratton. "He wouldn't have used those words at all; he would have said 'I felt my stomach knot'."

"Ok then," said Jennings. "If that's the case, which words or letters do we take out of the sentence?"

Stratton thought for a moment. "I guess the letters from the phrase 'go real tight'. The words 'I felt my stomach' would have been in the sentence anyway; the other words are the anomaly. So we've now got Kingston, go real tight and the letters r,r,l. Let's see what we can make of them."

"How do you know that there aren't any more clues in the text?" asked Stella.

"I don't," he replied. "But instinct tells me there's enough to go on. If we can't make any sense out of it then we'll have to go back again. Let's get our heads together and rearrange these letters into something that makes sense."

"Listen," said Jennings. "I'll go and get my laptop from the car. We'll log on to the Internet and go to one of those sites that does anagrams. It'll be a lot quicker than the three of us unscrambling the letters in our heads."

Jennings retrieved his laptop and five minutes later the three of them were crowded round the screen.

"What shall we start with?" asked Jennings. "Do you want me to use all the letters? Or do you want to take Kingston literally and just use the others?"

"Better put everything in to start with," said Stratton. "Let's see what comes up."

Jennings typed in the letters and a couple of seconds later a whole string of possible anagrams came up on the screen. The site indicated that there were over six thousand variations, and that was just using proper words.

"Fuck me! This is going to take a while," said Jennings as he began to scroll through the possibilities, proceeding slowly so that Stratton didn't miss anything. "What about this one?" he said, pointing to the screen seriously.

"Which one's that?" asked Stratton.

" 'Tring Shark on egg tit roll'. Perhaps we have to order a special dish from a Chinese takeaway in Hertfordshire; and then a mysterious Oriental man will bring out the box in a plastic tub," sniggered Jennings.

Stella and Stratton shook their heads.

Jennings chuckled again. "Or maybe 'Ring shark on egg tit troll'; meaning that we have to call a bloke called Shark on 34484887655, the corresponding numbers on a telephone keypad."

"You're a funny man Jennings. Ever thought of a career on stage?" said Stratton.

Jennings continued to scroll down the list quietly, keeping his amusement to himself. The other two were in no mood for any fun; that was obvious. After he'd gone through the whole list he went back to the top and started again.

"Stop there will you," said Stratton, halfway down their second viewing.

Jennings stopped scrolling and Stratton took a closer look.

"What is it?" asked Stella.

"It's this one here," said Stratton pointing to the screen. "'Great Rollright Kingston."

"What the hell is Great Rollright?" asked Jennings.

"It's a little village on the edge of the Cotswolds," said Stratton. "It's of no fantastic significance in itself, but just outside the village there's an ancient ring of megaliths; called the Rollright Stones. I remember it from a family day out when I was a kid. It's supposed to be a place of high energy where loads of ley-lines converge."

"Fair enough, but what the hell has it got in common with Kingston? They're hardly near each other are they?"

"No they're not. I don't know what the connection is yet, maybe there's a place on the map directly between the two locations that holds some significance."

Stratton went to the bookshelf in the hall and picked out the road atlas. He laid it out on the coffee table and turned to the relevant page. Using the edge of a piece of paper he made an imaginary line between the two locations.

"Anything?" enquired Stella.

Stratton shook his head. "There's nowhere on the line that suggests anything familiar. Woodstock, High Wycombe, Slough and Staines: none of them mean anything to me. It was only a hopeful punt anyway. We'll have to think of something else. Let's look up the Rollright Stones on the Internet, they're bound to have a website - I think they're part of the National Trust." Jennings googled 'Rollright Stones', and sure enough they found that the place had its own website. He scrolled down and stopped at the passage marked 'History of the stones'.

Stratton quickly read through the passage: *Legend has it that the stones are the cursed embodiments of an ancient king and his men. The king was on a quest to rule the whole country; he had reached the Rollrights when a witch appeared. She told him that if he took seven steps and could see the village of Long Compton then he would rule uncontested. He took the seven steps, but on the last one a mound rose up in front of him and totally obscured his view. The witch deemed him to have failed and he and his men were turned to stone. His men now form the stone circle and the king himself is the isolated King Stone.'*

"That's it then!" exclaimed Stratton.

"What's it?" said Jennings, looking perplexed.

"The King Stone," said Stratton. "He's buried it under the King Stone."

Chapter 24

Round the corner from Broomfield Park, Grady sat in his newly-rented Vauxhall Astra listening to the radio. He watched the blip on his portable screen with increasing indifference. It was ten o' clock in the evening and still Jennings' car hadn't moved. He had been waiting for eight hours. He would give it until midnight and then try and grab a bit of sleep.

The day had started well enough, considering. He had called in a favour from Brad Devereaux at the CIA's London station. Through his extensive network Brad had located Jennings with ease. He had also provided Grady with a state-of-the-art transmitter and screen, as well as a new gun. Grady had accepted the help gratefully. He had hired a car under a false name and made his way to Sunningdale. After fixing the transmitter to Jennings' car, he had parked himself in a lay-by and waited.

Grady was used to waiting for long periods; it went with the job. He was finding as he got older, that his boredom threshold was becoming shorter. This surprised him as he assumed that it should be increasing. Perhaps all the monotonous years of stakeouts were catching up with him, he thought. Maybe patience was a finite commodity, a store that gradually eroded over time, until one day it was gone; and you became a cantankerous old pensioner complaining about queuing and buses being late.

The main reason for his current restlessness though, was the fact that he had somewhere else he would much rather be. Over the years he'd avoided having any sort of meaningful private life. His job had been all that he needed: it had provided all the action, excitement and women that he could have wanted. Besides, any solid roots in the real world would have complicated matters. With the advent of Brooke, things had changed. These days his work was the complication. Hours spent watching an unchanging monitor, were hours that could have been spent with her; hours that should have been spent with her.

He banged the steering wheel in frustration. "Fuck you Miles!" he cursed aloud. He wished he'd never agreed to meet the guy in the first place.

It wasn't just Brooke that was bugging him though. He was none too happy at having to spy on Jennings and the other two again. He hadn't really wanted to leave them for dead in the cottage; it had been a necessary evil. When they had got out alive he had been almost relieved. They had treated him fairly and without malice. He felt ungrateful carrying out this new subterfuge. There was no room for sentiment in an agent's character, but what he was doing stank of betrayal. The universe had forgiven him for his sins and let him off scot-free; and now he was throwing that forgiveness right back in its face.

His one hope was that the whole situation could be resolved without any further recourse to violence. Theoretically it was simple: all he had to do was find the box and hand it over to Professor Miles; there was no need for anyone to get hurt. In reality though, he knew that whoever found the box first, it wouldn't be him. And nobody was going to hand it over without resistance.

His thoughts were broken by the monitor. The red blip that was Jennings' car had started to move. He waited for a couple of minutes and then set off in pursuit at a safe distance.

Chapter 25

Jennings drove slowly down the empty, unlit road, looking for the entrance to the stone circle. For almost an hour he'd been driving around blindly between the villages of Great Rollright, Little Rollright and Long Compton, searching for it. Stella sat next to him smoking a cigarette. Stratton was laid out on the back seat taking a nap. Conversation during the trip had been minimal. A long lay-by loomed up on his left-hand side and he slowed further. At the end of the lay-by was a green sign and he pulled in to read it.

"Well, here we are at last," he said. "I was beginning to think that we'd never find it."

Stella turned round and poked Stratton with her cigarette-free hand. "Come on sleepy head, wake up. We're here now."

Stratton sat up and stretched his arms wide and yawned. "That was quick," he said. "I thought I'd only just dozed off. What's the time?"

"Nearly midnight," said Jennings. "Near the witching hour."

Leaving the headlights on, they got out of the car. The cloud cover was thick, and there was no moonlight to pierce the pitch dark. Jennings opened the boot and removed the three torches and the shovel that they had brought with them. He handed out the torches and gave the shovel to Stratton.

"Digging's my job then?" said Stratton.

"Well, this *is* your show," said Jennings.

Armed with their torches they approached the entrance.

"No admission between sunset and sunrise," said Jennings, reading from the sign. "Sounds a bit ominous."

"According to the website, the stones come to life at midnight," said Stratton. "They turn back into the king's men and dance around in a circle, and sometimes they go down to Little Rollright spinney to drink. Apparently, anyone witnessing these scenes will go mad or die. Of course it's probably a load of old rubbish, but you never know."

"All right, there's no need to go on," said Jennings. "This place is creepy enough as it is without you filling my head with ghost stories."

A small black metal swing gate was all that covered the entrance. Beyond the gate was a dirt path. To the left of the path was an old corrugated-steel shed, painted blue, which served as the warden's hut. Jennings shone his torch on the front of the hut. There was a small slot on the door, and underneath it was a sign: indicating that a donation of one pound per adult should be made for the upkeep of the site. Another sign forbade sitting, standing or climbing on the stones.

"Do you think we ought to make a donation?" Jennings asked, turning to Stratton.

"Of course," said Stratton. He felt in his pocket and drew out some change. He extracted three pound coins and handed them to Jennings who dropped them through the slot.

"Do you think that everyone who comes here pays their pound?" said Jennings. "I mean; the system is open to abuse. You could quite easily get away with not paying if there's no-one to make you."

"I guess most people who come here are the sort of people who appreciate that the upkeep costs money," said Stratton. "The sort of idiot who would avoid paying wouldn't be interested in coming here anyway. They'd be more interested in going to the pub or buying drugs."

"Would that be the sort of idiot who'd do that?" Jennings said, pointing his beam to the two boarded-up windows on the hut. A sign underneath explained that the windows had been smashed by vandals.

"Yes, exactly that sort of idiot," said Stratton.

A thin mist hung in the air above the stones. Jennings felt a shiver travel right through his spine. As he approached the circle a grim sense of foreboding hit him. It didn't feel right that they should be there. He felt like a trespasser; not because the sign had said no admittance, but because unseen voices were telling him he was. It was almost as if the stones were talking to him; harsh repellent whispers, designed to warn him away from a place to which he was unwelcome.

Stella too, was feeling the atmosphere. There was something wrong about the place. It was creepy to the point of being sinister. Like Jennings she felt like they shouldn't be there; that they were intruding on a gathering to which they weren't invited; a gathering of the dead in which the living didn't belong.

"You two can feel it as well then," said Stratton, sensing their apprehension.

"Yes," said Stella. "This isn't right; I don't think we should be here."

"If it's any consolation, I don't want to be here either," he said. "There's an oppressive energy about this place. I don't think that the stones are going to spring to life at any moment, but all the same I reckon we should get on with the job and get out as soon as we can."

They walked to the centre of the circle and shone their torches around. The stones were of varying shapes and sizes; some tall and thin, some short and squat and some stocky and robust.

"Which one is the King Stone then?" asked Jennings.

"I think it's probably that one over there," said Stratton, pointing to a tall stone in front of a row of silver birch. "The one that looks like a thin oven glove. It's by far the tallest stone in the circle, it must be the one."

They walked over to the tall stone and, after determining with a compass which side of it was south, Stratton began to dig. A couple of deluges over the previous week had softened the earth nicely, and he wasted no time in making a hole two foot deep.

"How far down do you think we'll have to go?" asked Jennings.

"No idea," replied Stratton. "But any more than three feet would be ridiculous. To be honest I'd have thought we would have found it by now. I personally can't see the point of burying it any deeper than two feet."

He continued to dig, and in another ten minutes he had made a hole three feet deep and two feet square; there was no sign of the box.

"Are you sure we should be digging south of the King Stone?" said Jennings.

"Yes, of course I am. 'South Kingston' - south King Stone; it makes perfect sense," said Stratton.

Jennings wasn't satisfied. "But how far south of the King Stone should you be digging? It's pretty ambiguous isn't it? I mean, it could be anywhere in a straight line south."

Stratton began to get tetchy. "Look. There were no measurements indicated in the text so it obviously means that we have to dig directly next to the stone. It's as simple as that."

Stella, who up until then had been keeping out of it, broke into the conversation. "Of course, you could be digging under the wrong stone," she said.

"What?" said Stratton. "What do you mean, 'the wrong stone'? I think it's pretty obvious that this is the King Stone."

"I don't think so," she said. "It said in that history of the Stones that the King Stone was isolated from the rest of them. This stone is part of the circle. While you two have been arguing, I've been looking at the printout I took from the website. It turns out that the King Stone is fifty yards away; across the other side of the road. So I suggest we get over there."

Not wanting to leave a mess for the warden to clear up, Stratton quickly filled in the hole, and then they headed over the road.

The King Stone was situated in the middle of a small field. It was surrounded by a circular, spiked, black iron railing. Standing over ten feet tall, its top-heavy proportions made it look as if it would topple over at any second. Next to the Stone was an official sign saying something about the Minister of Works. Part of the placard had been snapped off by vandals, so the notice was unclear.

Wary of the damage that the spikes could do to his fertility if he slipped, Stratton carefully manoeuvred himself over the railings. Jennings passed him the shovel.

The base of the King Stone was covered on all sides by long, straw-like, grass; and this made the initial breaking of the turf difficult. After five minutes of hard graft, Stratton had cleared the awkward growth and was making steady headway down into the ground.

After another ten minutes, and eighteen inches down, his spade hit something solid.

"Here we go, I think we've got something," he said, and reached down into the hole. His hand gripped a cold solid object and he levered it out of the earth. It was a piece of slate.

"Excellent," said Jennings. "Perhaps we could start up our own roofing company."

Stratton picked up his shovel and started to dig again. Five minutes later he hit another object. He shone his torch down into the hole. Poking its head out of the soil was a piece of dirty white hessian cloth. He reached down and moved some more earth with his hands until he could see the whole of the package. He tugged at the cloth and, with a bit of force, dislodged it from its resting place.

"What is it?" said Stella, as Stratton dusted off the material and reached inside what was clearly a small sack.

From the sack Stratton produced an old biscuit tin: a large square one used to hold an assortment. He prised off the lid and got Stella to shine her torch inside. The magnificent sight of carved symbols greeted their eyes. They had found the box.

"Wow! It's beautiful," said Stella.

Stratton eyed the box with awe, years of expectation welling up inside him, his grandfather's legacy finally unearthed. With trembling hands he removed it from the tin and held it close, marvelling as two millennia of history flashed through his mind. "Yes it is," he murmured. "It's absolutely beautiful. The carving is exceptional. The symbols are really small, but the detail is incredible. This is real craftsmanship."

Jennings cleared his throat in agitation. "I hate to interrupt you David Dickinson, but can we get a move on? Let's fill in that hole and get the hell out of here. There'll be plenty of time for fawning over carpentry when we're safe and warm inside the car."

Stratton put the lid back on the biscuit tin and returned it to the sack. He gave it to Stella and filled in the hole. Handing the shovel to Jennings he lifted himself onto the railings.

"You want to be careful there. A man could do himself a nasty injury on those spikes," said a male voice. It wasn't Jennings.

Chapter 26

A couple of miles away Yoshima sat back in his seat and allowed himself some brief relaxation. The dot on his tracking screen hadn't moved for five minutes now, and he guessed that they must have found the place they were looking for. There was no need for haste on his part, he would sit and wait for them to recover the box and relieve them of it later. Sacred knowledge in the hands of the West was utterly unthinkable. They were totally incapable of tempering power with wisdom. Yoshima had witnessed with his own eyes the destruction that came from the witless use of devastating might...

...The morning had been tediously slow, with Yoshima constantly staring out of the schoolroom window wishing he was somewhere else. There was a time when he had loved Mathematics, but as he grew older, and the theories more complex, his enthusiasm had waned. His fourteen-year-old brain no longer craved material knowledge, he was above all that, his interests now lay firmly with the expansion of his soul. In particular he longed to join his soul with Haruko Tani the girl who lived next door. Every morning he would rise especially early and watch from his window as she carried out her pre-school chores in the garden. His heart would flutter erratically with just the slightest glimpse of her beautiful swan-like neck, or her perfect soft mouth. She was a year older than himself and probably thought him too young for a potential suitor, but he was determined that one day he would hold her hand and kiss those heavenly lips.

The urgent wail of the air-raid sirens dragged him from his reverie. They had been heard before in Nagasaki and all the children in the school knew exactly what to do. They filed out of class in an orderly fashion and headed out through the back of the building, making their way to the cave that the government had carved in the side of the hill for their protection. Yoshima lollopped along happily towards the back with his little brother Ichiro, knowing that the bombs would fall many miles away as they had done previously.

As they reached the cave Yoshima took one last look back over the city, expecting to see but a few distant pillars of smoke rising from unfortunate targets. What he actually saw would change his, and countless other lives forever.

There was a flash of light so brilliant that it obscured the landscape completely. Yoshima staggered back at its intensity and whipped his hands up to protect his eyes. Before he could regain his footing a mighty wind powered through and blew him into the cave, sending him crashing against the wall. He hit his head and passed out.

When he came to the world was dark. He was lying on the ground outside the cave with Ichiro hovering over him. "Yoshima!" he whimpered. "Yoshima! Wake up!"

Yoshima blinked a couple of times and sat up. "It is okay Ichiro," he said. "I am okay. What is going on?"

"I don't know!" cried Ichiro. "The light came, then the wind it came and burned us!"

Yoshima was suddenly aware of his own skin crawling with heat. He shot to his feet and grabbed Ichiro's hand. "Come with me," he ordered, and led his brother swiftly towards the river. The cold water was blissful and they stayed submerged for over half an hour.

After relieving their skin they joined up with the other children and began to walk down into the suburbs. The air was thick with choking dust and debris, the only source of illumination being the small scattered fires among the smoke. Ichiro grabbed Yoshima's arm. "Alligator!" he screamed.

Yoshima looked to where Ichiro was pointing and slowly walked over to investigate. He soon realized that the creature crawling along the ground was no reptile. It was a human, his or her skin reduced to black scales by the searing force of the blast. Its eyelids were gone and it stared up at them helplessly, its face charred beyond recognition and devoid of any discernible expression. Yoshima turned aside and puked.

As they progressed deeper in they saw many more 'alligators'. The children wailed, screaming '*jigoku*' (hell). When they finally reached Yoshima's street he knew that it was hopeless. The buildings lay in ruins with unidentifiable bodies littering the flaming rubble. He wandered over to where his house once stood and knelt in the ash reciting a prayer for the fallen.

With moistened cheeks he got to his feet and held Ichiro's hand. Through his tears a sudden flash in the greyness caught his eye. It was emanating from the hand of one of the corpses. He stumbled across the rocky waste and bent down to examine it more closely. Brushing the dust away, he removed the object from the corpse's grasp and held it up in the dimness. It was a silver pendant in the shape of a swan: it was Haruko's. He looked down at the disfigured cadaver and wept once again until he could weep no more...

...Yoshima slipped a hand inside his shirt and clasped the pendant tightly. The West must never again be allowed the power of life and death over his countrymen.

Chapter 27

Stella and Jennings shot around and shone their beams in the direction of the voice. Standing there with a gun in one hand and a flashlight in the other was Scott Grady. He had a rope looped over his right shoulder.

Jennings voiced his frustration. "Oh, for fuck's sake! Can't you leave us alone for five minutes? I thought you'd gone back to the States."

"Well I was going to go back, but then I had a change of plan. It seemed disappointing to come all this way and go home empty-handed. I figured I ought to finish what I started. Like they say: if a job's worth doing…"

"Ok. What do you want?" asked Jennings.

Grady sighed. "The box of course. So if you'll just hand it over then I can be on my way."

With no other options Stella handed the box over to Grady.

"Thank you very much. It's been a pleasure," he said. "Now I'm really sorry guys but I'm going to have to tie you up again. I need to get to the airport and onto a plane without any more hold-ups."

He made the three of them sit on the ground back to back in a triangle, and circled them with the rope six times, pulling it uncomfortably tight after each revolution. When he was finished they were locked fast together.

"Don't worry," said Grady. "Someone will find you tomorrow no doubt. It's not that cold either so you won't die of hypothermia.

"It's been nice knowing you." He gave them a little wave and walked off into the darkness.

"I can't believe he's stitched us up again," said Jennings, who was understandably disgruntled.

"Oh well, that's life I suppose," said Stratton, unconcerned.

Grady had left his car a quarter of a mile down the road. He trotted along happily, pleased at the ease with which he had secured the booty. He was glad that he hadn't had to shoot anyone. No mess, no fuss, everything was clean and clear. All he had to do now was get to the airport and get on the first plane to the States. Then he would meet up with Miles and hand over the box. After that he would use his large reward to take Brooke on the holiday of a lifetime. He'd always fancied going to one of those exclusive islands in the Caribbean, and now he was in the position to do so.

When he reached the car he threw the box onto the passenger seat and, after programming the SatNav, he started off for Heathrow. He'd only gone a few hundred yards though when he noticed a pair of headlights in his rearview mirror. He was surprised to see another car on the road and kept his eye on it. The car stayed at a respectful distance.

After another half mile he saw two pairs of headlights in the road ahead. At first he thought it was one car overtaking another, but as he got closer he realized that the lights were stationary. He started to feel uncomfortable. He could smell a trap.

He stopped the car fifty yards from the lights. It wasn't two cars blocking his way; it was four motorbikes.

He wound his window down and poked his head out. "What the fuck are you doing!" he shouted. "Get the fuck outta my way or I'll run you down."

There was no answer, but as his eyes became accustomed to the light he saw that each of the bikers was holding a shotgun. Meanwhile, behind him, another two bikes had rolled up. He looked back and saw that they too were brandishing weaponry.

He thought about his options, which were few. He either came out of the car with his hands up, or he tried to make it through the blockade. The latter would be possible if he kept his head down, but then there were the guys behind him to deal with as well. However many different scenarios he played in his head, it all came down to one thing; he was fucked.

"Ok boys, what do you want?" shouted Grady. "I can see you've got guns so I'm going to come out with my hands up."

He opened the car door and stepped slowly out with his hands in the air.

What appeared to be the main biker, a huge bull of a man with a great black beard, got off his bike and strode purposefully up to Grady. His shotgun in his right hand, he patted Grady down with his left. He removed the gun from Grady's shoulder holster.

"Ok, you've got my gun, now what do you want?" said Grady.

"I want whatever it is that you've just taken," said the biker. His voice was gruff but educated.

"I don't know what you mean," said Grady.

The biker whacked Grady in the stomach with the butt of his gun, and said, "Don't fuck me about Shaft."

The blow to his stomach made him double over. The biker was a powerful man. Grady decided not to fuck with him. "It's on the passenger seat," he spluttered.

After taking possession of the bag and its contents the biker forced Grady back into the car. From his bike he got several lengths of rope and proceeded to secure Grady to the driver's seat. By the time he'd finished Grady couldn't move an inch. Then, he ordered three of his gang over and they rolled the car onto its roof.

"Hey! What the fuck are you doing?!" Grady shouted.

There was no answer but Grady could hear one of them fiddling about at the back of the car. Out of the side window he saw a pair of booted feet walk past, with what looked like a rope trailing behind. He had no idea what was going on, but it didn't look good for him.

The main biker's face appeared at the side window. "I guess you're wondering what's going on," he said.

"Well, I am a little curious," said Grady.

"I'll bet you are," said the biker grinning. It was the grin of a madman. "The thing is, I heard through the grapevine that you like setting fire to things. A regular pyromaniac by all accounts. A friend of mine tells me that you burnt down his cottage. And what's more, he was in it at the time. It doesn't sound like a very nice thing to do to someone. What do you think?"

"I guess not," agreed Grady. He didn't like the way the conversation was headed.

"Anyway," the biker continued. "I thought it might be rather fitting if you yourself were to sample the delights of being burnt alive. I'm a great believer in karma. What about you?"

"Personally I think it's overrated."

The biker laughed and said, "Oh well, never mind But we're playing by my rules now. What I've done is connected this fuse here to the petrol tank," he pointed to the rope that led to the rear of the car. "It's a special slow-burning fuse. It'll take about half an hour to burn through the whole length; so you'll have plenty of time to think about things like karma and the meaning of life. It'll give you time to make peace with yourself, and maybe with God if you believe in that sort of thing. If you repent enough then perhaps you might even make it into heaven."

"Great," said Grady. "I'll be sure to give the big man your best wishes."

The biker produced a lighter from his pocket, lit the end of the fuse, and then, in a mock American accent, he said, "Have a nice day!"

The gang of bikers roared off leaving Grady alone. He squirmed and wriggled, trying to loosen the ropes that bound him, but they were too tight and after a couple of minutes he gave up. He laughed an ironic laugh of acceptance. After years of riding his luck, fate had finally caught up with him. This was the end of the road.

Chapter 28

Jennings struggled to break free of the ropes that bound them. He was determined that Grady wasn't going to get away with the box.

"I don't know why you're wasting so much effort," said Stratton. "We're not going to wriggle our way out of this, the ropes are pulled too tight."

"Ok then Einstein. What do you suggest we do?"

"I don't know. We'll just have to wait until someone finds us I guess."

"That's a great help," said Jennings. "By the time that happens Grady will be on a plane to the States and we'll never see that box again. I knew it was a mistake coming here so late at night."

"Well that's hardly my fault, is it?" said Stratton. "If your boss had given us permission we could have come here during the day with police to back us up. We didn't have any choice but to come here under the cover of night."

"You can't expect him to get a warrant to dig up National Trust land on a hunch, can you?" said Jennings, defending Brennan.

"No. But I'm not the one getting in a state about it am I?"

A roar of engines sounded in the distance and began to draw closer.

"What's that?" said Stella. "Sounds like a couple of tractors."

"I don't think they'll appreciate that," said Stratton.

"Who won't?" said Stella. "What is it?"

"It's the cavalry," said Stratton. "Before we left my parents' I took the precaution of calling for back up. I thought we might be followed, so I gave Oggi a ring. He said he'd round up his boys and keep his eye on the road for me. I guess that's them now."

A minute later the bikes stopped outside the field. Two of the bikers, both holding torches, came through the gate and approached the middle of the clearing. From the outline of his beard Stella could tell that one of them was Oggi.

"Having a bit of trouble old man?" he said to Stratton.

"Just a bit mate," said Stratton. "If you'd be so kind."

Oggi drew a large knife from his pocket. It was at least ten inches in length with a serrated cutting edge. Jennings looked up at it suspiciously. It was definitely illegal, but he let it pass. Oggi quickly cut through the bonds and they were free.

"Cheers Oggi," said Stratton. "I owe you one."

"I think you might owe me two," said Oggi. "I managed to stop your American friend. He seemed in a bit of a hurry to get away. There was an old sack on his passenger seat. I thought you might like to have a look at it."

Stratton smiled and said, "Excellent. That's saved us a whole lot of bother. Now we don't have to track him down. What have you done with him?"

Oggi broke into a broad grin. "Let's just say he's getting a taste of his own medicine."

Stratton frowned. "You haven't done anything too bad have you? He's not dead is he?"

"No he's not dead; well not yet. He will be in fifteen minutes, or so he thinks. He thinks I've attached a fuse to his petrol tank. I haven't of course; I just wanted to shit him up after what he did to you guys in Devon."

Stratton laughed and said, "Oggi, you're one sick mother-fucker."

Stratton walked with Oggi to his bike and Oggi handed him the bag. Stratton shook his hand and in return received a slap on the back. They smiled warmly at each other. Stella observed their body language with curiosity.

They were two very different people, that was certain, but they seemed to share an almost brotherly camaraderie. It was obvious that Oggi held Stratton in high esteem, and just as obvious that the respect was mutual. What she didn't understand was how this strange alliance had come about. There was Stratton, a born pacifist with a hatred of needless violence; and then there was Oggi, a brutish leviathan whom, she could tell from his eyes, would kill without a second thought. It was like watching God team up with the Devil.

"What do you want me to do with your friend from the States?" said Oggi, as Stratton prepared to leave.

"Just leave him there," said Stratton. "Someone will find him in the morning. I don't want him following us again tonight. Speaking of which," he said turning to Jennings, "I think you ought to check under the car for a transmitter."

"I'll do it in the morning when it's light. At the moment all I want to do is get some sleep. Like you said, he won't be following us tonight anyway."

After a small debate it was decided that, as it was the nearest place, they would spend the night at Jennings' flat in Oxford. As a rule he didn't like house guests but he was so exhausted that he had to make the offer. They couldn't go back to Stratton's parents' house, and Stella's apartment in Chiswick was too much of a drive.

Jennings' flat was the top floor of a converted three storey house in the Jericho district. The front door opened onto a spacious living area, with polished floorboards and a green three piece suite. The kitchen stood at the end of a long white hallway with doors on either side that concealed two bedrooms and the bathroom. The whole flat was exceptionally neat and tidy.

"'A place for everything and everything in its place'," Stratton said to Stella, when Jennings had gone to make them coffee.

"What do you mean?" said Stella.

"It's an old saying," said Stratton. "I think Jennings here has got a touch of OCD. Look how tidy the place is. The furniture's at perfect right angles; the CDs, books and DVDs are all alphabetized; and," he said running his finger along a shelf, "I'll bet you can't find a speck of dust in the entire flat. No wonder he was so edgy about us coming here; he thinks we're going to mess the place up. Notice the way he made us leave our footwear outside the front door."

"Well, to be fair, it was muddy. I don't think anyone would be happy with half a field being traipsed across their living room floor," said Stella.

Jennings returned with a couple of black coffees, one for Stella and one for Stratton. He himself just wanted to get to bed.

"Not joining us then?" said Stratton.

Jennings yawned and said, "No, I think I'll get some sleep. I want to be sharp in the morning. Brennan's going to want a detailed report of everything that's gone on, and he's never in a good mood on a Monday. He's not going to be pleased when he finds out that I completely disregarded his instructions and let you dig at the Stones. And he'll be even less pleased when he gets wind that Grady's still in the country. You two make yourselves at home. The spare bedroom is the door on the far left, you can argue amongst yourselves who has it."

After Jennings had bade them goodnight, Stratton removed the biscuit tin from the sack and opened the lid. He lifted out the box and held it up to the light, staring in fascination. Apart from the carved symbols it was very plain indeed. The unvarnished wood had started to crack with age, and the lid was attached by two simple hinges that looked as though they might give way at any second. It still had a certain ascetic beauty though, Stratton thought; and the intricacy of the symbols on the lid more than made up for the simple body.

"How old do you think it is?" asked Stella.

"No idea. I'm no archaeologist," said Stratton. "But it'd be interesting to find out. I think I'm going to have it carbon dated. I'm pretty sure that it's well over two hundred years old though, and that would certainly put the cat amongst the pigeons."

"Why's that?" asked Stella.

Stratton put the box down on the coffee table and said, "Well, if you remember, I told you that Reiki originated in Japan at the end of the nineteenth century - or so the story goes. If this box was made a lot earlier than that, then it puts Dr Usui's tale of seeing the symbols in a meditation under scrutiny. The four symbols used in Usui Reiki are all on this box; in fact they occupy the four corners of the lid, with the power symbol repeated again in the centre. So, if it pre-dates Dr Usui, then the actual origins of Reiki will have to be reconsidered."

"Why would he make up the meditation story though?" Stella asked.

"I don't know. He might not have made it up at all. I'm just saying that this box might open up a whole new history for the symbols. They could date back to..." he stopped, as if he was about to give something away.

"To when?" pressed Stella.

"A long time ago."

Stratton continued to examine the symbols. Each one was no more than a quarter of an inch square. They were carved in an almost perfect grid: twenty across and sixteen down. The Power Symbol directly in the centre was double the size of the others. Stratton figured that with the duplication of the Power Symbol, it meant that there were a total of 316 symbols carved into the lid. Taking off the four that he knew; it left 312 with, as yet, no clear purpose.

"There are a lot of symbols on there," said Stella, echoing Stratton's thoughts.

"There certainly are," Stratton agreed. "And I don't have a clue what any of them do, except for the four Usui ones."

"Any chance of telling me what they do? Or aren't you permitted?"

Stratton sat beside Stella with the box and explained. "This one," he said pointing, "'Cho Ku Rei', you know already. It's the Power Symbol and it increases the power that you are chanelling.

"The one in the top left corner is 'Dai Koo Myo'; this is the

Master Symbol, and roughly translated it means, 'great being of the universe be my friend'. It's used by Reiki Masters to attune their students. It also increases the power of the other symbols. Only a Reiki Master can use the Master Symbol.

"The one in the top right is called 'Sei He Ki', it means 'God and humanity become one'. It's used for mental and emotional healing. It clears blockages in people's heads. It can help with both addictions and relationship problems.

"Bottom left is 'Hon Sha Ze Sho Nen', it means, 'may the Buddha in me connect with the Buddha in you to create peace and harmony'. It's used as a long distance symbol; if you want to send Reiki to someone who is elsewhere then you use this symbol.

"It can also transcend time and space, so you can use it to send Reiki to the past or the future. You can send positive energy to an interview or a business meeting. Or you can send it back to a point where you fell out with somebody; the Reiki will heal the rift."

Stella took a sip of coffee. "Wow," she said. "It all sounds so...well, so unreal. I mean, can you really send energy through the air and across time and space, or is it all just psychological suggestion. Weak-minded people can be convinced of just about anything."

"Are you saying that I'm weak-minded?"

"No, sorry, weak-minded wasn't the word I should have used. What I mean is, that if someone wants to believe something is possible, and another person persuades them that it is, then in their heads it becomes a reality even if it's not. Like all these so called 'mediums' connecting with dead people. They pick on vulnerable people who are missing their loved ones, and prey on the fact that these people are desperate to know that the dead person is at peace. They'll use all sorts of tricks to get them to believe, but at the end of the day it's all psychological suggestion."

"Ok. I'll give you that one," said Stratton. "There are a load of charlatans in the medium business. But I'm sure that there are also people who genuinely can contact the spirit world. The secret is trying to distinguish between the two. And yes - people are open to psychological suggestion, myself included, but if you're implying that Reiki is all a psychological trick, and that I've fallen for it, then you really don't know me very well at all."

Stella thought about her next words carefully. "I'm not saying that you've fallen for anything," she said. "It's just a lot for someone like me to take on board. I live firmly in the real world. I was in the police for over ten years; I've learnt to deal in cold hard facts, not hearsay and speculation. All I have to go on is the statements of you and your grandfather. How do I know that any of that stuff happened to him - it may just be the fantastical ramblings of a senile old storyteller for all I know."

"He was not senile," interjected Stratton.

Stella apologized. "Sorry, that was a bit harsh. All I'm trying to say is that I need to experience this stuff for myself. How do I know that something exists if I can't see it or touch it?"

"You can feel it," said Stratton. "Like when we were at the stone circle. You felt that didn't you? You felt the energy repelling you."

"I guess so. I felt something anyway. Although it could have been the psychological effects of the darkness and the scare stories you were telling us about the stones coming to life."

Stratton sighed. "Ok, I can see that we're not going to get anywhere with this. I can't prove anything to you at this moment in time. If I channelled some energy into you right now, you'd still come back with the psychological suggestion argument, even if you did feel something. And anyway, what's wrong with psychological suggestion if it gets positive results? If a placebo makes a patient better, what makes it any worse than a real drug? And for that matter, what's your definition of reality? Everyone has a different reality. For all I know, you might not even exist, this whole world might not even exist, it might all be a figment of my imagination. All I can say for sure is, in the words of Descartes, 'I think therefore I am'."

"OK, ok," said Stella. "Let's not get into a deep philosophical discussion about this; we could be up all night. I just wanted to make a point. If you want the truth, against my better judgement, I do believe your grandfather, and I can feel things that I can't see. I call it intuition or a sixth sense, but it all boils down to the same thing doesn't it? It's all part of this unseen energy you're talking about, isn't it?"

"Absolutely," said Stratton, pleased that Stella was understanding. "Everybody has these abilities. We've all had times when our intuition has overridden logic, and been proved right. I don't think there's anyone in the world that could claim they'd never had at least one intuitive experience, however small. Instinct and gut feelings are all part of our connection to the cosmos. The more open your chakras are, the stronger and more frequent these experiences become. With Reiki, when a person is attuned and their chakras unblocked, they immediately develop a sharper perception of the world around them; it unlocks abilities that have lain dormant and untapped throughout their lives.

"Everybody has the innate ability to be psychic, it's just that some people are more able to harness it. As well as giving healing powers, a Reiki attunement opens up the part of the brain that contains these ancient cognitive capacities. It's almost like a rewiring.

"I'm sure that there's even a scientific explanation for it; if only science would look into it further with an open mind, rather than dismissing anything paranormal as fantasy. Apparently 80 per cent of the universe is made up of dark matter which we can't see. They expect people to believe this, and yet because there's no physical evidence of prescience or telepathy, they're brushed aside as nonsense. What if the dark matter we can't see actually controls these supernatural powers? What if dark matter contains the spirits of dead people? The problem is that we've advanced so far scientifically that we've lost all the natural gifts inherent in mankind."

"Like what?" she asked.

Stratton continued. "In ancient Egypt or India for instance, practices like the laying on of hands for healing would have been commonplace. Instinct and intuition would have been part of everyday life. People would go to seers and would take their prophecies as gospel. It was a spiritual society and communicating with the ether would have been normal. In fact, it still is in some parts of the world. But if you showed these people a television or a computer or games machine, they would find it absolutely amazing. The same way that we find the idea of communicating with the spirit world amazing. We've come so far technologically that we've lost, or forgotten, our fundamental capabilities. We have to rediscover these before mankind can evolve any further."

"So you think that everybody has psychic abilities, it's not just a talent you're born with," said Stella.

"Yes I do," said Stratton. "And I believe that everybody has the ability to heal themselves and others as well. You don't need any special powers to perform Reiki, you just have to be attuned and learn to channel the energy. I can do it, you can do it, anyone can do it.

"The problem is that some Reiki Masters are very secretive with their knowledge; it's almost as if they're scared of too many people learning what they know. They hold back information under the pretence that it's dangerous to learn too much about Reiki without understanding it properly. But I think the real issue is about power and control. It's human nature to want to keep yourself ahead of the pack, and I guess that some Reiki Masters don't want their students overtaking them."

"Isn't that a bit selfish though?" said Stella.

"Yes it is. But I think all human beings are in some way or other, even the very kind ones. The whole reason we're here is to advance ourselves. What the majority of the human race fails to realize is that we are all part of one big energy, and that by helping others to advance, we do in fact further our own souls. Slowly though, I think that people are realizing this."

Stella took a final swig of her now-cold coffee. She wanted to stay up and pick Stratton's brains some more, but it was three in the morning and the day's events were catching up with her. "I'd better get some sleep," she said.

"Ok, no problem," said Stratton. "You have the spare room. I'll make myself comfy on the sofa here."

"You're quite welcome to share with me," she said. And then added, "But I don't mean that in a funny way."

Stratton laughed. "I know how you meant it, but I'll be fine on the sofa thanks. I'll see you in the morning."

Stella wished him goodnight and went to the spare room.

Stratton sat with the box in his lap. He brought it up to eye level for a closer examination; he was sure that it held another secret apart from the symbols on the lid. If it didn't then why would Charles Mulholland been so protective over it? There must be a secret compartment, he thought. He realized that his grandfather and the others had checked for one with no success, but there had to be one - he just knew it. There was no other explanation for Mulholland's furtiveness.

He continued to study the box; inspecting every crack and groove in the wood minutely. His vision was tiring though, and after ten minutes he decided to call it a night and have another look in the morning with fresh eyes.

After turning off the light and making himself comfortable, he lay on the sofa meditating over the events of the previous few days. His thoughts kept on returning to his parents. Their lives had been taken for no reason. He was the one with the information that his grandfather had left; they had been almost nothing to do with it. They were just two normal people, enjoying a well-earned, happy, retirement. He felt guilty that he hadn't been there; and he felt guilty that he hadn't fully reconciled with them before they died. He drifted into an uncomfortable sleep.

Chapter 29

Outside the flat, in Walton Street, Yoshima watched the front window from his car. It had been ten minutes since the light had gone off. They would probably be asleep by now, he thought, but he would give it a while longer just to be safe. There were three of them this time and he had to be certain of catching them unawares.

He waited until three thirty and then slid out onto the pavement, closing the car door silently behind him. Looking left and right, he saw that the street was devoid of life, and made his way across to the large white door on the other side of the road. From his pocket he drew out two thin pieces of metal, both about four inches long, and inserted them into the lock. It was a standard Yale, and within seconds Yoshima had picked it and made his way through into the communal lobby. It was a far cry from the convoluted electronic security at Addington Hall, a job which had taken him weeks to plan: this was easy; good old-fashioned breaking and entering.

The hallway was dark, but a fragment of streetlight shone through the window above the door, giving him a glimpse of the stairs. With great stealth he tiptoed up towards the top floor. As he negotiated the second storey landing, a loud creak from the floorboards stopped him in his tracks. He waited for five minutes until he was positive that nobody had heard him, and carried on upwards.

By the top floor there was no light from the street filtering through. Along with his lock pickers Yoshima was forced to get out his pen light as well. Clamping the torch in his mouth, he shone the beam onto the lock, and skilfully manoeuvred the bits of metal until he heard the barrel click. He opened the door charily and poked his head round into the flat. The corridor light had been left on and he could just make out a figure sleeping on the sofa.

The body on the sofa stirred slightly as he entered the room. He stood still for a moment, but the body carried on breathing steadily and made no further movement. Standing beside the sofa he made a sign in the air above the slumbering man. He would now be disabled and Yoshima could get to work on the other two.

The first door he tried in the corridor was the bathroom and he swiftly moved on to the second. Inside the girl was sleeping soundly. He disabled her and moved along.

As he opened the door to Jennings' bedroom there was a squeak from the hinges. It wasn't particularly loud, but in the silence of the flat it echoed noisily. Jennings stirred and opened his eyes. He put his hand to his forehead and squinted into the hallway. "Who's there?" he said sleepily. "Stella? Is that you? Stratton?"

Yoshima quickly signed the air and Jennings stayed as he was.

A noise from the living room broke his concentration. He looked round and saw that the sofa was empty. He walked back down the hallway and positioned himself at the doorway in fighting stance. Edging forward inch by inch he tried to get a full view of the room. From his left side a boot came from nowhere and hit him full in the face. Clutching his nose he staggered back drunkenly. Before he could regain his composure another blow hit him in the stomach and he doubled over. The next thing he knew, he was lying face down on the floor with his right arm pinned behind his back.

"Not so easy when people fight back is it?" said Stratton angrily. His head was filled with the thought of his parents being tortured. "You're not dealing with harmless old pensioners now you sick motherfucker."

Yoshima raised his left hand and drew a sign in the air.

"Don't bother with that shit," said Stratton. "In case you hadn't noticed, it doesn't work on me. Just lie still." He patted

Yoshima down with his free hand. He felt the knife in his pocket and removed it. "You won't be needing this any more will you?"

Yoshima let his body relax. There was only one way out of this situation and that was to catch his assailant off guard. There was an angry young man pinning him to the ground; and his anger was creating adrenaline, which in turn was giving him great strength. But his anger would also make him vulnerable and open to a surprise counter-attack.

"Your parents died pathetically," Yoshima gloated. "They were begging and pleading. They had no honour."

Stratton brought his fist down onto the back of Yoshima's neck. "Just shut up you fuck! They had more honour than a sneaky, thief-in-the-night murderer like you will ever have."

Yoshima laughed. "Of course they needn't have died at all. They didn't know anything. But you do don't you? You know what this is about. It should have been you that died, shouldn't it? Do you feel guilty about their death? Does it bother you that maybe you could have saved them?"

Stratton raised his fist to strike Yoshima again. But as he did so, his grip on Yoshima's wrist loosened. Quicker than an eel, Yoshima slipped his hand from Stratton's grasp and rolled himself over. Stratton's fist came thumping down and missed his head by inches. Before Stratton had a chance to react, Yoshima landed a combination of sharp blows to his face which sent him backwards to the floor. In a flash Yoshima was on his feet and running for the door.

By the time Stratton had picked himself up off the floor it was too late; Yoshima had fled. He cursed himself for being so stupid. Yoshima had deliberately goaded him and he had fallen for it. Never lose your temper; he knew that; it was one of the golden rules of combat. And yet he'd allowed himself to be distracted, and now his parents' killer had got away.

In the spare bedroom he found Stella with her eyes open but unable to move. He laid his hands on her forehead and after thirty seconds she began to stir. "What the fuck's going on?!" she shouted, bolting up to a sitting position.

Stratton rested a reassuring hand on her shoulder and said, "Don't worry, you're ok now. You've been temporarily paralysed."

"How the hell did that happen? Did someone inject me with something? I didn't feel anything. Whatever was going on in the corridor woke me up; and I tried to move but I couldn't. I couldn't scream either. It was like a nightmare. I didn't think it was real."

"Oh, it was real all right," said Stratton. "And no, you weren't injected with anything. You were disabled by other means."

"Other means?" said Stella.

"I'll explain in a while. First of all I'd better see if Jennings is alright."

Jennings was sitting upright with his hand still shielding his eyes. Stratton had to restrain himself from laughing. He laid his hands on the crown of Jennings' head and mouthed some words. A minute later Jennings was able to move again. "Fucking hell!" he said. "What the hell just happened there? I saw some bloke in the doorway; he waved his hand in the air; and then I couldn't move or speak. What's going on?"

Stratton went to the kitchen and put the kettle on. He made two strong sweet cups of tea and carried them to the living room, where Stella and Jennings were sitting in dressing gowns, still bewildered.

"Are you two ok?" he asked as he handed them both tea.

Jennings answered first. "Yeah, I think I'm ok. I'm just a bit shell-shocked. I don't think I've ever been so frightened in my life. It was horrible, I can't really describe it. It was like being frozen in time I suppose."

"Yeah, it was," Stella agreed. "Like being a living statue. Who is that guy? How did it happen?"

"His name is Yoshima," said Stratton. "At least I think that's who it is. I can't be one hundred per cent certain. Anyway, when I was out in Tibet I heard about this guy who could apparently paralyse an opponent from across the room. He came from Japan and was an expert in the martial arts. He'd developed his inner energy, his chi, to such an extent that he was able to project it into another person's energy field and drain it. I'm pretty sure that's what happened to you two, as well as my parents and Mulholland."

Jennings gave Stratton an incredulous look. "So you're saying that this guy paralysed me with thin air."

Stratton corrected him. "Not thin air; energy. I can't explain to you how he does it because I don't know myself. But I've got a suspicion that he's using some of the symbols that are on the box."

"Why weren't you paralysed?" asked Stella.

"To be honest, I don't really know. I'm assuming that because I'm attuned to the Master Symbol, I'm somehow protected. I can't think of any other explanation."

Jennings took a sip of tea. His head was still in a spin. The events of the last few days had finally caught up with him. His entire world, his safe and familiar world, a world with long established physical laws, had been chewed up and spat out.

He was trapped inside an abstract reality, where everything he thought he knew suddenly counted for nothing. He was dizzy, he was flushed, but most of all; he was afraid.

"Try not to think about it," said Stratton seeing the look on Jennings' face. "I don't think he'll be back again tonight."

"It's not just him," said Jennings. "It's the whole situation. I feel like I'm way out of my depth. It's like I'm in the middle of a bad dream and I can't wake myself up. I don't know what's real anymore."

"I do understand," said Stratton sympathetically. "Like I said though; it's best not to think about it. You'll drive yourself crazy if you dwell on it too much. Believe me, I know. You're here in your flat and you're alive, that's the way to look at it. We know who the killer is now, I've got his knife and I'm sure it'll match with the victims' wounds, so the case is nearly closed. In a couple of months you'll have forgotten about all this shit."

"I doubt it," said Jennings, heavy with despondence. "This is the sort of thing that stays with you for a long time."

Stratton sighed and said, "Listen, you're tired. In fact we're all tired. I suggest that we try and catch at least a few hours' sleep. There's no point sitting up all night worrying about it. Yoshima won't be back tonight: his cover's blown now and most likely he's going to lie low for a while."

"What if he tries to leave the country?" asked Stella. "Shouldn't we put out an alert straight away to the ports and airports?"

"No point," said Stratton. "What are you going to tell them - 'stop all Japanese men trying to leave the country'; it's just not feasible. And besides, he's already killed three people in pursuit of the box; I don't think he's going to be going anywhere until he's got his hands on it. No, everything can wait until the morning; we can decide what to do then."

Chapter 30

The ninja waited silently in the shadows of the stones, alert and ready to spring. In the centre of the huge megalithic ring, several torch beams split the dark. Raised voices filled the air with acrimonious discontent. There were five figures in the stone circle and two of them came to blows. After a brief struggle one of the figures emerged clutching a rectangular object in his right hand. With a gun in his left hand, he backed away from the rest of the group. His bald head glinted in the rays of the torches. It was Sharlo Miles.

The ninja moved slowly out from the shadows, aiming to intercept Miles as he tried to get away. As he approached his target he drew his knife in anticipation. Miles turned away from the group and tried to make a run for it. The ninja, by now only feet away, leapt onto Miles' back and slid the knife across his throat in one swift, fell, movement. Miles dropped to the floor and lay still, his eyes lifeless and blood gushing from his throat…

Grant Romano woke with a start. The dream had become a regular occurrence, but its effect hadn't diminished. The macabre image of his friend's jugular-pumping demise still made him feel sick. A rivulet of sweat ran from his temple into the middle of his cheek. He reached for the glass of water on his bedside table and drank its contents down in one go. Still thirsty he got out of bed and made his way to the kitchen.

The kitchen clock told him that it was two in the morning. It felt much later. He thought he'd been asleep for ages, but it could only have been a couple of hours. Usually his dreams occurred in the morning, around seven o'clock, just before his alarm went off, and so didn't disturb his sleep pattern. Just recently though, he was finding himself waking up at all hours. He couldn't shake off the feeling that something was going to happen to Miles. He didn't know when, he just knew that it was inevitable.

He opened the fridge, pulled out a bottle of Evian water, and took a good drink. It didn't seem to matter how low he set the air conditioning, he would always wake up sweating with a bone-dry mouth. It was as if his body was running a marathon whilst he slept. He wondered if his dreams were draining him physically as well as mentally.

What to do about the Miles situation? That was the big question. Should he come right out and tell him about his dream? Or should he just leave it and hope for the best? As a friend he felt that he really ought to tell him. But also, as a friend, he didn't want to scare him needlessly. There were times when his dreams weren't entirely accurate; dreams were open to interpretation and couldn't always be taken at face value.

His dream of Miles' death could mean anything; it all depended what Miles represented in his mind. Miles was a trusted friend, so perhaps his death meant the death of a trust; perhaps someone, not necessarily Miles, would betray him. Equally though there were times when his visions were bang on the mark, and as the dream was recurring it was obviously important. He made up his mind to phone Miles in the morning and tell him all about it.

He needed to speak to Miles anyway, about another matter that had been bothering him. He was slightly irked at Miles' dismissive attitude towards his story of the box. He had divulged the information to Miles in all good faith, believing that if anybody would be interested then it would be him. And in the beginning he had been interested; asking lots of questions and appearing genuinely excited. But his initial curiosity had turned to an almost haughty indifference. It had got to the point where Romano felt stupid even mentioning it.

Of course Romano had no proof that such an object even existed. His only sources of reference were the tales his father had told him as a boy. Romano knew, even as a young child, that his father was full of it, and had a natural tendency to sprinkle his tales with a liberal dose of fiction. But there was something different in his voice whenever he mentioned the box. He spoke about it with such obvious reverence, that Romano knew in his heart the story held more than just a grain of truth. He was determined that Miles should take him seriously, and help him track down what he believed to be an item of great importance.

Chapter 31

The walls outside the consultant's office were covered with colourful pictures, drawn by youngsters from the children's ward. It brightened up what would otherwise have been a pitilessly aseptic waiting room. David Brennan sat on a blue plastic chair holding his wife's hand. He stared at the unpretentious paintings and wondered how the terminally-ill young artists who had produced them managed to be so positive. There were no images of sadness or depression; it was all smiley stick men and women, beaming and holding hands with their children, in impossibly green meadows, under impossibly yellow suns. Perhaps it was easier to be upbeat about life when it hadn't had time to grind the spirit out of you.

Dr James Burt, consultant oncologist, opened his door and bade Brennan and Anna to enter his office. He was a young man, early thirties, Brennan guessed, and was tall with dark brown hair. He looked like a ladies' man. He had obviously been fast tracked through the hospital hierarchy, but what he lacked in years he more than made up for in knowledge and experience. He was friendly and open and honest, and Brennan liked him a great deal.

"Well then, Anna, how are you feeling?" Burt asked, his eyes twinkling almost flirtatiously.

"Not too bad I suppose," she said. "The morphine's a great help."

Burt laughed. "I'm sure it is. What about you David, how are you coping?"

Before Brennan could answer, Anna interjected. "He's not. He's not coping at all. He's not sleeping properly for a start, and he won't do anything about it. He keeps saying that he will but nothing ever happens."

Brennan shook his head and sighed.

"Is that right David? You're having trouble sleeping?"

"Yes, I suppose so," admitted Brennan. "But I've tried loads of different pills and nothing seems to work."

Burt got out a prescription pad, scribbled on it, and handed it to Brennan. "There you go," he said. "It's a prescription for a drug called Temazepam. Take a couple of these before you go to bed and you should be sleeping like a baby in no time."

"Thanks," said Brennan. "But shouldn't we be discussing the real matter in hand. I'm not the one with cancer."

"Fair enough," said Burt. "But all these things help. You're a big part of Anna's life, and if you're not functioning properly then it puts needless stress on her. You can't expect her to beat this if she's worrying about you all the time. She needs peace of mind, as well as physical rest."

Brennan dropped his head like a scolded schoolboy. "You're right, I'm sorry. I'm just finding it hard to be rational at the moment."

"No need to apologize David; I'm here to help, not to judge you," said Burt, reaching for the brown envelope on his desk and pulling out a set of four scans. He clipped them to the light frame on the wall and turned it on.

"Right then, let's get down to business," he said, pointing to the first one. "This first plate on the left is the primary scan where, as you can see, there is a tumour about the size of a walnut. The second one after the initial chemotherapy shows a slight decrease in size. The third one, after further treatment, shows no change from the second. And that brings us to the most recent one, taken last week." He stopped and cleared his throat. "Unfortunately it appears that the tumour has in fact increased in size: it's now bigger than the original. It's gone from stage 2 to stage 3, which means it's pierced the wall of the lung. If it carries on the way it's going then the cancer will spread to the liver, and then I'm afraid it will be untreatable."

"So the chemotherapy isn't working then?" said Brennan.

"Well," said Burt, "like I said, it worked initially but its effect seems to have abated. This doesn't mean it's the end of the road, but we'll have to have a rethink."

"A rethink?" grumbled Brennan. "What the hell does that mean?"

Burt sat back in his chair, keeping his air of calm. "We'll just have to try radiotherapy. There's a relatively new procedure called CHART (Continuous Hyperfractionated Accelerated Radio Therapy). You would stay in hospital and have three doses of radiation every day for three weeks. This could work, but it would, unfortunately, put more stress on you Anna. You will feel very ill; much worse than the last treatments. What do you think?"

Anna shrugged. "I don't know what to think," she said. "I hate the chemotherapy and the way it makes me feel afterwards. If this other treatment is worse then I'm not so sure about it. But ultimately I want to live, so I don't suppose I have any choice, do I?"

"Well you do," said Burt. "But like you said, if you want to live then an increased treatment is the only thing I can recommend. And even then I can't guarantee that it'll work. It appears to be a very aggressive tumour. Perhaps you want to go home and think about it."

"What are the odds that this CHART treatment will work?" asked Anna.

"I won't lie to you," said Burt. "I'd say from experience in a case like yours that it's only about twenty per cent. But that's twenty per cent compared to zero per cent without it. I'm sorry I can't be more helpful."

"That's ok," said Anna. "It's not your fault. It's not anyone's fault; it's just life."

Brennan and Anna thanked Burt for his time and took their leave. They walked through the hospital hand in hand, neither saying a word. The news had not been unexpected, but there was always that small hope that maybe the tumour had begun to shrink again. The reality was that Anna's chances of surviving were one in five, and that was only if she agreed to more body-sapping treatment. Brennan looked across at her already frail body and wondered how much more she could take. He couldn't bear to continue watching her suffer.

They left the hospital and walked to the car park where Jerry was waiting with the Mercedes. He was standing outside the car smoking a cigarette, but he stubbed it out quickly as soon as Brennan came into view. Brennan took his mobile phone from his pocket and switched it back on. He speed-dialled a number.

"Who are you phoning?" asked Anna.

"Work," said Brennan. "I'm telling them to cancel my meeting this morning."

Anna grabbed the phone and cut it off. "Listen David, you don't have to do that. I know you've got a lot going on, and I don't want you to ignore it."

"Listen," said Brennan. "Work can go hang itself today. There are more important things in life."

Anna smiled and touched his cheek. "I know there are sweetheart, but to be honest I just want to be on my own today. I've got a lot to think about, and I'd rather have a bit of space. You do understand, don't you?"

"Yes, of course I do. I just don't want you to feel like you're fighting this thing by yourself."

"I know I'm not by myself, you've been fantastic. If I need you I'll ring. Ok?"

"Ok," said Brennan. "Make sure you do."

Chapter 32

Jennings sped down the fast lane of the M40 doing 90 miles per hour. Stella was in the passenger seat smoking a cigarette. Stratton lay across the back with his eyes closed in deep meditation. It was ten thirty, and the Monday morning rush hour was over. The road ahead was reasonably clear and Jennings felt confident that they would make their eleven thirty meeting with Brennan with time to spare. He felt a lot better than he had done the previous evening; five hours' sleep had done him good. It was also a lot easier to be rational in the daylight.

He had phoned Brennan at half past seven. As was usual on a Monday morning his boss had been gruff, even when Jennings relayed the news about the box and the killer to him. Far from being delighted, he had given Jennings a ticking off for disobeying orders and digging up National Trust land. Jennings hadn't yet filled him in with the details or told him about Grady. He thought that this was all best done in person.

"I wonder if Grady's out of that car yet," said Stella, making conversation.

"Probably," said Jennings. "Somebody will have found him by now. I expect he was found early this morning by one of the commuters from the village. He'll probably be trying to explain to the police why he was tied up and who did it to him."

"Why do you think he came back for the box?" she said. "He'd already got away with attempted murder. You'd have thought he would have counted his blessings and flown home to the States."

"I guess so," Jennings agreed. "But who knows what goes on in the mind of a spook...That's spook as in spy by the way," he added, seeing Stella's face cringe. "Maybe he's the sort of guy who has to see a mission through to the end, no matter what. He's a freelance so he probably gets paid for results. If he turned up without the box maybe he wouldn't get as much money."

"Yeah, but it's still a pretty big risk if you ask me. Money's not going to be any use if you're in prison."

"I know," said Jennings. "I'm only hypothesizing though. You did ask."

Stella finished her cigarette and threw it out of the car window.

"I don't know," said Jennings. "Whatever happened to 'keep Britain tidy'."

"Well, if you weren't such a nit-picker I would've put it out in the ashtray," countered Stella.

Jennings was about to say something else but decided not to bother.

In the back of the car Stratton roused himself to a sitting position. "Is there any chance of stopping off at the next service station?" he asked. "I need the toilet."

Jennings grunted. "I suppose so," he said. "But we're on a bit of a tight time schedule, so you'll have to be quick. Brennan's in a bad enough mood this morning as it is. I don't want to be late and make him even crankier."

"He seems to be in a permanently bad mood," said Stratton.

"I know," said Jennings. "But he's under a lot of pressure at the moment. The Prime Minister's breathing down his neck about this Mulholland business; the Americans are giving him grief about Grady; and then there're his problems at home of course...."

"What problems are they?" asked Stella.

"Forget it," said Jennings. "I shouldn't have said anything. It's not my position."

"Come on Jennings," she pressed. "What's wrong? Surely he's not having problems with Anna - they're the happiest couple in the world. I've never seen two people who were so in love."

"No, it's not like that. Anna's ill. She's very ill. She's got lung cancer."

"Fucking hell," said Stella. "That's awful. No wonder he's so stressed out. Why's he still at work?"

"He wants to keep himself busy," said Jennings. "There's nothing he can do about it, and Anna doesn't want him hanging around at home all day moping, so he just carries on working."

"How long has she got to live?" asked Stella.

"I don't know. He doesn't really talk about it a lot to be honest. You know what he's like - plays his cards close to his chest, doesn't he? And I don't really want to pry too much, it's none of my business really - he's my boss, not my best mate."

"I guess so," said Stella.

The first service station on their route was Heston on the M4 eastbound. After encountering heavy traffic on the M25 Jennings was loathe to stop. But when Stratton threatened to piss on the back seat of the car he decided that stopping off wasn't such a bad idea.

It was mid-morning and the service station was fairly crowded. Stratton weaved his way through to the toilets, with the box carefully tucked under his arm inside his jacket. Now that he had found it he wasn't letting it out of his sight. It wasn't that he didn't trust Stella and Jennings, far from it; it was just that he felt it was ultimately his responsibility and nobody else's.

He grabbed a cubicle and placed the box on top of the cistern. He stared aimlessly at it whilst the water flowed. A crack in the wood suddenly caught his glance. He had been examining the box nearly all night trying to find some hidden symbol or secret compartment, and maybe it was his fresh eyes, or maybe just the fact that he'd stopped trying so hard to look, but he noticed something in the crack that had previously escaped his attention.

He flushed the toilet and drew the box up to eye level. Halfway along the thin crack at the front, there was a small, almost imperceptible, knot in the wood. That in itself wasn't odd, but the colour of it was much lighter than any of the other knots that adorned the box. He reached into his pocket and pulled out a biro. He pushed the nib against the knot and it began to crumble. It was as he suspected; the blemish in the wood wasn't a knot at all: it was wood filler made to look like one.

He scraped away at the filler with the biro, but the nib was too thick to remove it all. The tiny gap was narrowing to a pinhole and he needed a slimmer tool to penetrate all the way through. He removed his house keys from his trouser pocket and quickly detached them from the flimsy metal ring that held them together. After uncoiling the ring he poked the end into the pinhole and dislodged the rest of the wood filler. He pushed the makeshift device in further and heard a quiet but definite click. He opened the lid of the box and looked inside and smiled to himself.

Five minutes later he left the cubicle and washed his hands. Aware that he had taken a long time, and that Jennings would be getting tetchy, he walked quickly out of the toilets, navigating his way through the idling clientele at speed, still buoyant from his discovery. His ebullience however was to be short-lived. As he approached the exit he felt a sharp pain on the back of his neck and his world went black.

A middle-aged woman was the first to notice Stratton tumbling to the floor. She knelt by the side of him and shook him lightly to try and bring him round. When he didn't respond she started to panic and shook him harder. She looked up at the small crowd that had started to gather, her eyes pleading for some help.

A hand rested on her shoulder. "Don't worry madam I'm a doctor," said a kindly voice. "I suspect the poor fellow has just fainted."

She looked to her side and kneeling there was a grey-haired Japanese man with a caring smile. He was smartly dressed in a charcoal pin stripe suit and looked every inch the professional. He felt Stratton's neck for a pulse and then opened up his jacket. "Can somebody get some water please," he asked the onlookers.

A young man handed over a newly-purchased bottle of Evian.

He opened the bottle and, lifting Stratton's head, he gently tipped water over his face. Stratton started to come round.

The 'doctor' handed the water bottle to the woman. "Keep his head up and give him a little of this to sip," he said. "I'll be back in a minute with my instruments to check him over."

Stratton slowly opened his eyes and tried to focus. He was lying on the floor looking up at a circle of blurred faces. Someone was tipping water into his mouth. He shook his head violently and his vision started to return.

"Are you ok?" asked the woman next to him holding his head.

"Yeah, I'm ok, I think. What happened?"

"I think you must have fainted. That's what the doctor said."

"What doctor?" said Stratton.

"The nice Japanese doctor who was here," she said. "He's just gone to get his medical kit. He said he'll be back in a minute."

Stratton sat himself up and felt inside his jacket. There was nothing there. He scrabbled around frantically on the floor.

"What's wrong?" asked the woman. "Have you lost something?"

"Yes," said Stratton. "A small wooden box. I had it in my jacket. Have you seen it?"

The woman said she hadn't.

Stratton crossed his arms and sighed. Yoshima and the box had gone.

Chapter 33

"Well that's fucked everything hasn't it?" said Jennings, as he drove out of the service station and rejoined the M4. "What am I supposed to say to Brennan now? He was pissed off with me as it was for digging up the box without his permission. He's going to blow a gasket when he finds out that we've lost it."

Stratton didn't say a word. The last thing he was bothered about was what Brennan thought. All that concerned him was finding Yoshima and getting the box back. He was mad at himself for having been so careless. He should have known that Yoshima wouldn't give up the chase. He should have been more alert. Instead, he'd been so pleased with his discovery in the toilets that his guard had dropped. Yoshima had crept up behind him and executed a near-perfect snatch. If he hadn't been so pissed off he would have admired Yoshima's style.

It was nearly quarter to twelve when they pulled up outside Scotland Yard. Jennings parked the car and hurried to reception with Stella and Stratton to get them signed in and hooked up with visitors' passes. He prided himself on his punctuality and he was already running fifteen minutes late.

The building was much as Stella remembered it; characterless and imposingly sterile. The only change was that Brennan now had a smaller office a few doors down from his old one on the top floor. On the 2nd October 2006, Special Branch (SO12), and Anti Terrorist Branch (SO13), had been restructured to form Counter Terrorism Command (SO15). Brennan was now in charge of Specialist Protection (SO1), covering, amongst others, ministers and foreign dignitaries. The restructuring had thrown all departments involved into a state of confusion, it had been nearly two years and still nobody really knew who was supposed to be in charge of what.

When they arrived at his office, Brennan was sitting at his

desk. Across from him sat a middle-aged man with a bald head. Neither man got up when they entered the room.

"Morning sir," said Jennings.

Brennan looked at his watch. "It's almost afternoon," he said without expression.

"Yes, sorry sir," said Jennings. "We hit a lot of traffic, and there was…well an incident."

Brennan glared at him and said, "Well come and sit down and you can explain yourself. It'd better be good though."

Jennings, Stella and Stratton each grabbed themselves a seat across from Brennan.

"By the way," said Brennan introducing the bald man, "this is Professor Sharlo Miles from America. He's the head of the National Institute of Paranormal Studies."

Miles nodded at them and smiled.

"So you're the one who sent that psychopath Grady over here," said Jennings.

Miles looked apologetic. "I'm sorry about that," he said. "I'm afraid our Mr Grady exceeded his remit. He was only supposed to track down the box; not hurt people. I was horrified when I found out that one of you had been shot. I'm afraid I've been a bit naïve about the whole thing. I'm not used to the world of espionage. I'm a peaceful man at heart."

Jennings looked at Miles suspiciously. His words seemed fair but there was a falsely obsequious air about him that Jennings didn't like.

"Anyway," said Brennan. "Before we go any further, I want to hear about what happened last night. I notice that nobody appears to be carrying a box of any kind."

For the next thirty minutes Jennings relayed, in detail, the events of the night before, including the episode at the service station. Stella occasionally interjected with information she thought pertinent, but Stratton kept quiet; his mind was busy with his own thoughts.

"Well that's a story and a half," said Brennan. "I said that it better be good, but I didn't mean for you to make it up. Do you really expect me to believe that some bloke paralysed you from ten feet away. I think your imagination's running away with itself. It was obviously some sort of trick."

"Maybe sir," said Jennings. "But if it was a trick then I have no idea how he did it. The point is, trick or not, this Japanese man is definitely the one who killed Mulholland."

"I agree," said Miles. "And I wouldn't be so quick to dismiss his claims about this man's powers either. I deal with this type of thing every day of my life, and believe me, there are people in this world who have extraordinary gifts far beyond normal comprehension. Why do you think the US government funds my institution? They wouldn't be giving me money for no reason would they? There's a hell of a lot going on in this world of ours that science just can't explain Mr Brennan; I suggest that you keep an open mind."

"Whatever," said Brennan, sounding unconvinced. "None of that makes any odds to me at the moment. All I'm concerned with is catching this Japanese guy - Yoshima or whatever his name is. We need to get a description of him out to the media. A photograph would be handy. Do you think the CCTV at the service station will have caught an image of his face?"

"I don't know," said Jennings. "It's possible. But the guy's obviously very clever - he would have thought about that beforehand I would imagine. He's probably either avoided the cameras or put his hand in front of his face. I suspect all that we have to go on is Stratton's description of him. We'll have to get a sketch artist to whip something up for us."

Brennan sighed. His day had started badly and was going downhill by the minute. After leaving the hospital and arriving at work he had been immediately confronted with the task of looking after Professor Miles. He had been instructed by the powers that be to extend him every courtesy. Miles was pleasant enough but he was an added complication to an already complex situation: Brennan was treading enough of a political tightrope without the Americans getting involved as well. And now Jennings had brought even more bad news; he wondered if things could get any worse.

"Ok then," he said. "I'll send Stratton down to the sketch artist, and I'll send someone over to Heston to get the CCTV tapes. You, Jennings, can get on with writing up a report of your movements over the last few days."

Jennings opened his mouth to speak but nothing came out, he knew Brennan well enough to realize that arguing was pointless.

"Is there anything I can do to help, David?" asked Stella.

"Not really," said Brennan. "We know who the killer is, so you can go back to whatever you do. Finding Yoshima is solely a police matter now."

Stella took a breath and said, "I just thought..."

"You just thought what," said Brennan. "You just thought that you could swan back in to the police force. You left remember. Perhaps you should have thought about it more before you decided to take the money and run."

Stella welled up with anger but bit her tongue.

"What about Grady?" said Jennings, changing the subject. "Is he going to get away again?"

"As far as I'm concerned," said Miles. "Scott Grady is now a rogue operative. He was specifically told to catch the first plane back to America. He disobeyed that order and, for reasons unknown, took it upon himself to continue searching for the box. If he is arrested again then you're quite welcome to him. He is no longer under the protection of the United States government."

Half an hour later Brennan sat alone in his office. He had dismissed Jennings, who would now be writing up a long report, and he had sent Stratton down to the sketch artist along with Stella. Professor Miles had gone back to his hotel, awaiting further developments. Peace and quiet at last, Brennan thought.

His stress levels had been rising all day.

Now that he was calming down he was starting to feel guilty at his treatment of Jennings and Stella. Jennings had done a good job really and had, at the very least, warranted some appreciation for his efforts. Stella too, had been instrumental in the operation, and hadn't deserved his barbed parting comments. He was losing his grip and he knew it. Perhaps he needed to get away for a few days; he could take Anna to one of those health spas in the country: a bit of pampering would do them both good. One thing was certain though - he couldn't carry on as he was.

A knock on the door broke into his thoughts. "Come in," he shouted.

The door opened and in walked Stratton.

"What do you want?" said Brennan. "I thought you were downstairs with the sketch artist."

"He's on his lunch break," said Stratton.

"Fair enough," said Brennan. "But that still doesn't explain what you're doing up here unaccompanied. This floor is for authorized personnel only; and last time I looked, you weren't authorized."

Stratton shut the door behind himself and said, "Ok you've got me, I'm not supposed to be up here. But to be honest nobody bothered stopping me - perhaps you should review your security. Anyway that's beside the point. I came up here because I think I can help you."

Brennan looked puzzled. "Help me with what?" he asked.

"Well, not exactly help you, more like help your wife."

"What do know about my wife?" said Brennan defensively. "Who have you been talking to?"

"It doesn't matter who I've been talking to," said Stratton, "what's important is that I know that your wife's ill, and I think I can help."

"What the hell can you do?" Brennan growled. "You're not a

doctor."

Stratton shrugged. "No, I'm not a doctor. But sometimes there's nothing that a doctor can do. Sometimes even a doctor can't prevent the inevitable. Medicine moves forward in leaps and bounds every day, but people still die, don't they?"

Brennan didn't answer.

Stratton continued, "Anyway, when a doctor says that there's nothing he can do, where do you go after that? Nowhere, that's where. And why? Because society has deified the medical profession. It's drilled into us from birth that doctors are gods, and that if a doctor or surgeon doesn't have a cure then it doesn't exist. The trouble is that once a doctor has said 'that's it' then most people give up and accept it, they don't bother looking any further."

Brennan interrupted. "I understand what you're trying to say. But I don't see how it's relevant to my wife's situation. What makes you think that she's beyond help?"

"I'm not certain that she is," said Stratton. "But judging from your mood today, the situation isn't looking good. I'm guessing that she's got a tumour and it's either getting bigger, or the chemotherapy isn't shrinking it."

Brennan gave Stratton a hard stare. The young man's accuracy was making him feel uncomfortable. "Listen," he said. "I'm sure that you mean well, but my wife's condition is none of your concern. Whether or not she is getting better is none of your business. And to be frank you've got a bit of a cheek coming in here and interfering. Whatever you think of doctors and the medical profession, they save millions of people around the world every day, and I for one have faith in their skill."

"You're taking what I said the wrong way," said Stratton. "I wasn't saying that the medical profession are unskilled idiots, far from it, they do a fantastic job, and you're right: they do help hundreds of millions of people every day. I was just making the point that, for all the great strides medicine has made in the last two hundred years, there is no 'cure all': people still die of disease - and cancer. There are alternatives to traditional medicine though."

Brennan gave a sardonic laugh and said, "And what alternatives are you talking about? Herbal tea? Leeches? Badger spleens? It's all a load of rot if you ask me. I've seen the documentaries on TV; with strange old women standing over people, waving a few crystals above their bodies, and chanting some stupid mantra in a language that they've probably made up themselves. It doesn't wash with me I'm afraid, I've met too many charlatans over the years to start believing in that crap now."

"I know what you mean," said Stratton, smiling in agreement. "There are a load of fakes out there; preying on the weak and infirm, trying to prise them away from their hard-earned cash. I find the whole thing disgusting. The problem is that people buy into it, so what can you do? My main worry is that these fraudsters are steering the general populace away from any alternative therapy whatsoever."

"Listen Stratton, I appreciate you coming up here to see me, but I don't want your help; and neither does my wife. I don't know exactly what it is you're selling, but you're not getting any money out of me."

Stratton laughed out loud. "Is that what you think? You think I'm trying to pull some sort of scam on you. Not at all. I don't want your money, I just want to help. Is that so hard to believe? Have all those years in the police force really made you that cynical?"

Brennan shuffled awkwardly and said, "I'm sorry. You're right; this job has made me extremely cynical. It's not just the job though, it's the world. We're living in an age of greed; an age where everybody wants a bigger slice of the pie; an age where the rich and famous are idolized, and every child in the land aspires to be like them. It's very rare for anyone to do something for nothing nowadays, so can you blame me for being suspicious?"

"No, I don't blame you at all. I understand completely. You're right, we do live in a material society, and most people are after anything they can get. You don't know me from Adam so you have every right to be suspicious. I can't force you to let me help, but I really think you should. Like I said, I don't want any money."

"Ok," said Brennan. "Let's say I agree to let you help. What are you going to do?"

"Have you heard of Reiki?" Stratton asked.

"Only in the last few days after we found that symbol. I've done a bit of research on the Internet. Sounds like a load of rubbish to me."

"Well it's not, I can assure you. But I can't change your mind just sitting here talking about it. You need to let me prove it."

Brennan looked noncommittal.

Stratton grabbed a blank piece of paper and a pen from Brennan's desk. "Here's my mobile number. Have a think about it and talk with your wife. If you decide to give me a chance then call me. Really you've got nothing to lose. It's not going to cost you anything, and if it doesn't work then your wife's no worse off than she was before."

"Thank you," said Brennan grudgingly. "I'll think about it. What I don't understand though is why you're so desperate to help."

Stratton smiled. "Because I can David. Because I can."

Chapter 34

Grady sat in the small café eating what the menu called a 'full monty'. It was basically a glut of fatty foods (sausages, bacon, eggs, chips, and black pudding) cooked in a hefty amount of grease. Baked beans were the only healthy thing on the plate, and they were limp and dry at that. It wouldn't have been his normal choice of breakfast, but after a night of being tied up he was starving.

He had been found early that morning by some yokel in a tractor. The guy had helped him out of the car and after Grady had indicated that a police presence wasn't essential, he'd flipped the car the right way up with the forks on his machine. Grady had thanked the guy profusely and slipped him a hundred pounds to keep quiet about the incident. He had then phoned Sharlo Miles.

Miles had been less than sympathetic, and told Grady in no uncertain terms that he was on his own: there would be no intervention from the intelligence services this time. Grady had shouted and cursed but Miles had just hung up. To compound his misery, the tyres on the car had all been slashed.

So that was it; it was game over. Miles had hung him out to dry. He'd known many agents that had been disowned by the government; he just never thought that it would happen to him. Of course, there was never any guarantee that you were going to be bailed out, but usually there was some trade-off or other to be made with the relevant country, and more often than not an agent would escape with no more than a bruised ego and a severe dressing-down. Unfortunately for Grady, his status as an UFA meant that he wasn't supposed to exist anyway, and that, coupled with the fact that Miles' last instructions had probably been without official consent, meant that he was totally and utterly fucked. He could see Miles now: putting on a show of innocence, claiming that Grady had been acting under his own steam; there would be no record of the phone call to Miles or the threats to Grady and Brooke.

Grady finished off the last of his meal. The food had filled a gap but he could feel the cholesterol chugging its way around his veins already. He called over the owner, a man who looked like he lived on 'full monty's', and ordered another coffee in an attempt to wash away the saturates. He pondered his next move.

There was only one person who Grady could turn to at this point and that was his friend Brad Devereaux, CIA London. 'Friend' was probably a strong word to use: you never really had friends in the world of intelligence; but there were people that you trusted more than others, and Brad was the one person that Grady knew wouldn't sell him down the swannee. He and Brad had both served in the same unit of the Marines in the eighties, when they were both just out of college. Grady had saved Brad's life in the Nicaraguan jungle; shooting a Sandinista in the head as he attacked and tried to slit Brad's throat. If anyone would help him then it was Brad.

Leaving his coffee to cool down, Grady stepped out of the café and onto the pavement. The café was situated in the town centre but not in a pedestrianized area, so there were few people milling about. It would be safe enough to talk.

Grady speed-dialled Brad's personal number.

After three rings a voice answered. "Hello, Brad Devereaux."

"Hey Brad, it's me Grady," he half whispered. "I'm in shit and I need your help."

"I know you're in shit," said Devereaux. "Deep shit."

"What do you mean? How the fuck do you know?" said Grady, keeping his voice low.

"That prick Miles has put the word about that you've turned rogue buddy. I don't know what you've done, but he's saying that he told you to get on a plane back to the States and you didn't. He's over here in Britain now; been sniffing around that Special

Branch guy Brennan, trying to ingratiate himself."

"That was fucking quick," said Grady. "He doesn't miss a trick, I'll give him that."

"Anyway," continued Devereaux. "This Brennan's either anti-you or anti-American, or both, because he's issued a warrant for your arrest. He's put your picture out nationwide. It's not exactly a manhunt or anything, but if some cop recognizes you then you'll be taken in; and there's no way you're going to make it out of the country: all the airports and ports have your photo."

"Fuck me man!" said Grady, forgetting to keep his voice down and getting a glance from a passer by. "I don't believe it. That lying motherfucker's done a real job on me. What the hell am I supposed to do now?"

"I don't know buddy, you'll just have to lie low for a while I guess. This'll all blow over in a while. In a year or so, when the heat's died down, you'll be able to get back to the States under a false identity."

"Great," said Grady. "That's just great. What am I supposed to do in the meantime? Hang around this piss-ant country eating fish and chips and drinking warm fucking beer? It'll drive me fucking mad. Is there nothing you can do to help me? You know - put a word in for me; get me out on a private jet or something?"

"I would if I could, you know that," said Devereaux. "My hands are tied though. You're hot property at the moment bud. Everyone knows that you and I go way back, and they'll be watching me like a hawk. I wouldn't be surprised if they're listening to this; it's supposed to be a secure line, but you know what they're like."

"Don't I just," agreed Grady. "Looks like I'll have to think of a way out on my own."

"Sorry Grady," said Devereaux. "There's just nothing I can do for you, unless of course you need money. I can get money to you."

"No, I'm good thanks. I've got plenty. Cheers Brad, I'll see you soon."

Grady hung up the phone and sighed. He walked back into the café and took a sip of his coffee. He consoled himself with the fact that he'd been in worse situations. None were coming to mind however. Perhaps Brad was right, perhaps the only thing to do was lie low for a while. If he went down that route he would have to go to London where a black American would be less conspicuous. In his current location, a small market town in the middle of Oxfordshire, he stuck out like a cold nipple.

Lying low was not in Grady's nature though. He was an innately proactive being who lived by the old adage that attack was the best form of defence. His mind set to work trying to find a way forward. There had to be a way of getting out of the situation. There had to be a way of clearing his name. Miles was the only person who could do this, but he wasn't just going to come out and admit that he'd blackmailed Grady. Grady needed to force it out of him. Grady needed leverage. Grady needed the box.

Chapter 35

David Brennan arrived home at six o'clock. He made a habit of never working too late on a Monday. Anna was sitting in the living room watching the news. He dumped his briefcase in the hall and went to join her.

"Hello sweetheart," she said. "How's your day been?"

"Well, apart from finding out my wife's not getting any better, and having to kowtow to the Yanks all day, it's been fine."

"Now, now," she said. "There's no need to be grumpy. Sit down and I'll make you a cup of tea."

"No, it's all right, I'll do it. You stay where you are."

Anna got off the sofa with fire in her eyes. "Listen David I'm not an invalid and I don't want to be treated like one. I'll make the tea. Now, sit down."

Brennan knew better than to argue and made himself comfortable in his chair and watched the news. He was pleased to see that the Mulholland murder was still one of the main stories, and that the sketch of the suspect was being broadcast to the nation. He hoped that there would be a sighting of him soon so the whole thing could be put to rest. He'd had enough of the case and he just wanted to get back to normality. If for no other reason than to get rid of Professor Miles, whom he'd taken an instant disliking to.

Anna returned with tea for them both.

"Lovely," said Brennan. "Just what I need. Anyway how's your day been?"

"It's been good actually," she said. "I've spent most of it on the Internet."

"Oh yes. What have you been doing? Playing poker and bingo?"

Anna laughed. "No, of course not. I've been doing some research on alternative medicine."

"What do you mean, 'alternative medicine'?" he asked.

"You know the stuff," she said. "Acupuncture, reflexology, herbal remedies - that sort of thing."

"Why are you doing that, it's all a load of rubbish. Just people trying to make a quick buck out of the old and sick."

"God you're an old stick in the mud," she said. "There's no need to be so dismissive of everything. I was only having a look, just to see what's out there. I hate to point out the obvious to you Chief Inspector Brennan, but the chemotherapy doesn't seem to be doing its job properly."

"Maybe not," he said. "But you heard the doctor, there's a chance that this new radiation therapy will work."

"There's also a chance that it won't," she replied. "And besides, I've had just about enough of conventional medicine. It makes me incredibly ill you know. Or hadn't you noticed? Maybe you should try a dose yourself and see how you feel."

Brennan put down his tea and leant over and grabbed her hand. "I'm sorry," he said. "I just want you to get better by whatever means possible. I know that the chemotherapy's been hell for you, and I don't like seeing you suffer, but I really want you to live. I want us to grow old together. I can't imagine a world without you in it." He looked in her eyes and his own began to moisten.

She smiled and squeezed his hand. "I know you want what's best for me sweetheart. I don't doubt it for a second. I guess I will have to try the radiotherapy. But I also want to look into other treatments, maybe as an addition to the CHART. Trying other things on top won't hurt will it?"

Brennan's thoughts immediately went to Stratton. The guy unnerved him for some reason, not in a sinister way - there was just something about him. And the way he looked directly into your eyes was discomforting. It was almost as if he was scanning your heart and soul and looking for guilty secrets. There was no malice in the guy however, and Brennan believed that he genuinely wanted to help. He didn't want any money; he'd made that clear enough, so perhaps there wasn't any harm in trying other therapies; purely as a complementary measure of course.

Brennan let go of Anna's hand, sat back in his chair, and took a sip of tea. "It's strange you should bring up the subject of alternative therapies tonight," he said.

"Why's that?" she asked.

"Well," said Brennan. "There's this guy who's been helping us with the Mulholland case, an ex-boyfriend of Stella's - you remember Stella who used to work for me don't you?"

Anna nodded. "Of course I do. I used to talk to her at all your functions. She was a lovely girl. Went to work for Henry Mulholland. You were really annoyed about losing her I seem to remember."

"Yes that's the one," said Brennan. "Anyway this guy Stratton…"

"Stratton?" Anna interjected. "I remember him. Nice enough bloke, bit of a charmer in fact, but a bit of an alcoholic as well. He got really pissed at your Christmas do one year - started dancing on the table; which wouldn't have been so bad if people hadn't still been eating. I remember him breaking Stella's heart."

"Maybe, I don't know. You seem to know a lot more about the lives of my staff than I do."

"That's because I take an interest in them David. Christ! I have to do something at these God-awful parties you take me to."

"Anyway," said Brennan. "Someone at work, probably Jennings, has obviously inadvertently let on about your situation. Because this afternoon he came waltzing into my office and started waffling on about this thing called Reiki. It's some Japanese healing art; something to do with life force energy."

"I've heard of it," said Anna. "It was one of the things I saw on the Internet today. I've ordered a couple of books on it. One of them is about this woman who has an inoperable stomach problem and has it treated by a Reiki Master. She gets better and then learns to heal people herself. There are loads of testimonies from people on the Net as well. It seems to help with nearly all illnesses, including cancer."

"Well. I've got Stratton's number. Do you want me to give him a call?"

"I don't know," she said tentatively. "I mean, he didn't seem like the type of person who'd know anything about that sort of stuff. To be honest he appeared a bit out of control; not all there if you know what I mean."

"It'll be ok, he's changed a lot I think," said Brennan, surprising himself with his defence of Stratton.

"Well if you're sure, then I suppose there's no harm in talking to him."

"Ok," said Brennan. "I'll give him a call."

Chapter 36

The Jericho Tavern had once been the launching pad for many an Oxford band, including Supergrass and the mighty Radiohead. That had been back in the late eighties - early nineties, when the city had produced a stream of groups that were the pride of the indie world. Following its demise as a music venue in the late nineties, the Jericho was under new ownership and again making a name for itself as a leading player on the Oxford scene.

Jennings remembered the glory days of the Tavern fondly. Back then, when he had studied at Brooks University, there was a real buzz about the place. Not only had it played host to the finest local talent, it had also managed to attract artists from all around the globe, such was its reputation. Of course it was only a small venue, but what it lacked in capacity it had made up for with kudos.

As he sat at the bar and looked around the place, he felt sad. It had never been the same since its downfall. The live music may have returned but, to him, the atmosphere had irrevocably changed. Maybe it was him getting old, or perhaps he just didn't understand the 'scene' any more. Whatever it was, he no longer felt at home there; not like he had done.

He knocked back a large swig of bitter and the truth hit him square in the face: the place was just too fucking clean. In the old days the bar had been laden with rickety old tables and chairs; the walls had been covered with ageing posters from the punk era and beyond; and the floor had been so worn that it was almost sawdust. But what it had lacked in comfort, it had more than made up for in character. Character was something sorely missing from the modern pub; refit, upon refit, upon refit, had seen to that. Once homely hostelries had, after many mutations and bastardizations, become plastic palaces of the prim and proper, and in the process had sold their souls to the suave and the staid. The Jericho had fallen into this trap years before and, however hard they tried, its vulgar beauty had been lost for ever, existing only in affectionate memories.

Jennings didn't exactly know why he was feeling so morose, but he imagined that it was a reaction to the events of the last few days. He might have been battered and bruised, and almost burnt to death, but the truth was, it was the first real action he'd seen for years. His job of protecting MPs and VIPs was fairly fulfilling, but very rarely did anything of note happen. He knew it was wrong, but secretly some days he longed for some lunatic to attack one of his charges, just to get his adrenaline flowing. The Mulholland investigation had by contrast been dangerous and exciting, and the thought of going back to personal protection filled him with gloom.

The Jericho Tavern reminded him of how sedate he, and his life, had become. Back in his student days he'd been so different: he'd survived on a healthy diet of wild parties, and sex and drugs and rock and roll. If there was a do to gatecrash or a drunken stunt to be pulled, then you could guarantee Jennings would be at the centre of the mischief. Now of course it was all change: he wore pin-stripe suits, hardly ever went out, lived on his own in an anally clean flat, and kept his CDs in alphabetical order. What the fuck had happened to him? Exactly when had he turned from Jennings the tiger into Jennings the pussycat? At what point had the establishment taken his soul away?

He eyed his suited reflection in the bar mirror with contempt. The pub had changed, but not as much as himself.

Now that he'd written his report for Brennan, his association with the Mulholland case was pretty much over. They knew who the killer was, so all that needed to be done was to put out his description nationwide, and wait for someone to call in with information concerning his whereabouts. This was easier said than done, but there was still no need for Jennings to be on the case full time, if at all. Even Brennan could take a back seat and get back to his real work. So, tomorrow morning it would be back to safeguarding the wealthy and corrupt from fates that so many of them desperately deserved.

He wouldn't have minded this return to normal duties so much if the case had been in any way resolved. They had discovered the killer's identity, but to Jennings so much remained unanswered. After his initial scepticism he had gradually become more interested in the box and its history. Now that he was off the case, he would probably never find out what secrets it held. Stratton also intrigued him, as did Yoshima and his ability to disable an enemy from a distance. He had been given a glimpse of a mysterious, perhaps life-changing, world, and now he had no good reason to continue exploring it. The next day, Brennan would assign him to protect some political muppet and that would be that.

He called the barmaid over and ordered another bitter. This was pint number four and he was starting to feel a bit tipsy. He didn't drink a lot as a rule, and particularly not on a school night, but it was one of those times when he needed to unwind and nothing but alcohol would do. And besides, it was still only nine o'clock, so he would have plenty of time to sleep it off before the morning.

He searched his head for possible reasons to stay on the case, but none came to mind. Perhaps if Brennan had been a bit more interested in the box and its history, then he could have persuaded him.

As it was, Brennan couldn't have cared less about the box or any significance it might have; all Brennan wanted was the killer found and the case put to bed. And he didn't need Jennings for that.

The only person in authority who seemed to want the box found was Professor Miles. Jennings imagined a scenario in his head whereby he suggested Brennan second him to help the American. This thought was immediately cancelled out by a picture of Brennan thumping his desk and breaking into an anti-American dithyramb.

As he proceeded further down his pint another thought occurred to him - he could carry on looking for the box in his own time. He knew for certain that Stratton wasn't going to give up the search, and he was pretty sure that Stella would carry on as well. If they teamed up, then between them they might get somewhere. He could keep them informed of any news regarding Yoshima, and they could follow it up, and he could help them when off duty. However, this idea was quickly dismissed, because if Brennan found out then Jennings would be read the riot act, and most probably lose his job for leaking information.

An hour and two pints later Jennings decided that discretion was the better part of valour, and left the pub and headed for home.

He walked down Walton Street quietly humming to himself and occasionally breaking his stride with a swift hop. He was merry, bordering on tilted, and happily oblivious to almost anything going on around him. He didn't see the man following him twenty yards behind.

At the door of his building he fumbled around in his pocket for the keys. He drew them out and squinted in the street light to find the right one. In the near dark with slightly blurred vision, they all looked the same. It took him two minutes and three attempts to get the right one. He entered the building with a stagger and nearly fell flat on his face. The fresh air had done him no favours and he was drunker than he thought. Behind him a shadowy figure slipped into the hallway.

Jennings placed his hand against the wall and felt for the light switch. The door shut behind him. A hand clamped itself over his mouth. He tried to struggle but another hand had clamped his arm behind his back. He was stuck.

"Jennings," whispered a voice. "It's me, Grady. I'm not going to hurt you; I just need your help."

Jennings gathered all the strength he had left and tried to extract himself from Grady's grip. The drink had taken its toll though, and he was too weak and uncoordinated to even move an inch.

"Listen Jennings, don't struggle. Like I said I'm not going to hurt you. I need you to be quiet though. If I take my hand away you're not going to cause a scene...are you?"

Jennings shook his head. Grady released his hand.

"You fucking bastard!" shouted Jennings. "I'm going..."

Grady covered his mouth again, and whispered, "Listen man, shut the fuck up. I told you, I need your help. I know we've got off on the wrong foot, but you seem like an okay guy to me, and to be honest I've got nowhere else to turn. I've been fucked over big time by an asshole called Professor Miles. Just hear me out will you. If you're still pissed at me after that, then you can take me in, ok?"

Jennings nodded. Grady relaxed his grip. He was taking a big risk approaching Jennings but, as the saying went, desperate times called for desperate measures, and this was a most desperate time. He hoped that he'd read the situation correctly and that Jennings wasn't the sort of person who would immediately go squealing to the authorities. He was a bit of a whinger and a moaner, but he seemed like the kind of bloke who you could trust to do the right thing.

"What the fuck do you think you're doing Grady?" Jennings said quietly. "There's a warrant out for your arrest; and you come barging into a police officer's house and assault him."

Grady let go of Jennings' arm and said, "Like I said, I've got no-one else. So can we talk?"

Jennings, being too drunk and tired to argue, agreed and led Grady up the stairs to his flat. He made two strong cups of black coffee and they sat down in the living room.

"Come on then Grady," said Jennings. "Explain yourself. But you'd better make it good. I don't trust you as far as I could throw you. The only reason you're here is because I've had one too many and I'm not thinking straight. And by the way - how the hell did you find me?"

"You didn't remove the transmitter I put on the underside of your car. I thought you would have checked for one," said Grady.

Jennings groaned. "I was going to this morning, but I was in a hurry and forgot. And besides, I didn't expect you to be roaming about still."

"Me neither," said Grady. "But here I am again."

Grady told Jennings exactly what had happened to him in the last few days, leaving nothing out. He even told him about Brooke and how much he liked her. He knew that the best way to get an honest man on your side was to be honest with him. He added the stuff about Brooke and his feelings for her, because he felt a bit of personal information might soften Jennings up and bring him round. If he saw Grady as a human being he would be more likely to help.

When Grady had finished, Jennings, who had been listening intently, clapped his hands and said, "Well done. A very touching story. Do you really expect me to believe you?"

"Listen man, it's the truth," said Grady.

"Maybe. Maybe not," said Jennings. "Either way, what do you expect me to do about it? I'm off the case now."

"That doesn't matter," said Grady. "I just need to know where that box is."

"Fuck me Grady! You've got a fucking nerve; after all that you've done. Do you really expect me to start giving you information?"

"Listen Jennings. You're a policeman. You're job is to find the guy who killed Mulholland. Neither you nor your department has any real use for that box. The only people who have any real interest in it are the killer, Stratton, and Professor Miles. And your boss is hardly going to give the thing to Stratton over Miles is he? If Miles wants the box then the British are going to give it to him, aren't they? All I want to do is get hold of the box so that Miles calls off the dogs. Then everyone's a winner, yes? You have the killer, Miles has the box, and I can get back to my life."

"And what's in it for me and my department?" asked Jennings.

"I'll track down the killer for you. And believe me I can."

"Well you've certainly thought it all through," said Jennings.

"Yes I have," said Grady. "I wouldn't have risked coming here otherwise."

"Unfortunately," said Jennings. "I have no idea where the box is. The killer stole it from Stratton this morning. Nobody knows where it is." He went on to explain the morning's events at the service station, and their meeting with Brennan and Miles.

"You must have a description of the killer now though. Right?" said Grady.

"Yeah, we have, but it's only a sketch. He kept his face well away from the CCTV cameras. A sketch of a Japanese bloke isn't going to be much help. You know what the public are like; they'll be reporting every Oriental from Lands End to John O' Groats."

Grady finished his coffee. It was bad news that the box had gone missing, but he felt the situation might have played into his hands. Now, if he tracked down the Japanese guy, he could kill two birds with one stone and get back in favour with the British and Miles.

"Listen Jennings," he said. "I can tell you're pissed off with the situation from your voice. You obviously want to stay on the case and catch this Yoshima guy. And if I'm not mistaken, you're kind of interested in the box as well. Am I right?"

Jennings shuffled uncomfortably but said nothing.

"I am right, aren't I?" Grady said smiling.

Jennings suddenly realized that in his stupor, he'd said and let on, far too much. Grady had taken advantage of his well-oiled state and got stuff out of him that he normally wouldn't say in a million years. He felt guilty and embarrassed.

"I think you'd better go," he said. "I'm drunk and I've said too much already. I'm bound by the Official Secrets Act for Christ's sake. I've just committed treason."

"Don't be so melodramatic," said Grady. "I'm not going to tell anyone what you've said. I told you, I think we can help each other. We're both just pawns in a much bigger game aren't we? Like I said, I've got nothing to lose now. If we work together then we can both come out of this looking like heroes."

Jennings yawned. "You're not going to let this go are you?"

"No, because I can't. I want my life back. I want to get out of this game and go back to the States and live happily ever after with my girl."

"No offence Grady, but at the moment I'm too drunk to think about this sensibly. I'm going to bed now, I'll talk to you in the morning."

Grady shrugged. "Ok man, whatever you say. Just remember, I'm throwing myself at your mercy."

"How could I forget," slurred Jennings, and stumbled to his bedroom to sleep.

Chapter 37

Stratton picked at the last of his lamb tikka and chewed on it thoughtfully. The day had been an unmitigated disaster, and it had been his fault. He knew there was nothing he could do about it now, but it was still preying on his mind. The idea of Yoshima having the box filled him with dread. He didn't have a clue as to Yoshima's intentions, but he was certain that they weren't for the good of mankind.

Still, he could take solace in the fact that even though Yoshima had the box, he didn't have everything he needed to access the symbols. Stratton had seen to that.

He looked across the dining table at Stella who was still devouring her take-away hungrily. He smiled to himself: even when she was shovelling food she looked beautiful. Sitting alone with her took him back to the days when they'd been together. He remembered those days fondly. If there was one time in his life when he could say that he had been truly happy, it was the first years of their relationship, before his darkness had set in. There was no one particular memory that stood out in his mind, just a blur of complete, exquisite joy. He wished he'd never caused her so much heartbreak.

Stella looked up from her food and caught Stratton's eye. "What's wrong?" she said.

"Nothing," said Stratton. "Nothing at all. I was just staring aimlessly."

"Oh, ok. You just looked a bit sad, that's all," she said.

Stratton nearly told her the truth but thought better of it. "I was just thinking about Brennan's wife," he said. "She's obviously in a bad way, and he seems completely devoted to her. It's just a sad situation."

"Yes it is. But you're going to help them aren't you?"

"Of course I am. But I'm sure there's tens of thousands of

people around the globe who are in the same position or worse. Who's going to help them?"

"I don't know," said Stella. "But you can't help everybody. All you can do is help the people that you meet on your way through life. I remember being told that once by someone. I think it was you."

Stratton laughed. "It certainly sounds like something I'd say."

Stella finished her food and cleared away the plates and plastic take-away cartons from the table. She left everything on the kitchen sideboard; it could wait until the morning. Her flat was a mess anyway; she hadn't been there for four days.

When she got back from the kitchen, Stratton had moved to the sofa and switched on the TV. She sat in the armchair to his left. "What's your plan then?" she asked.

"Plan for what?" he replied.

"Your plan to get that box back," she said. "I know that it's playing on your mind. There's no way that you're just going to let it go."

Stratton made a gesture of ignorance and said, "I don't know. I can't think of anything at the moment. I need to find Yoshima first - wherever he is, that's where the box will be. The problem being that he could be anywhere. I don't expect he will have managed to leave the country, but that won't help. Once he got hold of it he probably went to ground almost immediately. He's a ninja - if he doesn't want to be found then he won't be."

"So you're fucked then."

"I suppose so. He's got to show himself at some point though, and with a nationwide manhunt going on he's going to be spotted by someone. But even if he's caught I probably won't get the box back. Not with that Miles bloke hanging around anyway."

"But technically it's yours," said Stella. "Your grandfather was the last one to have it."

"Makes no odds really," said Stratton. "It's not really anybody's to be fair. If anyone has a claim to it, it's the family of that Indian guy Suri - that's if he had any family. If Miles wants it then I'm sure the government will make sure that he gets it. I'm just going to have to think of a way of finding Yoshima before anyone else does."

"Well, if you need any help then I'm here. I've not got anything better to do."

"What about your job at the house?" asked Stratton. "They'll still need security up there won't they?"

"Of course, but I'm supposed to be on holiday at the moment anyway. If they need me then I'm sure they'll ring."

Stella made them both a coffee and they sat watching the TV in silence. It was late and she was thinking about getting some sleep. She looked over at Stratton who seemed engrossed in the film. He was still good-looking, she'd give him that. In the years that had passed she'd forgotten how attractive he actually was. The image of him that she'd kept in her head was one of a twisted and ugly drunk. This had served her purpose well. Every time she even slightly missed him, she would conjure up that picture in her head and convince herself she'd done the right thing. Now that he was in front of her in the flesh, that representation of him had gone. What she saw was the man he'd been before the light had been taken from him. Yet he wasn't that man: he was a new man; a man she hadn't met before; a man who knew himself; a better man.

"I'm going to go to bed in a minute," she said. "What are you going to do? Go back to Peckham or stay here?"

Stratton looked at his watch. It was half past twelve, and the idea of getting across town by whatever means didn't seem appealing.

"Well, I do need to go back to the Angel to get some stuff, but it can wait until the morning. To be honest I'm a bit tired; if you don't mind I'll stay here."

Stella thought for a minute. It briefly crossed her mind to let him sleep in her bed. In her heart though she knew it was a bad idea: with all the emotional tension of the last few days, something was bound to happen; and it was something that she just wasn't ready for.

"You'll have to make do with the sofa I'm afraid," she said. "It's quite comfy though. I'll go and get you a duvet."

Stella got him a duvet out of the airing cupboard and made herself ready for bed. She was glad that he'd decided to stay. There was part of her that needed him there. The last few days had scared her more than she cared to admit, even to herself. If Stratton had gone back to the pub, she didn't know if she'd have been able to sleep properly. Although logic dictated that she was now out of danger, her imagination was still seeing ghosts round every corner. On her own in a dark flat she suspected that she might flip. With Stratton there she felt safe. In fact she felt safer than if the whole of SO1 was protecting her. There was something about him that inspired confidence. It was as if he was invincible.

She finished brushing her teeth and took one last peek in the living room. He was still watching the film. She smiled to herself and went to bed to dream sweet dreams.

Chapter 38

Jennings opened his eyes and immediately closed them again. The sun was thrusting its head through the curtains, its rays like hot pokers. His forehead was pounding with the beat of jungle drums. His mouth felt like it had been coated in creosote, and his stomach could have turned milk to butter. He remembered now why he didn't drink on a weekday.

An overwhelming feeling of guilt slapped him in the face. The previous evening came gushing back like a burst hydrant. He couldn't remember exactly what he'd said, but he knew deep down that it was bad, and that he'd betrayed the trust placed in him by Her Majesty's government.

He tried opening his eyes again, this time only squinting. His digital clock indicated that it was seven thirty am. He had forgotten to set the alarm and he was going to be massively late. Brennan expected him in at nine o'clock sharp for a briefing on his next assignment. With a huge effort he launched himself out of bed and hastened to the bathroom to freshen up. When he got there the door was locked. It occurred to him that Grady hadn't left.

He banged on the door. "Grady! Is that you in there?" he said, knowing that it couldn't be anyone else.

"Yeah man, it's me."

"Listen Grady, I need to have a shower and get ready for work."

"I hear you man," Grady hollered. "I'll only be a few minutes - I'm just dropping the kids off."

Jennings felt his stomach twinge. "That's a bit too much information mate. Just hurry up will you."

Jennings went to the kitchen and put the kettle on. What the hell had he been thinking the night before? How could he even have entertained the idea of letting that madman into his flat?

The thing was, he hadn't been thinking, and now, to say the least, found himself in a bit of a spot: he was harbouring a fugitive; and it certainly wouldn't look good on his previously unblemished record.

He made himself a strong black coffee with two sugars and took a couple of tentative sips. There was only one way out of his predicament: he had to take Grady in. Grady had said that if Jennings didn't want to help him then he would come quietly. Of course that may just have been flannel. But even if Grady did acquiesce, could Jennings really trust him not to let on about the information that he'd let slip. Grady could really drop him in it if he wanted to.

He heard the click of the bathroom door and Grady walked out and into the kitchen. "I wouldn't go in there for a while if I was you," he said.

"Charming," said Jennings.

"Ooh coffee," said Grady rubbing his hands. "Don't mind if I do."

Jennings stood and watched as Grady helped himself to coffee.

"So what's the plan then boss?" asked Grady, as he unsuccessfully searched the fridge for milk.

"What do you mean? 'What's the plan?'" said Jennings. "I'm planning to have a shower and get to work as soon as I can. You can do whatever you like."

"So you're not taking me up on my offer of help?" said Grady.

"I don't know Grady," he said putting his hand to his forehead. "I've got a stinking hangover and my head hurts like hell. I can't think straight at the moment. I don't know whether to take you in, or let you go, or what. You've put me in a real position here."

"Hey, I'm sorry man," said Grady sympathetically. "I know I've backed you into a corner. But like I said last night - I've got no choice. I needed to get to someone on the inside of the investigation, and you were the only one I could find, because of the transmitter on your car. If I had my choice I'd be over in the States now."

Jennings swallowed a mouthful of coffee; it wasn't making him feel any better. "Look, I appreciate your predicament. But like I said, I can't think properly at the moment. I'm going to take a shower."

Jennings went to the bathroom and Grady took his coffee in to the living room. He was beginning to regret approaching Jennings at all. The guy was all right, and underneath he could sense a spirit of adventure, but he was a panicker who worried too much about dotting the 'i's' and crossing the 't's'. He was the sort of guy who would progress through the ranks of his chosen profession at a steady pace, maybe marrying along the way and having a couple of kids, but he would never experience the freedom of being his own man, or the mischievous exhilaration of bucking the system. It was too bad really because Grady was almost starting to like him.

After Jennings had showered and changed he joined Grady in the living room.

"Feeling any better?" Grady asked.

"Much better thanks," said Jennings. "I could do with some food though. But I haven't got time."

"You should make time. So what if you're a bit late. Nobody's going to die are they?"

"Well actually they might," Jennings countered. "My job is to protect people, and if I'm not there then they could very well die."

"Point taken," said Grady. "So what are you going to do with me? Are you going to take me in?"

"No I'm not. Well not yet anyway. I don't particularly trust you and I don't know if your story is true, but that Professor Miles is definitely up to something. I took an instant dislike to him, and if taking you in is what he wants then I'm not going to do it. It doesn't mean that I'm going to help you though."

"Fair enough," said Grady. "But have a think about it. Remember, with the right information I'll find this Yoshima guy for you. Nobody would have to know."

"I'd know," said Jennings. "And that's enough."

Chapter 39

Two hundred feet above the ground, in the clear blue sky, a hawk circled with predacious grace. His keen eyes were locked onto the patch of grey, hopping slowly along the field two feet from the hedgerow. Occasionally the grey thing would stop and nibble at some foliage. This is when he would make his strike. He began to circle lower, using the branches of the trees to mask his presence. The rabbit continued on his lolloping journey, unaware of the impending danger.

At sixty feet, just above the tops of the trees, the hawk held his altitude. Soon he would have to break his cover, and then it would be a race. If the rabbit saw him too quickly then it would be in the hedgerow before the hawk could even unfurl his deadly talons. If, however, the rabbit idled, then the hawk would dine well. There was a split-second difference between hunger and satiety.

At the edge of the trees the hawk hovered for a second, gathering himself for his fell swoop. Then with terrifying speed he dived for the rabbit. Fifty feet, then forty, he sped bullet-like towards his prey. At thirty feet the kill was almost certain, but, at that moment, a twitter from the hedgerow alerted the rabbit to his vulnerability, and realizing his peril he darted for cover. Just ten feet away the hawk extended his talons ready to fasten upon his unfortunate prey. It was too late. The rabbit had escaped into the bushes and the hawk was forced to pull out of his dive.

From the farmhouse Yoshima watched the episode with cool detachment. He wasn't quite sure who he had been rooting for: the hawk or the rabbit; the hunter or the hunted. As a rule it would have been the hawk, the hunter; the majestic killing machine of the air, skilful and swift and deadly. Today though, he wasn't so sure, he was also admiring the rabbit's vigilance, and the lightning-quick reactions that had taken him to safety.

He felt a surge of empathy with the creature, because he, like the rabbit, was now the hunted.

He sat at a big oak table in the farmhouse kitchen sipping green tea. He'd just finished a light breakfast of mackerel and scrambled egg, and was waiting for his paymaster to arrive. The box lay on the table just in front of his empty plate. He eyed it inquisitively and wondered what secrets it held. He recognized the four main Reiki symbols and a couple of others, including the one he'd altered to disable people. But that was as far as it went - the rest were a complete mystery. It shouldn't have concerned him really, he'd been paid to do a job and he'd done it, but he couldn't help being curious. He was, after all, an expert in symbols and their properties.

The sound of a car engine broke him from his thoughts. Instinctively he left the chair and dropped to the floor. He crawled along the floor to the sink. He poked his head over just enough to get a view of the dirt track that served as an approach to the house. A dark green Range Rover was making its way down to the yard. The driver was alone.

After the vehicle had passed the window, Yoshima got up and made his way to the front door. He opened it a couple of inches and peered out. The vehicle matched the description he'd been given, but, as he hadn't seen his employer before, he was going to be cautious. After initial contact had been made in Tokyo through a third party, communication between the two of them had been limited to written instructions and phone calls. This would be their first face to face meeting.

The Range Rover stopped just outside the disused stable. The driver got out of the car. He was medium height and was wearing a green barber jacket, light grey trousers and Wellington boots. On his head he wore a grey cap. Even to Yoshima's eyes he looked like a cliché. What surprised him the most though was that the man was white: in all their phone calls they had conversed in Japanese and Yoshima expected an Oriental.

The man walked up to the door and Yoshima opened it slightly further. The man saw him and lifted his hand in greeting.

"The weather is very fine," said Yoshima in Japanese.

"Yes, but the vultures hover," replied the man in the same language.

Satisfied with the man's answer Yoshima bowed, and the gesture was reciprocated. The two men walked through to the kitchen.

The man's eyes lit up as soon as he saw the box. "Excellent," he said, still using Japanese. "I never believed that I'd see it again - not in this lifetime anyway."

"I told you that I would find it," said Yoshima.

"Yes, you did. And I am eternally grateful for your efforts," said the man, picking up the box with care. "I appreciate that it was no easy task."

"Not easy, no. But no task is beyond Yoshima."

The man admired the box for a moment, savouring its feel in his hands: he had waited many years for this. He rotated it slowly, his eyes lingering on every last knot and crack. Then, from his jacket pocket, he produced a paper clip. He unravelled the metal and poked the end of the clip into a barely perceptible hole at the front of the box. There was a small click and he opened the lid. Inside, the false base of the box had lifted up, revealing a wafer thin compartment. The compartment was empty.

The man looked puzzled. "Have you done anything to the box?" he asked Yoshima.

"No. I just took it from the boy and brought it back here - like I was instructed to."

The man's look of puzzlement turned into a frown. "Well, there should have been some parchment in here," he said. "Somebody's taken it."

Yoshima took the statement as a personal slight. "Well, it's not me," he said indignantly.

"I apologize Yoshima. I didn't mean to imply that it was you," said the man. "I was merely thinking aloud."

Yoshima accepted the apology with grace. He was suitably impressed with the man and his manners. What particularly pleased him was the fluency with which the man spoke Japanese. Even though he was Caucasian he spoke Yoshima's tongue like a native.

"You speak Japanese very well for a Westerner," said Yoshima.

"Thank you," said the man.

"I must admit that I was expecting you to be someone from my own country," said Yoshima. "I was given that impression from our phone conversations. Not just because of your excellent language skills, but because of the distaste you seemed to have for the West and their greedy ways. You appeared very passionate about retrieving this artefact so that its power would not be abused."

The man put the box down and said, "I am very passionate that it should not be abused, Yoshima, believe me. Like you I believe that most people in the West tend to use anything sacred as a fashion item. They go to yoga classes, and use Reiki and the like, but they have no real idea as to the sanctity of these practices. It's just something for the middle classes to impress their friends with. If it wasn't fashionable to do these things then they wouldn't bother."

Yoshima looked deep into the man's eyes to see if he was telling the truth or just paying lip service. It was hard to tell, but he didn't appear to be concealing anything. "Absolutely," he said eventually. "All these things belong in the East where there is honour and respect for them."

Yoshima boiled the kettle and made the man a cup of green tea, which he accepted gratefully.

"It is perhaps not my place to ask," said Yoshima. "But what exactly is missing from the box?"

"To be honest Yoshima, I don't exactly know myself," said the man. "It was only recently that my research uncovered the fact that it had a secret compartment. The compartment is only thick enough to house paper, so I'm assuming that it contained details on what the box actually is, and how to use the symbols. I can't really think of anything else."

Yoshima frowned. "So the box is useless without these instructions?"

"I think so," said the man.

"We must find them then," said Yoshima. "The boy must have removed them. I will hunt him down and retrieve them."

The man put down his tea and raised his hand. "No Yoshima, you cannot do that. You're a wanted man now. If you show your face outside of this place then the chances are that you'll be recognized and caught by the police. Your description has been all over the television and the newspapers."

"I will not get caught. I am a ninja; I am an expert in evading my enemies. And even if I did slip up, it is my problem not yours, I would never disclose any information about you."

"I know you wouldn't," said the man. "You are a man of honour, I am fully aware of that. But I will need your help for another task once we have found the missing instructions. I can't risk having you incarcerated."

"I appreciate your concern," said Yoshima. "But I will find the boy and the missing items. It is a matter of personal pride to me. My job needs to be completed fully or I will not be satisfied."

The man gave a sigh of resignation. "Okay Yoshima, go and find the boy."

Chapter 40

Stella sat alone at the bar of the Angel, eating the bacon sandwich that Stratton had bought her from the local greasy spoon. It was ten o'clock in the morning and the pub was not yet open. Lenny the barman was clattering about in the corner, sweeping up shards of broken glass. Stratton was upstairs in his flat with Oggi. Stella had not been invited to join them. It was apparently a 'private matter'. She had no right to be annoyed by this, but she was anyway. It felt like a slight on her personality; that she couldn't be trusted. It also smacked of sexism: the two men discussing important stuff that a woman couldn't possibly understand.

She knew underneath that Stratton did trust her and that he wasn't sexist, but it didn't stop her getting wound up about the situation.

She finished her sandwich, which was delicious, and lit herself a cigarette. The smell of smoke was a welcome relief from the hum of stale beer that permeated the post-party air. She wondered what the two of them were up to in the flat. She was a naturally curious person and not knowing what was going on was driving her crazy. It was really none of her business, Stratton was no longer part of her life, and yet she needed to find out.

"They have a strange friendship," she said to Lenny, who had finished cleaning the floor and was now bottling-up.

"Who?" he said.

"Stratton and Oggi," said Stella.

Lenny continued to stock the fridges.

"Well..." pressed Stella.

"Well what?" said Lenny.

"What do you think?" she asked. "They don't seem likely friends do they? I mean, there must be some reason for it. How did they meet for instance?"

"I don't know, I'm just a barman," said Lenny. "Whatever happens between the customers is their own affair. It's not good to ask too many questions in this place. And it's not good business either. People come here because it's discreet."

Stella took a sip of her rapidly-cooling coffee. "Of course they do," she said. "But I only wanted to know a little bit about it. I don't need anybody's life story."

Lenny stopped his work and turned to face Stella. "Listen lady," he said. "I know that you're a friend of Stratton's, but that doesn't mean anything to me. If you want to know about him and Oggi why don't you just ask him? If he wants you to know then he'll tell you himself. This place is my livelihood, and I'm not going to jeopardize that by telling tales out of school."

Stella took the hint and finished her coffee and cigarette in silence. She should have known better than to ask too many questions in a place like the Angel.

Five minutes later Stratton and Oggi came back downstairs. Oggi left through the back door and Stratton sat next to Stella at the bar.

"You all finished with your little boys' meeting?" she said, barely disguising her irritation.

"Yes thanks," said Stratton, and sensing her mood he added, "It wasn't anything personal you know. I needed to speak to Oggi in private. There's stuff we had to do. Things that are just between me and him."

"What are you? A couple of bum bandits?"

"There's no need to be like that is there? Just because you're not getting your own way you don't have to start getting facetious. You're acting like a spoilt brat."

Stella poked her tongue out at him and he laughed.

"Shall we make a move then," he said. "I told Brennan we'd be round at eleven. We don't want to keep them waiting."

Stella's car, a black Toyota MR2, was parked at the back of the pub. After she had checked that none of her tyres had been slashed, they set off for Brennan's house in Wimbledon.

"Your car was perfectly safe out the back there," said Stratton.

"What do you mean?" asked Stella.

"I saw you checking your tyres. Trust me; there is no way that anyone would dare touch any vehicle that was parked at the Angel."

"Well, you can't blame me. Peckham's not exactly a crime-free zone is it? And the Angel's hardly the Ritz."

"Maybe not," said Stratton. "But I know where I'd rather leave my car."

Stella ignored the comment and concentrated on her driving.

After a couple of minutes silence, Stella decided to bring up the subject of Oggi again. "You still haven't told me how you know Oggi," she said.

"I don't believe you've asked," he replied.

"Well, I've hinted enough times but you keep changing the subject," she said petulantly.

"I just know him from the pub."

"There's more to it than that," she said, lighting a cigarette. "There's something funny going on between the two of you. When I first met him, he said that he owed you one. What did he mean? What does he owe you?"

Stratton opened the window for some fresh air and said, "He doesn't owe me anything as far as I'm concerned. I helped him out once, that's all."

In front of them a van stopped without warning. Stella hit the brakes sharply. "For fuck's sake Stratton! Will you stop avoiding the issue and just tell me what's going on between the two of you?!"

"Calm down Stella," he said, resting his hand on her shoulder. "It's not that I don't want to tell you. I just can't; it's not really my place. I promised Oggi that I wouldn't mention it to anyone. If you really want to know then you'll have to ask him. But let me tell you, he's highly unlikely to give anything away."

Stella took a drag of her cigarette, put the car into first, and drove off again. She was angry at herself for having pushed Stratton so hard. It was unfair of her to do so. If he had been able to tell her, then of course he would have. He had made a promise to Oggi and he was going to keep it; she had to respect that.

One of the reasons she had loved him so much was his discretion. There was nobody in the world that she would trust more with her deepest secrets. If you told Stratton something in confidence, then that's where it would stay, and he would never use it against you.

"I'm sorry," she said eventually. "I shouldn't be so nosy, should I?"

"Don't worry about it," he said. "If I was in your position I'd be curious as well."

"You could tell me one thing though," she said. "That's if you're allowed."

"What's that then?"

"There's a badge sewn on the front of Oggi's jacket that says 'Filthy Few'. What does it mean?"

"If you see that on a biker's jacket, it means that he's killed a man," said Stratton.

"Fucking hell!" she cried. "So Oggi's killed someone!"

"I couldn't say. I'm just telling you what the badge means," said Stratton diplomatically. "Would it really surprise you that much if he had?"

"Well yes...I mean no...I don't really know. He looks vicious, but when you talk to him he's kind of all right. He seems sort of gentle, if you know what I mean?"

"Yes I do know what you mean," said Stratton. "But I wouldn't be fooled by it. There's two sides to Oggi and God help anyone who gets on the wrong one."

The traffic lights up ahead turned red and Stella slowed down. "That's one thing I don't understand though," she said. "You're a pacifist, or at least you were; you hate violence. And you hate people who lie and people who steal. You're basically a good man Stratton, so why are you living above a place that's so obviously inhabited by thieves, psychopaths, murderers and drug dealers? Why are you friends with people like Oggi?"

"Well you've certainly kept an open mind about the place," he said laughing. "But, in answer to your question: I stay there because it's safe, and I trust the customers. There's an unspoken rule in the Angel, about not pissing on your own doorstep. It's like a little club, and what goes on between its walls stays between its walls. It's like holy ground for the criminal community. If you fuck up in the Angel then you'd better get out of town - fast."

"Ok, I get it," said Stella, pulling away from the lights. "But it still doesn't really answer my question. By staying there it's like you're condoning their actions."

"I'm not condoning their actions," said Stratton. "I'm not there to judge people, I'm there to…Well, I'm not there to judge people. The line that separates us and them is a lot thinner than you think. Nobody's perfect. Like I said to you before, we're all capable of destroying others. If pushed far enough, most people in the world are capable of some malevolent act, however small. Have you never heard of the phrase 'there but for the grace of God go I'? Everyone has their limits."

"Maybe," said Stella. "But you're never going to be an armed robber or a murderer are you?"

"I wouldn't be so sure," countered Stratton. "Remember that night in Windsor? I might have killed that kid if you hadn't stopped me. I may have seen sense on my own, but I can't be sure. It doesn't matter that the guy was waving a knife in my face, the fact would be that I'd killed someone, and I wouldn't be any better than any other murderer."

"Okay, point taken. But you're not a thief are you?"

"No I'm not," said Stratton. "But I've been lucky enough to lead a life where I haven't had to steal. People do what's needed to survive. I can't say for certain that I wouldn't steal food if I was starving on the street."

Stella pulled out another cigarette and gave him a swift glance. "Don't try that one on me," she said. "I know for a fact that you wouldn't steal anything. If you were starving you'd either ask for food or not eat. I know that some people are more fortunate than others, but not all poor people decide to go into a life of crime. Look at me for instance: I didn't exactly have an easy life, as you well know, but instead of taking the easy, destructive, route, I decided to make something of myself. Everyone has a choice; it's just that most people decide to take the easy option."

"Okay, you've got me," said Stratton. "I'm just trying to justify myself." After a brief silence he added, "Do you want to know the main reason I stay there?"

"Go on then, tell me," she said.

"It's because the people are interesting," said Stratton. "They don't conform. Who wants to spend their time with people who don't have a mind of their own? To the rest of society they may seem like scum, and some of the things they do are disgraceful. But most of them are free thinkers, and by and large most of them are intelligent and, believe it or not, kind. I'd rather spend my time there than at church with the hypocrites. You can learn a lot about people in a place like the Angel. There are no masks or facades; what you see is what you get."

"Interesting," said Stella, stopping the car at Brennan's gate. "But we'll have to carry this on another time, because we're here now."

The gates opened and Stella drove up to the house. She'd been there once before, years ago, when she'd had to pick Brennan up for an early meeting. She didn't remember the place being so big. He hadn't done badly for a policeman.

She parked the car on the gravel frontage and they walked up to the front door. After a couple of minutes it opened, and Anna

Brennan welcomed them.

"Hi Stella," she said. "Lovely to see you again. Sorry to keep you waiting, but I was having a doze."

They entered the house and Anna led them to the large living room.

"Have you met Stratton before?" asked Stella, gesturing towards him.

"Yes," said Anna. "I believe I have. It was at a Christmas dinner. You'd had one too many if I remember rightly."

"Possibly," said Stratton. "It certainly sounds like me."

"Is David not here?" asked Stella changing the subject.

"No he's not," said Anna. "He wanted to stay of course, but I wouldn't let him. He'll just keep butting in and questioning everything. I know that he means well, but I want to make my own mind up about things. He's a great support but sometimes he can get suffocating." She laughed. "God I must sound awfully ungrateful."

"Not at all," said Stella. "Everybody needs their own space."

Anna gestured for them to sit down. "So Stratton," she said. "I hear that you might be able to help me."

Chapter 41

Grant Romano stood patiently in line at passport control. The woman in front of him turned round and gave him a quizzical stare. For a moment he thought that she'd recognized him and was going to say something. Fortunately her children began tugging at her sleeves, and she turned back round to attend to them.

Romano was pleased with himself; he'd managed to get all the way from LA-X to Heathrow without anybody clocking him. He'd only bleached his hair and put on a pair of glasses but it had been enough to throw people off the scent.

He walked up to the window and handed his passport over.

"Could you take your glasses off please sir?" the official asked politely.

Romano removed the thin-rimmed spectacles.

The official looked closely at him and then back to the passport. He repeated the action a couple of times. He then handed the passport back. "Thank you Mr Atkins," he said. "Enjoy your stay."

Romano smiled and walked through the gates. He wondered if the official realized who he was. Usually, when he wasn't travelling incognito, officials would recognize his face and question him because the name on his passport didn't match the handle that they knew him by. His real name, Gary Atkins, was not common knowledge. It was one of Hollywood's best-kept secrets; if, of course, there was such a thing as a secret in Hollywood.

He walked up to the baggage carousel and waited for his luggage to appear. Standing among the crowds in his thin disguise, he felt like a spy or a fugitive. His travel routine wasn't normally so cloak and dagger, but for this trip he wanted as little attention as possible. He wasn't in England to publicize a film, he was in England to get some answers.

Sharlo Miles hadn't returned his calls for three days. Romano had got so fed up that he'd called one of his friends in the CIA to find out what Miles was up to. His source had told him that Miles had flown to the UK on government business. Romano didn't believe this. He was near certain that Miles was in the UK on the trail of the box.

Eventually his luggage made it onto the carousel. Typically, it was one of the last items to be dispatched. The large green rucksack came round to him and he whisked it off the conveyor. He had chosen this particular item for his gear as he felt his set of Gucci valises might draw unwanted interest.

Outside the terminal he grabbed a black cab. Using a German twang for cover, he asked the driver to take him to the Astoria in Covent Garden. It was a decent enough place to stay, but not somewhere that the paparazzi had a habit of frequenting.

"Business or pleasure?" asked the cab driver as he drove off.

"A bit of both hopefully," replied Romano.

The cab driver stared at Romano in his rear view mirror. "Don't I know you from somewhere?" he said.

"I don't think so," said Romano, thickening his accent slightly more.

The cabbie shrugged his shoulders and carried on driving.

At the Astoria, Romano checked in and went to his room to grab a shower. The room was a standard double. Nothing too flash, but comfortable enough for him. He may have been Hollywood royalty but he was no prima donna.

After showering he lay on the bed for a while, deciding on his best course of action. He knew that Miles was staying at the Dorchester, his source had given him that information, but he didn't know how best to approach him. Should he try ringing again? Should he let Miles know that he was in the country? Or should he just go over to the Dorchester and surprise him? If the past few days were anything to go by, then there would be no point phoning. So the only thing to do was to try and get a face to face meeting.

After slipping on some clothes: blue jeans, black jumper, sneakers and a black leather jacket, he made his way to Covent Garden tube station. He took the Piccadilly line to Green Park and then the Jubilee to Bond Street. It was three in the afternoon and the trains, although busy with Christmas shoppers, weren't packed to bursting point as they would be in a few hours' time. Romano was glad to have a bit of breathing space: he was claustrophobic, and to him there was nothing worse than the London Underground at rush hour.

After leaving Bond Street station he headed for Park Lane and the Dorchester Hotel. The Dorchester was where Romano usually stayed when he was in the UK. He liked its luxuriant blend of tradition, trend and technology. He hoped that he wouldn't be spotted by an eagle-eyed member of staff.

He approached the reception desk. "Hi," he said to the pretty young brunette. "I'm here to see Professor Sharlo Miles." He kept at the German accent.

"*Welche zimmer nummer?*" asked the girl, picking up on his accent.

Romano stared blankly for a moment, and then said, "No, no. You must speak English. It is goot for me jah." The thought hadn't occurred to him that anyone would try and converse with him in German.

The girl smiled. "What room number Mr Romano?"

Romano hammed it up some more. "Vot do you mean. I vant Professor Miles. Who is zis Romano?"

The girl started to giggle. "You're not going to be winning any Oscars if you keep putting on performances like that," she said.

Romano looked around, there was no-one in ear shot. "Ok, you've got me," he said. "But can you keep it quiet. I don't want anyone to know I'm over here in England."

"Well, I don't know about that," she said. "The world's

biggest movie star hovering around the Dorchester pretending to be German: there must be a saleable story in there somewhere."

"Yes, there is. But I'd appreciate it if it didn't get out. How much do you want?"

"Let me think," said the girl. She looked serious. Two seconds later she started to laugh and said, "Don't worry, I don't want anything. I won't tell anyone I've seen you."

"Thank you," he looked at the girl's name tag. "Thank you Lucy. I really appreciate it."

"No problem, I like a bit of subterfuge," she said. She looked up Miles' room number and rang his phone. A minute later she hung up and said, "There's no answer I'm afraid, Mr Romano. He must be out. Do you want to leave a message for him?"

Romano thought for a minute. "No, not really," he said. "The thing is, I really want to surprise him. If you could let me know when he gets back, then I can go up to his room. Is that ok? Or will it get you into trouble?"

"It's not really the done thing to be honest. But seeing as it's you, I don't see any harm in it. I mean it's not like you're up to anything sinister is it?"

"Thank you," said Romano. "I'll go and have a drink in the bar. I'll give you my mobile number, and if you could call me when he gets back I'd be very grateful."

"How grateful?" she said, her eyes sparkling playfully.

Romano felt something stir. The girl was sexy. But this was neither the time nor the place for it. Business first. He handed over his mobile number, smiled, and headed for the bar.

He ordered himself a large cognac, took a copy of The Times from the rack, and sat down at a table in the corner with the newspaper obscuring his face. After the episode with the receptionist he wanted to keep out of the way. If she recognized him, then he could be sure that others were likely to as well.

He checked his phone was switched on and started to read the paper. Immediately his attention was grabbed by the main headline - 'Mulholland killer unmasked'.

A photo fit of a Japanese man filled most of the front page. What interested him though, was the name Mulholland. He had no idea who Henry Mulholland was, he hadn't been famous in the States, but the name was definitely familiar. He cast his mind back trying to place it. Did it have something to do with his father? Maybe. He couldn't be sure.

He lowered the paper slightly and picked up his balloon of cognac. Out of habit he swilled the liquid round and took a deep sniff. Then he took a large sip. Over the top of the glass his eyes fell upon a well-built man with dark, slicked-back hair: it was Mel Gibson. In one swift movement Romano put down his glass and raised the paper back up to cover his face. Much as he loved Mel, he really didn't want to get into a conversation with him right now. The two of them, in a bar together, in the afternoon, could only go one way.

His phone rang and, keeping the paper high, he answered it. It was Lucy, the receptionist.

"Hello, Mr Romano," she said. "He's just gone up to his room."

"Thank you Lucy."

Romano peeked over the top of his paper. Gibson was at the bar with his back to him. He drank the rest of his brandy quickly and, keeping his head down, strode out into the lobby. Miles' room was number 218 on the second floor. Romano took the stairs.

He knocked softly on the door. He waited for a minute but there was no answer. He knocked again, this time a bit louder.

Thirty seconds later Miles came to the door. "Can I help you?" he said, without recognition.

Romano took off his spectacles. "It's me Sharlo. It's Grant," he said.

For a good ten seconds Miles just stood and stared. Then he said, "Grant, how good to see you. What the hell are you doing here? And why the disguise?"

"Why don't you let me in and I'll tell you," said Romano.

"Of course. Come in, dear boy."

Miles led him in. It was a large room with a double bed at the top, covered by a green eiderdown, and a mahogany table in the middle. Two high back green leather chairs stood each side of the table. In the left-hand corner there was a writing bureau. The walls were magnolia, the carpet cream, and the fittings florid.

"Would you like a drink?" asked Miles. "We've got the mini-bar here, or I can order us up a bottle of something?"

"Yeah, a drink would be good," said Romano. "How about a cognac?"

"Okay," said Miles. "I'll get them to bring up a bottle of Hennessey XO, that's the one you have, isn't it?"

Romano nodded his approval and Miles rang room service. He gestured for Romano to sit down, and they took a chair each at the table.

"Well I must say it's good to see you," said Miles. "A welcome friendly face in a strange land."

Romano remained impassive. "Why haven't you answered my calls Sharlo?" he asked. "I've left five or six messages on your phone and you still haven't got back to me. It's almost like you're avoiding me."

"I'm sorry Grant. I have been meaning to call you back, but I've been incredibly busy."

Romano studied Miles' face carefully. He might be some dumb actor but he knew when somebody was hiding something.

"Listen Sharlo," he said. "You're a good friend and I don't want to fall out with you, but there's something you're not telling me. You might well have been busy, but you've been busy before and it's never stopped you getting back to me. My instincts tell me that you're hiding something from me; and they tell me that it's something to do with that box I told you about. And before you answer, remember how accurate my instincts are."

"Really Grant," Miles said innocently. "Are you feeling all right? Are you sleeping properly? It seems as though you've become quite paranoid. I told you only last week that I hadn't uncovered any information about that box. Don't you believe me?"

"Quite frankly: No," said Romano. "The way you act whenever I mention it has made me suspicious. And I've had dreams about you Sharlo; dreams about you and the box; dreams where..." He stopped himself from giving too much away. "Well, dreams anyway."

"Dreams can often be influenced by our subconscious," Miles countered. "If something is troubling you, then it tends to manifest itself in bad dreams."

"Okay Sharlo. Cut the bullshit. These dreams started before I even became suspicious of you, so they haven't been influenced by anything. You're definitely up to something or you wouldn't be over here in the UK. I know how much you hate the place."

There was a knock on the door. It was room service. They had brought up a bottle of Hennessey XO and two balloons.

Miles poured out two large measures of brandy and handed one to Romano. "You're right; I don't like the UK that much, particularly at this time of year: it's too cold. But I had to come over on government business."

"The whole thing smells Sharlo. I told you, my instincts are rarely wrong," said Romano. "And another thing's just hit me. I was reading in the paper about that industrialist who was murdered the other day. I thought I recognized the name from somewhere, and I've just remembered - Mulholland was the name of one of my dad's war buddies. There's too much coincidence."

"You're not going to let this go, are you Grant?"

"No Sharlo. I'm not."

"Very well then," said Miles with a sigh. "I suppose I'll have to come clean. You're right, I am after the box. When you first told me the story about your dad being saved from death by an Indian mystic, and acquiring some ancient box with magical powers, I must admit to having been slightly dubious. Particularly in the light of your father's habit of telling a tall story or two."

Romano laughed and said, "Yes, he did come out with some rare stuff."

"Anyway," continued Miles. "After thinking about it for a while I decided to check out your father's war record. You were somewhat vague about the details."

Romano interrupted. "The thing is Sharlo, my father told me these stories when I was a kid. By the time I was old enough to appreciate or remember anything, he was a gambling drunk who didn't even know the time of day. All I knew is that he got saved; him and his friends found this box; the box had mysterious symbols on it that he said could work magic and heal people."

"Of course. Well like I said, I checked out your father's war record and then I got a private investigator here in England to do a little more digging. I won't bore you with the details, but eventually, through fact and hearsay, I discovered that there may well have been a box like your father said. Although the information I received was, to say the least, fuzzy, from the description of the symbols I concluded that they must have derived from some form of Reiki. Have you heard of Reiki?"

Romano nodded and said, "Yeah, it's become quite fashionable recently in LA."

"I thought it might," said Miles. "Anyway, at the institute we've done many studies on Reiki over the years. And although we still haven't got to the bottom of it, there is a pile of evidence as to its effectiveness. Some of the results we've had from experiments have been startling. The symbols really do seem to be connecting people to a higher source of power. Personally I think they could be the key to the biggest breakthrough that mankind has ever known. I think they're the key to connecting us with what people call God."

Romano sat back in his chair. "Wow!" he said. "Do you really think so?"

"Absolutely," said Miles. He took a large sip of cognac and continued. "I see a lot of strange things at the institute, as you can imagine, but most people have talents that they're born with and remain unexplained. With Reiki the gift is not inbred, so we know why people are able to do what they do: because they've been attuned. Anybody can be attuned to it, which is what makes it exciting. And not only does Reiki give people healing powers, it improves their intuition as well. People who have been attuned seem to develop much higher levels of ESP than they had previously. Think how far the human race could go if everyone was attuned. We could turn ourselves into a race of telepathic super beings."

"And how do you think the box fits in to this?" asked Romano.

Miles, who had become quite animated in his enthusiasm, took another drink to calm himself down. "I've read many books on the subject of Reiki; some good, some bad, some indifferent. But a common thread of belief seems to be that there are a host of lost symbols. The story goes that they are hidden in a monastery in either Tibet or India. I believe that the symbols on the box that your father and his friends found could well be these lost ones. Who knows what they could do? They may help to rid mankind of disease and give human beings powers that they never thought possible."

Romano was silent for a moment, thinking about what Miles had told him. Eventually he said, "This is all well and good Sharlo, but it doesn't explain why you've kept me out of the loop. Why the hell haven't you told me all this before?"

Miles got up and put a hand on Romano's shoulder in a fatherly fashion. "The only reason I've kept you in the dark, Grant, is because I didn't want to worry you, and I feared that if you knew too much you would want to get involved; thus putting yourself in danger. You read in the paper about Henry Mulholland didn't you? Well, he was killed because of the box. Two more people have been murdered since. All relatives of your father's friends."

"But surely if people were being killed over this thing then you should've warned me."

"Not really," said Miles. "Nobody knows what happened to your father: that he moved to America to start a new life. As far as his old friends knew, he had gone abroad for adventure and died childless. There was no link between you and the box - unless of course you got involved and made one."

Romano sank further into his chair. He felt guilty and stupid.

"I'm sorry Sharlo," he said. "I should have trusted that you were doing the right thing. I just got flustered. And what with these dreams as well. I just wish that you'd answered my calls, then we could have avoided this."

"No need to apologize Grant, it's all water under the bridge now, as far as I'm concerned," said Miles, sitting back down. "I wouldn't mind hearing about these dreams you've been having though. They sound quite intriguing."

Romano poured himself another cognac and relayed his dream to Miles.

Chapter 42

Anna Brennan was travelling through space. Not dark empty space; but bright, vivid, multicoloured space. She was flying through a tunnel enclosed by a rainbow of nebulae. In front of her, surrounded by shimmering stars, was a swirling cloud of orange gas that circled like a cyclone around a disc of purest white. The disc had the same inescapable power as a black hole, but instead of infinite gravity it was emanating infinite light and love. It was pulling her in at what seemed like a million miles a second, but, tantalizingly, however fast she went she didn't seem to draw any closer. And although part of her wanted to reach the light and dissolve into it, she knew in her heart that it wasn't yet time.

The tunnel and the light gradually disappeared and were replaced by gentle mists of blue and green. She was floating slowly back to earth.

Her breath was slow and rhythmical. She became aware of her physical being once more. Her entire body pulsed with energy, and where there had been pain before, there was now just a warm glow.

"Are you ok?" asked a faraway voice.

Anna wanted to answer but found herself unable to do so. She was too happy, too peaceful, to talk. She needed a few more minutes to herself.

"Anna," said the voice softly. "Are you ok?"

Anna opened her eyes and smiled. She stayed silent. For a while she stared at the ceiling.

"I'll go and get you a glass of water," said the voice. "I'll be back in a minute."

Anna continued to gaze straight up. The room seemed incredibly foggy, shrouded in a haze of heat. She closed her eyes for a few seconds, and then opened them again, hoping to regain some visual clarity. The haze remained.

"How do you feel?" said the voice.

Anna turned her head sideways. Stratton stood next to her holding a glass of water. "I'm good," she said. "In fact I'm more than good. I feel like wow! Like I haven't felt before. What have you done to me?"

"Given you a dose of pure energy," he said. "Here, have a drink of water, you'll probably be thirsty."

Anna sat up on the massage table and took the glass from Stratton. He was right, she was really thirsty. She'd been feeling so good that she hadn't noticed before, but now that he'd mentioned it, she realized that her mouth and throat were incredibly dry, as if she hadn't drunk in days. She drank the whole glass down in one go.

Stratton went back to the kitchen to get some more water for her.

"The room seems very hazy," said Anna when he returned.

"You've generated a lot of heat," said Stratton. "A lot of power's just gone through you. Not only that, but you're also in tune with the energy of the universe. You're relaxed and better able to perceive it at the moment. You'll probably feel a bit light-headed for a few days while your body adjusts, and after that... Well we'll have to see. But don't worry about it; everyone feels a bit dopey after a Reiki session. The more power you take on board, the more stoned you feel."

Anna drank some more water. "I just can't stop smiling," she said. "It's absolutely amazing. I feel like going out and giving the world a great big hug."

Stratton smiled. "Well that's good news at least," he said.

Anna twisted herself round and sat with her legs dangling over the edge of the table. "I have to admit, there was a point where I nearly asked you to stop," she said. "When you had your hands above my lungs, I thought I was going to scream. I was in real agony for a few minutes. But then suddenly the pain stopped and I felt like an incredible weight had been lifted from me. My mind started to drift into weird and wonderful places."

"I did say that you might experience a bit of discomfort," said Stratton. "The pain was a blockage being removed. I was impressed that you stuck with it, it's just too much for a lot of people."

"Was it not painful for you as well?" she asked.

"No, not painful," said Stratton. "But it certainly made me sweat. When someone has something seriously wrong, it takes a lot of power to shift it. There was a massive amount energy flowing through me. I have to admit, it was almost too much for me as well."

Anna thought for a moment. "When you say 'shift', do you mean that you've shifted my tumour?"

"I wouldn't go that far," said Stratton. "It's hard to tell what's happened to the tumour. All I can say is that there was a blockage, and now there isn't one. It's blockages in the lymphatic system that cause tumours. The blockage is now gone, but I don't think the tumour will have disappeared immediately. It's a physical object so it has to go somewhere. Don't be surprised if you start to cough up a load of phlegm in the next few days."

Anna looked horrified. "Are you saying that I'm going to cough up my tumour?" she said.

Stratton put a reassuring hand on her shoulder. "Don't look so worried," he said. "I'm not saying that it will happen, but it might. If a lot of Reiki is taken on board for a serious condition then there tends to be a strong reaction. The body begins to purge itself of poisons. Coughing up phlegm sometimes happens, as does diarrhoea. I'm just letting you know what to expect. The thing is not to panic, you might be a little bit ill for a few days as you clear it out, but after that you should feel much better."

"I feel better now," said Anna. "Do you think it'll really get rid of my cancer?" She was hopeful and incredulous.

"I don't know," said Stratton truthfully. "But it's not going to make it worse. Ideally I'd like to come back and see you another couple of times. If you want my honest opinion, then I think it'll work if you want it to."

"What do you mean, if I want it to?" said Anna. "Of course I want it to work, who wouldn't? Nobody wants cancer. Nobody wants to die. Do they?"

"Well you wouldn't think so would you?" said Stratton. "But some people are, by nature, self-destructive. I know this for a fact because I used to be one of them, maybe I still am. Take alcoholism for instance. Alcoholism is a disease, but it's a disease you can choose not to have if you really don't want it."

"Are you comparing cancer with alcoholism?" Anna said, her voice bordering on anger.

"No, of course not," said Stratton. "But the premise of beating the disease is maybe the same. Alcoholics know they're killing themselves and yet they carry on regardless. Some say they want to beat it, and they do. Some say they want to beat it, and they don't. The difference is that the ones who conquer it are the ones who really want to. The failures, whatever they say, have a secret desire to self-destruct. It's all about looking deep inside yourself and discovering what the illness is really about. Deep-seated anxieties, and bitterness and hatred, tend to manifest themselves in physical form at some point in life. You have to search long and hard to find the true root of an illness before you can cure it."

Anna became more irate. "So you're saying that my cancer is due to a secret desire to self-destruct?"

Stratton sensed that the conversation was heading to a bad place. "I'm not here to judge you Anna," he said. "I'm just telling you about a theory that's been around for thousands of years. There's an old saying attributed to Buddha that says, 'Every human being is the author of his own health or disease'. He also says 'Peace comes from within. Do not seek it without'. But I don't want to get into some big philosophical debate about it. All you need to take from what I'm saying is that you will get better if you truly want to. And if you ask me, I believe that you truly want to."

He smiled at her with candour, and rested his right hand on her forehead.

Immediately Anna was calm again. "I'm sorry," she said. "I know you're only trying to help me. And I think you have already. I feel better than I did on morphine."

"Good," said Stratton. "But remember, you still need some more sessions really. And you should still visit your consultant however well you feel. You need to know if the tumour's actually shrinking or not "

"Ok," she said. "No problem." She hopped off the table and they went downstairs to the living room where Stella was waiting.

"Wow! That's put some colour in your cheeks," she said, looking to Anna.

"Well I certainly feel good," Anna beamed. "I don't know exactly how, but Stratton here has definitely worked some sort of magic on me."

After a quick coffee Stella and Stratton took their leave. They were both hungry and decided to grab themselves a late lunch. They stopped off in Wandsdworth at a pub that did food all day. It was clean and modern, part of a big chain.

"I couldn't believe how well Anna looked," said Stella as they waited for their food. "Before you took her upstairs she looked so frail and ashen that I thought she'd keel over if you prodded her. When you came back downstairs she was positively glowing. She looked like people do when they've just had sex."

Stratton laughed. "What are you trying to suggest?"

"Not that. You're not that good in bed," she said grinning. "I was just gobsmacked, that's all. I know this stuff appears to work, but I didn't realize it worked that well. She looked and acted like a totally different person."

Stratton took a sip of red wine. "She was a different person," he said. "People who have a Reiki session, and actually take to it, are never the same again. It starts you off on a journey: a journey to find who you really are. You begin to look inside yourself and question your actions more deeply. For some people it can be a painful process, full of incredible highs and unfathomable lows. Once someone starts searching their soul intensely, they can uncover all manner of thoughts and desires that they didn't know existed. The secret is to find these deep-seated feelings and deal with them."

"Okay, but wasn't the point to help her with the cancer?" suggested Stella.

"Yes, of course it was," he said. "But, as I explained to her - physical illness is a manifestation of what's going on in your mind and soul. The Reiki will help with the physical action of shrinking the tumour but it will also get to the root of it in her head. Something in her psyche has caused the illness and unless that's addressed then it'll return."

Stella tutted. "She was a heavy smoker Stratton; that's what caused the cancer. Not some fucking childhood memory."

"Okay, but what made her smoke in the first place?" he countered.

"I don't know," she replied. "Why does anyone smoke? Because they enjoy it I suppose. Because they're addicted to the nicotine."

"Fair enough, if that's what you think," he said knowingly.

The food arrived and his statement was left hanging. They had each ordered a rare rib-eye steak with fries, salad and pepper sauce. They ate hungrily and in silence. Stratton's silence was contented. Stella was still thinking about the patronizing tone of his last comment. She ate her fill and went outside for a cigarette.

When she returned Stratton had finished his food and was swilling the last of his wine around the bottom of the glass, meditating on its movement.

"Okay then smart ass," she said. "Why do people smoke then? I know you're dying to tell me."

Stratton continued to play with his wine. "Because of a desire to self-destruct."

"So you're saying that I want to destroy myself?"

"I guess so," he said. "You might not be conscious of it though. It's a way of blocking things out, just like excessive drinking or taking drugs; or even excessive exercise. The smoking takes your mind off what you should be dealing with. The longer you smoke, the deeper the problem buries itself, eventually eating away at your body. It's easier to destroy yourself than address painful issues. It's like a slow suicide."

Stella looked incredulous. "Are you saying that it's not actually the smoke that's causing cancer, but the problem that it's hiding?"

"I think they go hand in hand, it's like a vicious circle. The best thing is to deal with the problem in the first place," he said. "Anyway, we're getting away from the point. You know that smoking can kill you don't you? And you're a human being with your own free will?"

"Yes," she said. "So what?"

"So, you choose to smoke of your own free will, therefore you must have an inner self-loathing that makes you want to self-destruct."

"Okay, point taken," she said, not out of agreement but because she was fed up with the lecture. Even if he was right, she didn't want to hear it.

Stratton sensed her mood. "Well you did ask," he said. "You know better than anyone about my history of self-destruction. I'm not sitting on some pedestal looking down on you and telling you what to do. I'm the last person to take the moral high ground. I'm talking to you but really I'm giving advice to myself. I'm trying to get rid of my own demons."

Stella finished her wine and looked across at Stratton. He

gave her a tender smile. "What do you want to do?" she said. "Do you want to stay here for another drink, or shall I take you home?"

"I don't think another drink's a good idea for me is it?" he said. "And you're driving, so it's no good for you either. Perhaps you ought to take me back to Peckham."

They left the pub and walked down the road to Stella's car. Part of her was upset by the fact that they hadn't stayed longer. She knew that once she dropped him off, there was a chance she might not see him for a while. She was getting used to him being around. All she had to go back to was an empty flat.

She could ring one of her friends and go out with them, but it wouldn't be the same. She felt as though their little adventure was coming to an end. It wouldn't be long before she wished it had.

It was six o'clock when she pulled up at the back of the Angel to drop him off. "Well, I guess I'll see you when I see you," she said.

"I guess so," he conceded. And then, as if reading her mind, he added, "You can call me any time, you know. We don't have to be strangers any more. I realize that we can't go back to the way we were, but it doesn't mean we can't talk does it?"

"No, it doesn't," she said smiling. She kissed him on the cheek.

Stratton got out of the car and wished her goodnight.

"By the way," said Stella as he turned to go. "She lost a child."

"What?" he said. "Who lost a child?"

"Anna. About 20 years ago she had a miscarriage. She was five months pregnant and there were complications. After that she couldn't have children."

"Oh, I see," he said. "Why are you telling *me*?"

"I thought you might be interested," she said. "It kind of backs up your theory. It was just after that when she started chain smoking. Blocking things out and all that."

"See you soon," he said and waved goodbye.

He watched her pull out of the car park and drive down the poorly-lit street. He smiled and yet he felt strangely empty. He'd devoted so much time to his own self-reliance that he'd forgotten the simple pleasures of companionship. He knew that he couldn't depend on somebody else for his own happiness, but maybe he'd taken it too far. Perhaps it was time to free himself of his disciplined philosophies; perhaps it was time to just go with the flow.

Stella's car disappeared from view and he turned towards the back door of the pub. Of the four street lights in the car park, only one was working, and that was inevitably the one furthest away. He pulled his keys from his jacket pocket and squinted to find the one that fitted. He tried all of them one after the other but none would turn the lock. Systematically he tried them all again. Still the door wouldn't budge. He knocked loudly to try and grab someone's attention. There was no answer.

He started to walk round to the front of the pub. After only a few steps his phone rang. He grasped into his pocket and pulled it out. It never reached his ear.

Chapter 43

Stella lay in bed staring at the ceiling. It was ten o'clock in the morning and as a rule, she would by now be up and dressed. Today though, she didn't feel much like getting out of bed. There was nothing for her to do, so why bother. She had just phoned Mulholland's PA who'd told her that everything at the house was fine and to enjoy her holiday. After the adrenaline-pumping weekend she felt impotent and deflated.

She wondered what had possessed her to give up her job with Special Branch. She knew the answer of course - it was money. But money always came at a price, and now she was paying it.

She reached over to her bedside cabinet, grabbed the remote control, and turned on the television. It had been years since she'd had the opportunity to watch daytime TV and she wondered if it had improved any. A five minute flick through the channels gave her the answer - a resounding no. Cookery, antiques, property; the staple diet of the scheduler. Was there nothing for the discerning viewer before six o'clock?

She was just thinking about going back to sleep when the buzzer to her flat rang. Who the hell was it? She hadn't invited anyone over; and her friends always called before turning up. She decided to ignore it. Thirty seconds later it rang again. This time it was a lengthy, sustained buzz. The type that grates.

Stella got out of bed and slipped on her dressing gown. As she made her way to the intercom it buzzed again.

"All fucking right, I'm coming!" she cursed.

She pressed the button. "Hello?"

"Stella?" said a gruff but familiar voice.

"Yes."

"It's me Oggi, can I come up?"

Without thinking she said, "Yeah sure, just push the door when you hear the buzz."

Oggi? What the hell did he want? How the fuck did he know where she lived? Maybe Stratton had sent him over; but then why hadn't Stratton come himself.

She opened the door to her flat and was greeted by the sight of a grim-faced Oggi. "Hi Oggi, come in" she said. "What's up?"

Oggi strode into the flat. "Is Stratton here?" he asked.

"No, I haven't seen him since last night when I dropped him off at the pub. Why?"

"Because I think something's happened to him. I think he's been kidnapped."

He reached into his pocket and pulled out a mobile phone. "I found this outside the back of the pub this morning. It's Stratton's."

"Maybe he just dropped it," she said hopefully.

"Well it did occur to me," said Oggi. "But firstly, it's not like him to mislay things. And secondly, nobody's seen him since you left him last night. He never made it into the pub. This was the only place I thought he might be."

"Well he's not here," she said. "And how did you get my address anyway?"

"Stratton gave it to me yesterday. Just in case."

"In case of what?" she snapped, angry at Stratton giving out her personal details.

"In case something like this happened," said Oggi. "He wanted to make sure you had protection if he wasn't around."

"Well, thank you for coming over, but I don't need protecting thank you very much," she said haughtily, her pride having taken a blow. "I'm an ex-Special Branch officer. I've done close protection for the royal family for Christ's sake. I think I can handle myself. The last thing I need is a murderer as a bodyguard."

Oggi held up his hands and said, "Hey Stella, don't have a pop at me. I'm only doing what Stratton asked. If you want to go it alone that's fine by me. I just thought that you might be able to help me find him."

Stella calmed herself down. "Sorry Oggi," she said. "I'm pissed off at him, not you. Why don't you sit down? I'm going to make some coffee. You can smoke if you want, there's an ashtray on the table."

"Well, if you're sure you don't mind having a *murderer* in your flat," said Oggi pointedly, giving her a stern glance.

While the kettle boiled she got dressed; putting on a pair of jeans and a loose-fitting black cashmere sweater. She made the coffee and sat down in her armchair. Oggi was on the sofa and took up both seats.

"What did you mean when you called me a murderer?" he asked, not impolitely.

"Sorry about that," said Stella. "It just came out."

"Ok, but where did it come from. What's Stratton been saying?"

Stella could feel Oggi's eyes boring into her. She shuffled awkwardly and said, "He's not said anything really. He just told me what that badge on your jacket means - the one that says 'Filthy Few'. He didn't expand on it; in fact, if you must know, it's like getting blood out of a stone whenever I ask him anything about you. He's more likely to take a bullet in the head than give anything away. To be honest it pisses me off a bit, there used to be a time when he'd tell me anything, now it's like he doesn't trust me."

Happy at Stella's ignorance, Oggi relaxed. "It's not that he doesn't trust you Stella. It's just not his place to tell you," he said. "Stratton's a good man, a far better man than me, and he's also a trustworthy man. Really, you should appreciate his silence. It means that if you ever tell him anything then it'll be safe. I never trust anybody who's willing to give up another person's secrets, it means that they'll do it to you too."

"I guess so," she said. "I shouldn't have been so nosy in the first place really. I was just curious about your friendship. You've got to admit you're not the most likely of mates, are you?"

"I guess not," Oggi conceded. "But let's not dwell on it. You know all that you need to, and that is that Stratton's my friend. What we should be doing is trying to find him."

Stella took out a packet of cigarettes and offered one to Oggi, who accepted it. "I agree," she said. "But where the hell do we start? We don't even know who's taken him."

Oggi lit Stella's cigarette, and then his own. "That's not strictly true," he said. "I think he's been taken by that Japanese bloke, Yoshima."

"What makes you think that?" she asked. "What would Yoshima want with him? He's already got the box."

"I know he has. But the symbols on it are useless if you can't activate them. He needs Stratton to show him how."

"You seem to know an awful lot about it," she said curtly, again secretly hurt that Oggi knew more than she did.

"I only know what Stratton told me. And to be honest it wasn't a lot. He just said that he didn't think Yoshima had all the information he needed, and there was a possibility that he might come for him."

Stella studied Oggi's expression. It was deadpan, but she was sure he knew more than he was letting on. "Ok then," she said. "Let's say Yoshima has taken him. How the hell do we find Yoshima? I don't think he's in the phone book."

"No, I've already looked - it goes straight from Yorke to Young," quipped Oggi. "The only thing we know is that he was attacked at the back of the pub where I found his phone. Perhaps we should start there. Maybe ask around, see if anyone saw anything. You should know, you're the ex-copper."

"Yes I am. And speaking of coppers, why don't we phone them? I'm sure we can get a crack squad onto this if I tell David Brennan what's happened."

At the mention of police Oggi became nervous. "I don't think we need to involve the police at the moment," he said. "We haven't got any real evidence that he's been kidnapped, have we? And he's only been missing for about fifteen hours. They're hardly likely to approve a full-scale manhunt."

"I guess you're right. But I'm going to phone Brennan anyway."

Before Oggi could stop her she'd picked up her mobile. She went to her room and returned five minutes later with a despondent look.

"No joy then?" said Oggi.

"No," she said gloomily. "He was polite, but he said that the case was out of his hands now, and that I should phone the new officer in charge. I did that, and he said the same as you; that Stratton hadn't been missing for long and that there was no reason to suspect foul play. He said that Yoshima was hardly likely to come out of hiding with the whole country looking for him. I can see his point of view."

"Oh well," said Oggi, trying to hide his relief. "We'll just have to get on with it ourselves."

Chapter 44

Stratton opened his eyes but still he could see nothing. He closed them then opened them again: there was no difference. As far as he could tell in his disorientated state, he was lying face upwards. There was some sort of material in his mouth, probably covered by heavy-duty tape, and ropes bound his arms to his body. His legs too were tied fast. He felt like a mummified body.

He didn't know what time of day it was or how long he'd been out for. What he did know was that he'd been drugged, because his head felt like it had been filled with wet sand. The last thing he remembered was pulling his phone out of his pocket.

He rolled himself over a couple of times. The floor was cold and damp, indicating that he was either in a cellar or a shed. He assumed, because of the pitch darkness, that it was the former.

There was no doubt in his mind who had taken him. It was obviously Yoshima, eager to get his hands on the attunements that Stratton had lifted from the box's secret compartment. Unfortunately Yoshima was out of luck, because there was no way that Stratton was going to divulge their location, not even in the face of death. If a psycho like Yoshima activated the symbols it would be catastrophic.

Stratton tried to wriggle inside his biting bonds, hoping that he could maybe loosen them slightly to make himself a bit more comfortable. They were expertly tied however and after a couple of minutes he gave up. But it did give him some satisfaction to think that Yoshima considered him such a danger that he had to be gagged and bound.

He wondered whether anybody in the outside world had missed him yet. It could be days before anyone started to question where he was. Even if they had, how would they find him? Yoshima was anything but sloppy; he wouldn't have left a Hansel and Gretel trail leading up to his lair. No, nobody would find him; it was just his own will and skill pitted against Yoshima.

Above him, seemingly far away, he thought he could hear voices. Perhaps it was the TV, although he wouldn't have put Yoshima down as a TV sort of person. He strained his ears to see if he could make out what the voices were saying. For a moment they stopped and he began to think that he'd imagined them. But then they started again, this time much closer. There was definitely a conversation going on, but not in English.

He looked to his right where he thought the voices were coming from. The outline of a door had appeared, surrounded by yellow light. A key rattled in the door; it opened, blinding Stratton's eyes.

Chapter 45

Stella jumped off the back of Oggi's chopper and removed her helmet. She had wanted to take her car but he had insisted that she ride pillion. She had the unnerving feeling that he wasn't going to let her out of his sight.

Apart from Oggi's motorbike, the only other vehicle at the back of the Angel was an old VW Golf Mk II in red. Stella recognized it from the night before when she'd dropped Stratton off.

"Where do we start then?" asked Oggi.

"I don't know," said Stella. "I guess we've got to try and find somebody who may have seen something last night. Something odd."

"That'll narrow it down a bit," he said. "There's not many odd things going on around here at night."

Stella gave him a petulant look. "There's no need for sarcasm," she said. "I'm just trying to think logically."

"Okay," said Oggi. "Well, thinking logically, did you notice anything strange when you dropped him off? He was obviously attacked just after you left, before he could get in the back door; because that's where his phone was. If Yoshima was on his own, which I suspect he was, then he's not going to have wanted to carry a body too far. Even if he had help, you don't want to be lugging a body around the streets; it's going to draw a lot of attention. He was either parked here or just down the road, no more than twenty yards away."

"You're right," Stella agreed. "The problem is, I can't remember all the cars that were here. That one was here," she said, pointing to the Golf, "but as for the rest - I'm really not sure."

"Roughly how many cars were here?" asked Oggi.

"I'd say about five or six maybe," she said racking her brains. "It was dark though. Perhaps if it had been light I would have remembered more. I've got an idea though. Who owns the Golf?"

"I don't know to be honest; I've not seen it before. But I'm sure Lenny will know. Why?"

"Well. Am I correct in assuming that it's just customers who use this car park?" she asked.

"Not just customers," said Oggi. "But only people who are known locally."

"Just what I thought," said Stella. "The thing is that this is a tight little community, if community is the word I'm looking for. You lot are quite literally thick as thieves, aren't you?"

Oggi shrugged and said, "Yes, I suppose so."

"Well then, I reckon that somebody's going to have noticed a strange car hanging around. All we have to do is find the owner of the Golf and ask him if he saw a car he didn't recognize parked here last night."

Oggi agreed that it was a good idea and they went in to talk to Lenny, who pointed them in the direction of the back room, where a couple of young lads were playing pool. They were in their early twenties, and both wore jeans, trainers and sweat-shirts. Their names were Troy and Assif. Oggi knew them well. "Hello lads," he said. "How's it going?"

Assif looked nervous. "Good thanks Oggi," he said. "Look, if it's about that coke I sold your friend the other night, then it's nothing to do with me. I got it off this bloke and I didn't have time to test it, you didn't give me a chance to explain."

Oggi cocked his head slightly and gave Assif a stern look, then he smiled. "No, the coke was fine as far as I know," he said. "I just need some information from you. I'm led to believe that the red Golf parked out the back is yours. Is that correct?"

"Yes," said Assif, still wary. "I bought it the other day. Dead cheap it was."

"How long's it been out the back?"

"I parked it out there about five thirty yesterday afternoon. I had a drink last night and left it there."

"Okay," said Oggi. "When you parked up, did you notice any strange cars out the back?"

Assif shook his head. "I couldn't say really, it was dark. There were a few cars out there but I wasn't really looking. The only car I remember is Suzanne's because I parked next to it."

"No problem. Thanks for your help," said Oggi. He led Stella through the bar and out of the pub.

"Where are we going now then?" asked Stella.

"To see Suzanne of course."

Stella followed Oggi round to the back of the pub and up to a Victorian terrace that stood fifty yards past the car park. Three doors down Oggi stopped and walked up the path. He knocked on the door. No answer. He knocked again. A minute later a woman poked her head out of an upstairs window. She was young and pretty with blonde hair. Her hands were covering her breasts.

"What do you want Oggi?" she shouted down. "I'm kind of busy at the moment. If you know what I mean."

"I need to ask you something," Oggi yelled back up. "It won't take a minute. It's really important. Stratton's gone missing."

"Okay, I'm coming down."

Suzanne opened the door. She was wearing a white silk dressing gown. "What's happened to Stratton then?" she asked, not inviting them in. She gave Stella a quick once over.

"He's been kidnapped," said Oggi. "I think he was attacked at the back of the pub last night. I need to know if you saw any unfamiliar cars parked there last night."

Suzanne nodded and said, "I did as it goes. There was a silver-grey Mondeo parked in the corner. I only noticed it because it was the only car there that wasn't over ten years old. You know what it's like around here; a load of old rust heaps most of the time. You don't often see a new car parked out the back of the Angel."

"What time was this?" asked Oggi.

"About four o'clock I think." She thought for a minute. "Yes four definitely. I had a customer at quarter past, and there was nowhere to park out here, so I went up to the Angel."

"Was there anyone in the car?" he asked.

"Not that I saw."

"I don't suppose there's any chance you saw the registration number," asked Stella, none too hopeful.

"Of course not. I'm not a fucking snoop or a memory man, am I?"

Oggi thanked her for her time and they left. Stella's heart sank. She began to doubt if she'd ever see Stratton again.

Chapter 46

Stratton turned his head away from the light. He stared at the wall. It was white, with flaking paint revealing grey stonework. The floor was bare concrete. A spider scuttled into the corner and disappeared into a crevice.

"You're awake then," said a voice, it didn't sound like Yoshima's: the English was too good.

Stratton turned his head back round. A man looked down on him with piercing blue eyes. His hair was silver, and his face was slightly wrinkled. Stratton put him in his early fifties. He was tall with a light frame and wore grey trousers and a white shirt. On his feet were Wellington boots. Behind him stood Yoshima, his arms folded and his face without expression.

The man bent down and ripped the duck tape from Stratton's mouth. The cloth stayed halfway in and Stratton spat it to the floor. He said nothing.

The man continued to stare at him, Stratton held his gaze firmly. Eventually the man spoke. "You don't look much like your grandfather," he said amiably. "Although your silence indicates that you share his stubbornness."

"How the hell would you know my grandfather?" croaked Stratton. His throat was raspingly dry.

The man put a thoughtful finger to his mouth. "For now, let's just say that we shared a common interest in spiritual artefacts," he said. "An interest that you yourself seem to have inherited."

Stratton said nothing.

"I'm sorry about all the bondage," said the man. "I expect it's quite uncomfortable for you. But I'm reliably informed that you're too dangerous for any other course of action. I can't have you injuring myself or Yoshima here can I? By the way, my name's Augustus," he paused, looking for recognition in Stratton's eyes: there was none. "And I think Stratton is what people call you, am I correct?"

Stratton nodded.

Hands behind his back, Augustus paced to and fro in front of him. "Well Stratton," he said. "I think you know why you're here and what I want from you."

"No idea," whispered Stratton.

At a nod from Augustus Yoshima walked up to Stratton. He brought his right foot crashing down onto Stratton's stomach. He was wearing heavy-duty boots. Stratton gasped with pain. He wanted to double over but the ropes made it impossible.

"Ouch," said Augustus. "That looked painful. I wouldn't want to be in your shoes. Of course, you can save yourself any further pain by telling me what you've done with the parchments that were in the box." He looked hopefully at Stratton. "Well?"

Stratton caught his breath. "I've got no idea what you're talking about," he said. "What parchments? There's only one thing parched around here and that's my throat."

Augustus chuckled. "Very witty," he said. He nodded to Yoshima. Again his boot connected with Stratton's abdomen, right on the solar plexus.

Stratton's eyes trickled water.

Augustus grinned. "I'm sure Yoshima could go on all day if I let him. But I doubt if you could. Why don't you just tell me what you've done with the parchments?"

Stratton cleared his throat. His eyes were defiant. "I told you, I have no idea what you're talking about. I unearthed the box, and before I had a chance to study it properly, your man Yoshima here stole it from me. I never even knew there was a secret compartment. You might be making it up."

"We both know that's not true," said Augustus. He walked out of the cellar and returned a few minutes later with the box. He opened it and showed Stratton the compartment.

"Interesting," said Stratton. "But how do you know there was anything in it? And if there was, what makes you think that I removed it? It could have disappeared hundreds of years ago."

"It could have. But it didn't."

Stratton was perplexed. How did the guy know so much about the box? Even he hadn't known about the secret compartment until he'd happened upon it in the service station toilets. Yet Augustus knew about both the compartment and the fact that it held ancient writings.

"You seem to know a lot about it," he said.

Augustus smiled. "Yes, I do," he said. "I've spent many years researching its origins. It wasn't easy I can tell you. Very few people even know of its existence. I've travelled most of Asia trying to find out its history. How much do you know about it?"

"Not as much as you, obviously," said Stratton. "All I know is that my grandfather and his friends came across it in the war, one of them used it for his own devices. My grandfather took it and hid it. I know the symbols are Reiki symbols but I have no idea what they do."

"So you know nothing about where it came from?"

"No."

"Well then, I'll give you a brief history - or as much as I know," said Augustus. "Unless of course you've got something better to do?"

"No," said Stratton drily. "I seem to have an opening."

"As I've said," Augustus started. "I spent many years travelling Asia in search of anyone who knew anything about, or had even heard of, the box. I knew the story of the four friends being saved in the jungle by a mysterious healer, so I started my search in Burma. I must have visited nearly every temple from Rangoon to the Kabbaw Valley, but although some of the monks knew something about Reiki and a few symbols, nobody knew anything about Suri or the box. The problem is that a lot of monks in that part of the world are itinerant and move from temple to temple and from country to country.

"After Burma I went to Tibet, where, as you are aware, a lot of

Reiki legend is derived from. Again I had no luck. Eventually I ended up in India, it's a country I had visited before, in my younger days. I concentrated my search in northern India near the Himalayas as to me, it felt right - if you know what I mean."

Stratton nodded.

"Anyway, to get to the point, I eventually found someone who did know something about the box. He was an old Indian man of about 70 or 80. I met him in a temple in Simla. He was a travelling Buddhist priest. When I described the box he immediately grabbed my arm in earnest. And when I mentioned the name Suri, his eyes went wild. His intensity was such that it scared me.

"I calmed him down and asked him to tell me what he knew. At first he would say very little, so I told him the story of Suri and how the box had been taken to England and that it was now hidden. He told me that the box was very important and very powerful and that it should be returned to India. I asked him to explain. He told me that for over a thousand years the box had been guarded by a secret order of monks. With war in Asia being commonplace, the box was moved sporadically to different locations. When Burma was invaded by the Japanese, it was decided that the box should be moved again. Suri took the responsibility and made his way to India with it. You know what happened to him of course."

"Yes," said Stratton. "But where did this other guy fit in?"

"He had been a pupil of Suri's in the Burmese temple. He had just been initiated into the order when Suri went off on his journey. When Suri disappeared they assumed the box had been lost forever."

"Why would he tell you about the secret compartment though?"

Augustus gave a malicious grin. "Let's just say I coaxed the information out of him."

"You fucking bastard!" Stratton shouted hoarsely, his stomach aflame with anger. "The guy was a priest for Christ's sake! How can you justify hurting a peaceful Buddhist priest!"

"Now, now, don't work yourself up about it. He's still alive and in one piece. I just had to find out how to activate the symbols. You would have done the same thing."

Stratton grunted. "You've obviously got the wrong impression of me then."

"Whatever," said Augustus dismissively. "The thing is, I need the information that was in the compartment."

"Well, you're not going to get it. I don't know where it is. And even if I did I wouldn't tell you. I'd rather die."

"Really?" said Augustus. "This should be interesting then."

He nodded to Yoshima.

Chapter 47

David Brennan looked across at his wife. She was quiet; too quiet. He'd been home half an hour, yet she'd hardly said two words to him. Normally she would at least ask how his day had been, or whether the roads had been busy. Today she had said hello and that had been about it, apart from thanking him when he'd made her a cup of tea. It didn't take a detective of his experience to realize that something was up. She had been the same the night before. He suspected it was something to do with Stratton; he knew he should never have let the man anywhere near Anna.

"Is everything ok?" he asked.

"Yes, I'm just a bit tired that's all," she replied. "That Reiki session has sent me a bit dopey. He said I might feel like this for a few days. I'll probably be ok tomorrow."

"Fair enough," he said and turned his attention back to the television news.

Anna's eyes were fixed on the television too, but her mind was elsewhere; as it had been since her session with Stratton the day before.

What he'd said about mental problems manifesting themselves in physical form had made her think. And with the amazing amount of energy that had been pumped through her body as well, she was in a state of turmoil. There was something going on within her that she really didn't understand. It was as if Stratton had released all her demons at once and they were now running amok, creating unholy havoc like a posse of pernicious pixies. He'd said that she might feel unwell, but this was more than that, he'd unleashed a divine storm.

Without thought she began to drift back through her life, her subconscious desperately seeking the cause of the tempest. Perhaps there was something in her childhood that had caused all this bitterness to swell inside her. She flicked through her memory bank trying to pinpoint some formative hurt or trauma that may have affected her more deeply than she cared to remember. There were playgrounds, roundabouts, grass-stained knees; teachers, schools and boys that teased. But there was nothing more distressing than the usual adolescent angst, and nothing that seemed to correlate with her current state.

She moved forward to her twenties: a couple of bad relationships had perhaps tainted her slightly. But then she'd met David and any previous heartache had been washed away by his overwhelming love and unconditional kindness. Their life together had been happier than she could ever have imagined, they were perfect for one another, and they were just as in love now as they always had been. It was not the yearning of lost love that was eating away at her.

She continued to watch the TV, detached from the war that raged inside.

She moved forward to the recent past, to when she had contracted the cancer. Her parents had passed away in quick succession the year before she was first diagnosed. Could this have triggered enough emotional stress to make her ill? It was true, she had been hit very hard by their deaths, but they had gone peacefully and there had been no bad feelings left hanging. She had grieved for them well, letting her tears flood out at their passing. There was no unfinished business with her parents.

She went backwards and forwards again and again trying to hit upon a link. It was in there somewhere. Her brain was sending out messages at the rate of a million a second, a barrage of lightning bolts attempting to connect with the eye of the storm, all of them being deflected by a seemingly impenetrable wall of pent-up emotion. Bang! Smash! Crack! Crash! The onslaught continued, hammering away in a bellicose frenzy. Still the wall didn't show any weakness. But then, almost imperceptibly, the ferocious salvo began to break down the concentrated barricade.

Anna became aware of a dull ache in the right side of her chest. It stretched from her breast all the way through to her back, just below the clavicle. The TV still blared away in front of her but nothing was registering, the images were a distant blur.

Her mind had regressed 22 years. She was in the hospital. There was an insufferable stabbing in her abdomen. She was screaming with pain; a pain that she'd tried hard to forget. 'It didn't happen! It didn't happen!' her head screamed. But it had happened. And it had continued to happen, playing in a continuous loop deep in her psyche.

Years of suppression welled up inside her. The pain had moved to the centre of her chest and became increasingly acute. Her eyes were watering and she began to shake. Her mug of tea trembled in her hand.

Brennan, who had been engrossed with his own thoughts, looked across at his wife and realized that something was wrong. "Anna," he said. "Anna. Are you ok?"

She began to choke.

Brennan leapt out of his chair and went to her aid. He removed the mug from her hand and knelt in front of her gently holding her shoulders. He tried to stay calm. "Speak to me Anna," he pleaded. "What's wrong? What's happening to you? Good God, shall I call an ambulance?"

Anna was unable to speak. Tears rolled down her face. Her mild choking had become a hacking cough. Her eyes were lit with an alien madness. Brennan started to panic. He tried to hold her more tightly, but as he did her arms flailed violently and pushed him away. She fell to the floor in convulsions.

Lost and afraid, Brennan watched helplessly as his beloved wife writhed wildly across the carpet. He knew he should be doing something but he was paralysed with shock.

Eventually her psychosis began to ebb, but the coughing was getting worse. She pulled herself up onto her hands and knees. She struggled for breath. With every splutter, something was making its way slowly up her windpipe. She coughed some more, deliberately now, desperately trying to dislodge the obstruction. It carried on its upward journey, every spasm drawing it nearer to her mouth and expulsion. With one final, lung-bursting, effort, she coughed harder and louder than she ever thought possible. A jet of acrid phlegm hit the back of her throat and discharged into her mouth, filling it completely. She spat the vile substance onto the floor, and, weary with the effort, she blacked out.

When she came to, she was lying flat on her back. David was kneeling above her gently slapping her face. "Anna," he was saying softly. "Anna, wake up."

Anna focused on his kindly face and smiled at him. "I'm okay," she said. "Just let me lie here for a minute. You can get me a glass of water if you like. My mouth tastes foul."

When he returned with the water she was sitting up and staring at the large black, sticky pool that she'd coughed up. "What is it, do you think?" he asked.

She smiled peacefully and said, "It's 22 years of hurt sweetheart. But it's gone now. It's gone forever."

Chapter 48

Jennings sat in his chair by the door of the hotel suite reading Viz. It was years since he'd bought a copy of the comic and he was glad to reacquaint himself with it. He was pleased to see that many of the characters he remembered were still there. It took him back to his student days when life had been a lot more carefree.

Since his visit to the Jericho Tavern two nights before, he'd been doing a lot of thinking. Was police work really his calling in life? He'd only joined up because it was that or the dole queue; then he'd just cruised along moving up the ranks, finally reaching Special Branch. It wasn't that he didn't enjoy his job, a lot of the time he did, it was just that there wasn't a lot of room for creative flair. There were rules in close protection, and they had to be followed precisely or people would die.

There were times however when the job threw up an unexpected bonus, and yesterday had been one of those times. Thanks to the alcohol, Jennings had been late for work. He'd wandered in at eleven o'clock, citing heavy traffic as his excuse. Brennan hadn't bought it, and was about to give him some tedious admin work when the phone rang. On the other end was Professor Miles demanding that Brennan send an officer to protect him. He claimed to be worried about the possibility of 'rogue agent' Scott Grady coming after him. Brennan had tried to fob him off, and suggested that perhaps it was the CIA's job. Miles had countered by saying that it was the duty of SO1 to look after foreign dignitaries. Brennan eventually had to back down and knowing that Jennings disliked Miles, he had given him the job, as a punishment for being late.

Jennings had pretended to be annoyed at the assignment, but underneath he'd been secretly pleased; it kept him close to the Mulholland case; and more importantly, close to the action.

When he'd arrived at the Dorchester mid-afternoon, there had been another surprise waiting for him. Sitting in Miles' hotel room sipping brandy was none other than Grant Romano. Occasionally Jennings' job did involve contact with people from the world of show business, but he'd never been in such close proximity, or spoken to, anyone as big as Grant Romano. The guy was a living legend; Hollywood royalty. And when Miles persuaded Romano that it would be safer if he stayed with him at the Dorchester, that was just the icing on Jennings' cake. To make things more comfortable for the three of them, Miles had taken a suite on the top floor.

Jennings looked up from his magazine. Romano, who had been having an afternoon nap, walked into the room. He was wearing dark blue tracksuit bottoms and a white T-shirt. His hair was still dyed blond.

"Hi Jennings," he chirped. "How's it going? I guess you must be bored sitting there all day."

"I'm used to it, Mr Romano," replied Jennings. "I'm ok as long as I've got something to read."

"I told you before - call me Grant. You don't have to stand on ceremony with me," said Romano. "I was just about to watch a DVD, why don't you join me? It's the new Tom Hanks one. It hasn't even been released yet in the cinemas over here."

"Remember Grant - DVD piracy is a crime," said Jennings drily.

"Very funny. It's my own copy. I'm a star. I'm sent these things. The studios give the newest releases to me. So do you want to watch it or not?"

Jennings thought for a moment; he did fancy watching a film but he was on duty. If Miles came out of his room and saw him idling in front of the TV he'd probably kick up a stink. He voiced his concerns to Romano.

"Don't worry about old Sharlo," said Romano. "I'll deal with him. And let's face it, nobody's really going to try to break in here and get him, are they? He's just being paranoid if you ask me. What do you think?"

"Probably not," said Jennings. He knew very well that no-one was going to be breaking in. The only person who would want to was Scott Grady, and Jennings knew exactly where he was: safely tucked away in his flat in Jericho.

They watched the DVD, Jennings enjoyed the film almost as much as the fact that he was watching it with one of the most famous people on the planet. Not one to be star-struck, there was still something undeniably cool about sitting in a suite in the Dorchester watching movies with Grant Romano...movies that weren't even out yet on general release. All that was missing was a bottle of beer.

Just before eight o'clock Miles appeared from his room. Jennings was back at his post by the door, keeping up the pretence, and Romano was watching TV.

"Do you know if they've got any more leads on that Yoshima fellow yet?" Miles asked Jennings.

Jennings carried on reading his magazine. "I told you. I'm nothing to do with the investigation any more."

"I know that," said Miles. "I just thought you might have heard something. I'm sure that word gets around in big cases like this."

"I suppose so," admitted Jennings. "But you're more likely to hear about it than I am at the moment. You're the one that's got the government at your feet and the police eating out of your hands. I'm only a pawn in this game." There was more than a hint of disdain in his voice.

"Maybe so," said Miles. "But I want to make sure I'm kept in the loop on this one. I know how tight-lipped you police can be."

"Give the guy a break Sharlo!" hollered Romano from the sofa. "If there was anything to tell, he'd tell you. Why don't you come and have a drink?"

Miles left Jennings in peace and joined Romano, who poured

him a glass of brandy.

"There's no need to be so tetchy," said Romano. "Like Jennings said - if there was anything to tell, you'd be the first to know. Just relax. Don't be so up tight - it's not going to help anyone."

Miles sighed and shook his head in frustration. "I know Grant," he said. "The thing is, I'm under a lot of pressure at the moment. There's a lot riding on this box. I need to find it and unearth its secrets or the institute is history."

"What do you mean?" asked Romano.

"Just what I say," said Miles. "You may not be aware of this, but the institute's main funding comes from the defence department. We do have the occasional private backer, such as yourself, but 90 percent of our money comes from the defence budget."

"The defence budget?" questioned Romano. "What has the institute got to do with defending the country?"

"A good question," said Miles. "And one that I'll answer after we've organized dinner." He phoned room service, ordered some food, and continued. "Where was I?" he said. "Oh yes - the defence budget. Well, during the 1970s there was a spate of people across America claiming to have paranormal powers. Whether this was brought on by suggestion and the media hype surrounding people like Uri Geller, I don't know, but anyway, more people than ever before were claiming to be telepathic and to have telekinetic powers. Under scientific conditions, most of these people were proven to be fraudsters. I don't know if you remember that guy who pretended to be able to move pencils and paper with just the power of thought?"

Romano shook his head.

"Well, it doesn't matter, but this guy was actually just blowing a super-thin jet of air through his tongue. He did it so well that nobody noticed. He did it live on TV and still nobody caught on. But eventually he was found out by an eagle-eyed scientist, and his fame was shot, so to speak.

"Anyway, amongst all these conmen there appeared some people with real abilities. Once they had proven they were genuine, these people were quickly whisked away from the limelight by the government. They helped the FBI to locate murderers. The CIA used them to pinpoint spies and in some extreme cases, they used them to read minds. The upshot of this was that in the early 1980s someone high up decided to take things further. They saw that the powers these people had were still in their infancy, and that if they were researched properly and explained, then their potential was unlimited. I suspect that whoever it was envisaged an army of patriotic 'super Americans', using their paranormal skills to destroy the filthy march of communism."

Romano laughed. "I guess it was like that in those days," he said.

"Yes it was," said Miles. "So much so that any advantage over the Soviet Union had to be looked into. That's why they started the institute. All the research into ESP and telepathy was spread across the country at that time. They needed to centralize all the scientists under one roof to progress any further."

"And you were one of these scientists?"

"Yes, I was. I had started out in quantum physics, but my spare time was taken up with studying paranormal phenomena; I was obsessed with it. I strongly believed then, as I do now, that mediums and people with telepathic abilities held the key to the secrets of the universe. When I heard about the institute I immediately put my name forward, and I was lucky enough to get a job there. Ten years later I was the director."

Miles was interrupted by the light rapping of room service. Jennings looked through the eyeglass and, satisfied that it wasn't Charles Manson, let the bellboy in. Romano came over and gave him a tip as he left.

Romano set up three places at the elegant dining table and

laid out the plates of food. Miles had ordered a simple meal: a selection of roast meats and some seasonal vegetables. All three helped themselves. Jennings sat at the table. Miles gave him a stare but said nothing.

"So carry on then, Sharlo," said Romano, helping himself to some new potatoes. "I want to hear why they're going to cut your funding."

Miles finished a mouthful of beef, took a sip of red wine and continued. "So after ten years I became director of the institute and I have been since. That's fifteen years now. The problem is that we're not making as much progress as the government would like. We've studied thousands of mystics over the years and still we're no nearer to finding out what gives them their abilities. It's a force that we just can't see or detect as yet. Maybe it's super strings, or maybe it's dark matter, who knows? But until we have a machine to measure these theories then we're just flying blind."

"But surely the government can see that it's important to carry on the studies," said Romano.

"Yes they do," said Miles. "But they want to downsize the operation significantly. Although we've helped nurture many people who've gone on to be intelligence agents, we haven't produced what they really want - which is answers. I'm sure if we could deliver them an army of men like this Japanese fellow Yoshima, then they would be more than happy, and how we got them wouldn't matter. But we have neither the army of agents with mystic powers nor the answers to training them."

Romano cut into a slice of beef and said, "What about private backers? Perhaps they could invest more."

"Unfortunately," sighed Miles, "like the government, they too want results. The institute's been going for 25 years now, and in that time we have only made limited progress in our understanding of the paranormal. I can't blame anyone for becoming frustrated. We need a breakthrough; and we need it soon.

"That's why the box is so important; it's our one chance of establishing a link between humans and the unseen energy of the universe. Without it, my research will be confined to a couple of men with a computer in a portacabin."

He took a sip of wine and his face turned grave. "So it's essential that I find this box at all costs."

Jennings studied Miles' face. When he said "at all costs" he looked like he meant it. It looked as though Grady might be telling the truth, and that Miles had set him up. Much as Grady had pissed him off, Jennings could see he was still being made a scapegoat. Everything that had happened to himself and the others had been at Miles' behest. Grady had been a pawn in the game, like the rest of them.

Jennings sense of justice started to kick in. He couldn't see a man's life destroyed just for following orders. He'd seen it all too much in his career: the men at the top assigning blame to an expendable minion. This time it was going to be different. He didn't know how, but he was going to make sure that Miles paid the proper price for his duplicity. He kept his face impassive as he pushed his food round the plate.

"What about this Yoshima guy?" asked Romano. "If you could study him it'd be good wouldn't it?"

Miles played with his food thoughtfully. "Of course it would," he said. "But I suspect that Mr Yoshima would be highly uncooperative. If he wanted to share the secret of his power with somebody then I'm sure he would have already done it. Even if he was willing, he would probably only open up to one of his own people. Some Orientals are extremely partisan with their knowledge. They believe that the West will use their traditions for capital gain and not for the good of mankind. They believe that we have no respect for the sanctity of their rituals. I have to admit that to some extent I agree with them."

Jennings finished eating and left them talking. He went back to his chair at the door. Everything Miles did was grating him now, from his words right down to the expression on his face. He couldn't understand why a good guy like Romano would put up with him, let alone have him as a friend. Obviously Romano didn't know what he was capable of. Although he'd soon find out if he somehow got in the way of Miles and his goal.

He needed to expose Miles, not only for personal reasons, but because he was making a mockery of national security. He didn't know how to go about it, but he knew a man who would. That man was Scott Grady.

Chapter 49

Stratton lay doubled over on his side. He couldn't remember ever having been in so much pain. It felt like he'd been trampled by a herd of wild mustang. He was still tied up in a cocoon of ropes and, now that Augustus and Yoshima had left, he was again staring into blackness.

Yoshima had given him the working over from hell. He'd patently spent most of his life dedicated to the study of inflicting pain, because he was certainly no amateur. Stratton had been punched and kicked, and pinched and poked until his body had turned numb. Every single pressure point on his body had been expertly located and manipulated until he screamed. At various points he'd passed out, only to be woken again by water in his face.

He shivered with cold. The temperature in the cellar had dropped appreciably since they'd left, and the adrenalin of his beating was wearing off. He rolled about on the floor to try and generate some heat. It was doing his battered body no favours, but he felt that if he just lay there then hypothermia would set in. Surely they would have to check on him soon.

There was no way they were going to let him die; not while he still held the secrets of the box. If he passed away then so did any hope of Augustus finding the attunements.

Who was Augustus anyway? The name rang a bell somewhere in the back of his mind but he couldn't pinpoint it. If he was sitting comfortably in a nice warm room then it would probably hit him in an instant, but what with the cold and the pain and the stress, it was impossible to get his head around anything apart from survival.

A light came on outside the door. Twenty seconds later Augustus walked in. In his hand was a tray. On the tray was a slice of baguette and a bottle of water.

"Still alive then I see," said Augustus breezily. "Good job."

He set the tray down by Stratton and, kneeling, lifted him to a sitting position. After opening the bottle, he held Stratton's head and carefully tipped water into his mouth. Never before had any liquid tasted so good. He had been deprived of food and drink since his capture. The water soothed his cracked lips and trickled like a heavenly stream down the back of his sandpaper throat.

Augustus held up the slice of baguette, it was dry and hard. "Something to eat?" he offered.

Stratton shook his head. It would be physically impossible for him to take even a small bite. His face was so swollen that he could hardly open his mouth, and his gums were sore and bleeding from the loss of three teeth. Augustus was using the bread as a cruel torture.

"You should eat something really," insisted Augustus. "You'll waste away otherwise."

Stratton stared at him through slit eyes. The swelling around them was so bad that they would soon close over. He couldn't think of anything to say.

Still on his knees, Augustus poured some more water into Stratton's mouth. "Well, if you're not going to eat then this should keep you alive for a bit longer," he said. "A man can survive lengthy periods without food, but not without water. And I need you around long enough to tell me what you've done with those parchments."

Stratton gulped down as much water as his weakened state would allow. When he'd finished, Augustus said, "Of course, all this is quite unnecessary. If you'd just tell me what I need to know then you can go. There's no point being a martyr. I shouldn't imagine you want to take another working from Yoshima, do you? The last one was quite horrific. I had to look away in the end."

Stratton coughed up some blood and spat it out onto

Augustus' shirt. "I'm not going to tell you anything," he mumbled, his voice hardly a whisper.

Augustus looked down at his shirt without emotion. He raised himself up and smiled. "I have to admire your bravery," he said. "But what's it all for? All I want is to find out the secrets of the box, just like you do. I believe that the symbols contain tremendous healing powers. Is there something wrong with wanting to heal? Surely the whole world should have access to this information, not just a selfish few like yourself."

Stratton choked up more blood. "I'm not being selfish," he gasped.

"Really?" questioned Augustus raising his eyebrows. "Well I don't see why you're being so guarded about the whole thing - unless of course you think that it holds other secrets as well? Maybe you think that my intentions go beyond its health benefits? Maybe you think I want it so that I can gain power like Charles Mulholland did all those years ago?" He paused and looked Stratton in the eye. "Well don't worry. All I want is to tap into its healing powers."

"Why's it so important?" choked Stratton.

"Never mind that," said Augustus. "Are you going to let me have the information or not?"

Stratton thought for a moment. Maybe Augustus did just want to utilize the healing powers of the symbols. But if this was the case, why had he killed so many people to get to it? Power in the hands of someone who treated human life with such disdain was unthinkable, however good their intentions. It would be a dishonour to his parents and mankind if he gave this man what he wanted. There would be no bargain.

"Not in a million years," he said.

"Fair enough," said Augustus calmly. "It's your choice. I'm sure Yoshima will be pleased. He's champing at the bit to get going again. It's a pity really; you don't look like you're going to last much longer." He began to walk to the door, then he turned and said, "You're very arrogant you know, thinking that it's your duty to keep the symbols hidden from other people. What makes you think that you're any better than I am? What gives you the right to keep the information to yourself? You're acting just like your grandfather did, treating everyone else like a child." With that he left to get Yoshima.

Stratton lay down and attempted to calm himself for the imminent beating. He steadied his breathing and tried to clear his mind. It was no use though, Augustus had got him thinking. Why had he mentioned his grandfather again? And why was he so angry with him. Stratton could almost taste the venom in his words.

He went through it in his fast-waning mind. Grandfather - Augustus, Augustus - grandfather, he repeated, over and over again. His brain was aching, he couldn't think. Then he relaxed, and it hit him straight in the face. He knew where he'd heard the name before, and he knew who Augustus was. But surely it couldn't be? It just wasn't possible.

Chapter 50

Stella added some more water to her stew. It had been years since she'd cooked anything from scratch and she was unsure of the correct amount. She wouldn't have been cooking at all if it wasn't for Oggi. He hadn't left her side for two days. Even when she went to the toilet he was waiting right outside the door. Making a stew had given her an excuse to get some time on her own. It wasn't that she didn't like him, he was palatable enough, but she was starting to feel suffocated.

"Are you sure you don't need any help in there?" Oggi hollered from the sofa.

"No, I'm fine thanks," she yelled back.

She had tried politely to tell him that she didn't need protection, and then she had told him impolitely, but neither approach had worked. He had obviously made some sort of promise to Stratton and, short of killing him, there wasn't a lot she could do about it. She hoped that Stratton would turn up soon.

Since the day before, their efforts to track Stratton had been fruitless. They had asked everybody in the pub, and all the residents within two hundred yards, if they had seen anything suspicious. Nobody had seen a thing, not Stratton, not the Mondeo, nothing. He'd vanished into thin air.

She put the stew in the oven and joined Oggi in the living room. He had commandeered the remote controls and was watching 'The hairy bikers' cookbook'. She poured herself a glass of wine and lit a cigarette.

"Are they friends of yours?" she asked, gesturing towards the TV.

Oggi laughed. "No, I just like cookery programmes. As you can probably tell, I like my food," he said, patting his huge belly.

His phone rang and he answered it. After a minute of sporadic grunts he put it down. "Well. It sounds as if we might have a good lead," he said.

"Who was that then?" asked Stella.

"That was Lenny at the Angel. He said that he's found someone who saw the Mondeo driving away last night. They even caught part of the registration apparently. We've got to go and meet them."

Stella jumped out of her seat. "Well, what are we waiting for?" she said excitedly.

Oggi stayed still. "Calm down. We'll eat first," he said. "There's no hurry with this one. I need to think about it."

Stella raised her hands in frustration. "What the hell is there to think about?!" she remonstrated. "Stratton's in trouble and we've got a chance of finding him. He could be dying for all we know."

Oggi stared at her with cold eyes. "We'll eat first," he commanded.

Stella went quiet. She briefly held Oggi's gaze then looked away. This was not a man to argue with. Half an hour later she dished up the food. They ate in silence. It was clear that Oggi didn't want to talk. After clearing his plate Oggi downed a glass of water and said, "Thanks Stella that was lovely."

"There's more if you want it," she said.

"No thanks," he said politely. "I don't want to bloat myself out. I need to be alert tonight." He paused to light a cigarette. "I'm sorry about earlier. I didn't mean to snap at you. It's just that the situation isn't quite as clear cut as you think. The person who claims to have seen the Mondeo isn't exactly a friend of mine. In fact I'd go so far as to say he hates me."

"Why's that?" asked Stella. "What have you done to him?"

"It's not what I've done to him; it's what he thinks I did to his brother. He thinks that I killed him."

"And did you?" pressed Stella.

"It's complicated," said Oggi. "And it's neither the time nor

325

the place to talk about it. All you need to know is that there's history between us. I'm worried that he might be laying a trap for me."

"If you're that worried why don't you just phone the guy? You don't need to meet up with him to get a registration number."

"No, of course I don't," agreed Oggi. "Well not in an ideal world anyway. The problem is that he's insisted on a face to face meeting. He wants money for the information and he won't talk until he's got it."

"How much does he want?"

"Five thousand pounds."

Stella looked incredulous. "Five thousand pounds?! Just for a fucking registration number! That's fucking criminal!"

"Quite," said Oggi. "But it could have been a lot more. He thinks I killed his brother, remember."

"Where are we going to get five thousand pounds from at this time of night?" she asked.

"Don't worry about that," said Oggi. "I've got the money covered. I just hope he's not using this as an excuse to get me alone. Either way I've thought about it and I've got to take the chance - I owe it to Stratton."

Chapter 51

Larry Jordan was a self-made man. One of a litter of seven boys, he had grown up on the streets of Lewisham. His father was a bin man, driving the refuse lorry, and his mother had stayed at home, keeping order with a sharp tongue and a rolling pin. They were a close-knit family, and over the years the boys had gained themselves a reputation in the local community. Nobody fucked with the Jordans.

As the youngest, Larry had grown up in the shadow of his siblings; he'd been a hard man through expectation rather than disposition. He tried to fit in with his brothers' dodgy dealings but his heart wasn't really in it.

In his early twenties he decided to go it alone, forming a legitimate company and showing a natural flair for business. Now in his early forties he owned a string of nightclubs, and commercial property dotted around the capital.

He was a family man these days with a wife and three children. His early years of loan-sharking and leg-breaking were a distant memory. But he was still fiercely loyal to his brothers.

Oggi had met Larry Jordan only once. That was just after Jordan's brother Frank had been killed. Frank had been shot twice, once in the head and once somewhere else. Larry heard rumour that Oggi had pulled the trigger in anger at a business deal gone wrong. He had confronted Oggi in the Angel and warned him that if he found the rumours to be true then he was a dead man.

"So he's got no evidence that you killed his brother then?" said Stella, as they walked up Lewisham High Street towards Jordan's club.

"No. None at all," said Oggi. "Just a lot of idle gossip. Me and Frank were business partners at one point. I won't tell you what in, but needless to say it wasn't exactly legal. Anyway, a couple of days before he died, we had a bit of an altercation in the back room of the pub; harsh words were exchanged, and Frank stormed out. Two days later he was dead. So Larry assumed that it was me."

"That's one hell of an assumption," said Stella. "It's a big step from arguing to killing."

"Try telling that to Larry Jordan."

Bella's was just off Lewisham High Street. It had been Larry Jordan's first nightclub, and he'd named it after his mother. It occupied the top floor of a converted warehouse and was accessed on the outside by two flights of metal steps.

At the entrance Oggi and Stella were greeted by a couple of burly bouncers. Oggi informed them that they were here to see Mr Jordan and, after a brief exchange on the radio and a swift patting down, they were led in. It was ten o'clock and still early for club land. They were guided through the near-deserted bar, disco lights rotating over the empty dance floor, to a hallway at the back. Their chaperone knocked on a door marked 'Private'. After a short wait the door opened and they were ushered through. The doorman stayed behind them, guarding the exit.

Larry Jordan sat behind a large, ebony-effect desk in a black leather swivel chair. He was a handsome man, with dark hair and strong features. Converse to his standing, he wore blue jeans and a black T-shirt. His fingers were templed in front of his mouth. He looked up and eyed Oggi with detached interest. His eyes were brown and severe.

"I hear you might have some information for me," said Oggi, unfazed by Jordan's icy glare.

"I might do," he said. "But it's going to cost you."

"I know. I've already been told," said Oggi. "Five thousand isn't it?"

"Maybe. Maybe more. I haven't decided yet," said Jordan. He pivoted side to side in his chair, then stopped and lowered his hands. "I mean, how important is this guy to you? Is he just a mate, or is he like a brother?" He emphasized the last word and let it hang in the air.

Stella shuffled awkwardly. Oggi had told her not to come, and she was beginning to wish she hadn't. The atmosphere in the room was dark and filled with menace. The friction between the two men was palpable. They stared at each other like gunslingers. Each one waiting for the other to make a move.

Eventually Oggi broke the silence. "Listen Jordan, you've got no proof that I had anything to do with your brother's murder. So why don't you just give me the registration number of that car, I'll give you five grand, and everyone's a winner."

"Except for my brother," said Jordan. "I don't think you understand how close our family is. You can't off one of us and expect to get away with it."

Stella looked across at Oggi. His eyes were starting to glaze. He was becoming impatient. "For fuck's sake Jordan. Let's leave this for another time. I need to find my friend. I need that number."

Jordan remained calm. "Not until I get some answers," he said. "I want to know what happened to him. If you didn't kill him then you must know who did. I want the truth."

Oggi walked up to the desk and slammed his fist down. Stella felt the shudder in her belly. "You don't want the truth!" he shouted. "All you want is someone to fucking blame for your brother's death! The truth is that your brother was a fucking cunt! He got what was coming to him. There was only one person to blame, and that was himself!"

For a brief moment Jordan looked shaken. He wasn't used to anybody questioning his authority, let alone having the balls to shout at him. But he quickly regained his composure. "I want to know what happened to him," he said flatly. "It had to be you Oggi. You, Frank, and that Steve Hurworth - you were all in business together. They both end up dead and you survive: it doesn't take a genius to figure it out."

Stella swallowed nervously. She shouldn't have come; she was in way above her head. She knew the name Steve Hurworth, as did nearly everybody who watched the news. He was the policeman who'd died a hero's death while single-handedly tackling a crazed gunman. Or at least that's how the story had been told. Perhaps there was more to it.

Oggi calmed himself. "Look Jordan," he said. "Your brother's dead, and nothing's going to bring him back. Give me the registration number of that car and I'll give you five grand - it's a simple business deal. Let's not complicate it with baseless grudges. Let it go."

Jordan looked past Oggi and nodded to the doorman behind. Oggi heard a familiar click. He didn't need to look round: the doorman had a gun.

"I'm not letting anything go until I've got some answers," said Jordan. "The longer you drag this out, the less chance you have of finding your friend. If you don't start talking then I'm going to have to assume that you killed my brother, and that means I'll have to kill you - and the girl here too." He waved a hand at Stella. "So, if you value your lives you'd better start singing."

Stella looked over at Oggi, her entire being screaming at him to tell Jordan what he wanted to know. Oggi felt her gaze. "Okay Jordan," he said. "Have it your way. But you're not going to like it; not one little bit."

Jordan sat back in his chair. "Try me," he said, and gestured for Oggi to sit down opposite.

Oggi took the seat and began. "Well, as you quite rightly pointed out, myself and your brother were business partners. We started off by bringing lorry loads of cheap cigarettes and booze into the country, and then we expanded the operation, bringing in DVDs, CDs, weed and coke, and even guns. Steve Hurworth, who was local CID, caught wind of our little operation, but instead of trying to catch us out he decided to blackmail us for a slice of the action. I didn't like the guy, he was a real slime - the sort who could ooze right under a door, but we had no choice; we had to let him in.

"Anyway, after a while, your brother started to distance himself from me. He was spending more and more time with Hurworth and I began to suspect that they were up to something behind my back. I confronted them several times about it, but they said I was being paranoid. Begrudgingly, I let it go.

"A few months later, one of my lads who helped out with the DVDs gave me a ring and asked me to come and see him. He'd taken a couple of discs home to watch, and discovered something disturbing. He put one of the discs on and I was nearly sick: it was child pornography. I snatched the DVD from the player and took it to Frank and Hurworth, asking for an explanation. They denied any knowledge of it and said that it must have got in there by accident. I didn't believe them and I stormed off.

"Two days later I got another call from the lad who tipped me off about the DVD. He said that he'd seen two of Frank's boys escorting a couple of girls off the back of one of our lorries. He said they couldn't have been over ten years old. I went mad, and armed with my shotgun, went round to Frank's house. I knocked on the door but there was no answer. In my rage I kicked the door off its hinges and went in. I heard noises coming from the basement. I took that door out as well and headed down.

"When I got down there I found four young girls. They were all huddled together on a bed in the corner; they looked terrified beyond belief. I tried to calm them, but they were foreign and couldn't understand what I was saying. Then I heard shouting from upstairs and realized Frank had come back. He came down to the basement and tried to placate me. He said that it wasn't what it looked like.

"I looked over at the girls, and then I looked back at him. His eyes betrayed him. I knew at that moment exactly what he was and what he was up to. I raised my gun and shot him between the legs. Then, after leaving him screaming for a while, I shot him in the head."

Jordan leapt out of his seat and slammed his palms down on the desk. His eyes blazed with fury. "You fucking liar!" he shouted. "My brother was a good man! He would never have anything to do with sordid shit like that!"

Oggi stayed calm and stared Jordan down. "I didn't want to believe it either," he said. "But it's true."

"Well it's the first I've heard about it," said Jordan waving his hands. "Surely it would have been in the papers. I would have at least got wind of it."

"In normal circumstances you would," said Oggi. "But you've got to remember that his partner was a cop. Hurworth kept the whole thing hushed up. He didn't want too many questions being asked: not with his heavy involvement in the operation. If he got caught then his life would have been over. He wouldn't have survived prison - not with being a dirty cop and a nonce."

Jordan sat back down in his chair, unsure what to do. "So what happened between you and Hurworth then?" he asked.

"Hurworth came after me. I was the only one outside of their little ring that knew for sure what they'd been up to. He waited for me one night, in an alleyway by the side of my girlfriend's house. I had to walk down there to get to my bike. He stepped out in front of me, and before I knew it he'd shot me twice in the chest. I went down, but I had enough strength left to pull out my gun and I shot him twice in the back as he walked away."

Jordan laughed darkly and said, "You really expect me to believe that? If you were shot twice in the chest then you would have been in hospital. The police are automatically called when someone turns up with a bullet wound. You would have been placed at the scene. Your whole story is bullshit!"

Oggi gave him an icy stare. "Are you calling me a liar?" he said.

"Yes I am."

"Well I'm not lying. It happened exactly like I said. I didn't go to the hospital. I went to...Well let's just call him a back-street doctor. We all know them Jordan. Don't deny it. If you move in the circles that I do, you have to know someone who'll fix you up - no questions asked."

"Very true," admitted Jordan. "But why the big press coverage about his 'hero's death'. Surely they must have found out what he'd been up to."

Oggi shrugged. "Even if they did, they're hardly likely to have advertized the fact. Admitting that one of their own was head of a paedophile ring wouldn't exactly be good publicity, would it?"

Jordan looked at Oggi thoughtfully. "Well then. What do I do with you?" he said. "Even if what you're saying is true, it still doesn't take away the cold, hard, fact that you killed my brother. Whatever he did, I still loved him. You don't get away with killing a Jordan."

"Do what you fucking want," said Oggi defiantly. "The guy was scum, and so was Hurworth. I'm glad I killed them."

Jordan reached into the desk drawer and pulled out a Browning 9mm fitted with a silencer. He let off the safety, stood up, and pointed the barrel at Oggi's nether regions. Stella looked on in horrific anticipation.

"Well Oggi," said Jordan steadying his aim. "You're about to find out how my brother felt."

Chapter 52

Jeremy! Thought Stratton. That's who Augustus was. He was Jeremy! He couldn't quite believe it. Augustus Jeremy would be at least 85 years old. Yet here he was looking hardly a day over 50.

Augustus walked back into the room, closely followed by Yoshima. Both looked severe.

"You've got one last chance to tell me," said Augustus. "Otherwise it's more of the same I'm afraid."

"Fuck you Jeremy!"

Augustus smiled. "So, you've figured it out then," he said. "I didn't think it would take you this long to be honest. Although I do look good for my age - don't you think?"

Stratton said nothing. Augustus nodded to Yoshima.

Yoshima booted Stratton hard in the stomach. He repeated this motion twice more. Stratton struggled for breath. The ropes that bound him were constricting his lungs.

"This will only go on as long as you want it to," said Augustus. "You can stop it at any time."

Stratton stayed silent. He was in pain, but he was becoming accustomed to it. He tried to concentrate his mind. If he could focus properly, the pain would subside and become a dull background noise.

Yoshima continued to kick and punch away; not at full power but just enough to tenderize his victim. He found that a sustained attack was much more effective than a short violent one. Eventually the boy would plead for him to stop.

He turned Stratton over and began to work on his spine, applying pressure at sensitive points. He knew from experience that this torture was more than most people could bear.

Stratton was barely conscious. His mind had started to drift into sweet oblivion. He dragged up the happiest memories he could. Thoughts of Stella consumed him. The sharp jabs in his spine turned into pinpoints of pleasure, rapidly spreading over his entire body, until he was wrapped in a blanket of bliss. Nothing could hurt him anymore. Nothing. He was flying away to a place beyond imagination. Lights flashed in front of him and he started to rise.

Augustus looked down on Stratton. His body was limp like a rag doll. There was a contented smile on his face. "Enough Yoshima," he said. "We're not going to get anything out of him."

Yoshima stepped away. Augustus bent down and checked Stratton's pulse. It was faint, but it was there. From his pocket he drew a small bottle of smelling salts. He waved them under Stratton's nose. Stratton didn't respond.

Augustus slapped him hard in the face and tried the salts again. This time Stratton let out a hushed groan.

Augustus bent down and said in his ear: "You're obviously not going to give me what I want, so I'm going to have to resort to different measures. I wonder how stubborn you'll be when someone you care about has to suffer. Let's see how much the girl can take."

Stratton registered the words but continued to smile. They wouldn't get to Stella. Oggi would see to that.

Chapter 53

Stella winced as Jordan squeezed the trigger of his gun. But instead of the whiz of a bullet, there was an empty click. She sighed audibly. Oggi looked understandably relieved.

Jordan laughed and lowered the gun. "I'm not going to kill you Oggi," he said. "There would be no justice in it. And besides, I really don't want to have to go through the whole rigmarole of disposing of bodies and covering my tracks. No my friend, I'm going to hand you over to the police. I'm sure they'll have fun with you - I hear they're particularly nice to cop killers!"

"If the police had any evidence they'd have arrested me by now," said Oggi. "With a good lawyer I'll be out in 24 hours."

Jordan sat down in his chair. He put the gun back in his desk, and from the same drawer he withdrew a slim black electrical device. "This," he said, "is a digital recorder. It has picked up our entire conversation. It's as good as a confession don't you think?"

Before Jordan could react, with a speed that defied his heavy frame, Oggi thrust out his hand and snatched the recorder. He threw it on the floor and stamped on it. After twisting his heavy boot a couple of times he lifted his foot to reveal shards of broken plastic and metal. "Where's your confession now?" he said.

"It doesn't matter," said Jordan with nonchalance. "I'm sure my testimony along with Gary's," he pointed to the doorman behind, "will be enough to convict you. The broken recorder will come in handy as well: proof that you said something incriminating and tried to hide it."

Oggi weighed up his options. He could make a run for it, but he suspected that the doorman wouldn't hesitate to shoot him in the back: he had that look about him. Also, he couldn't really leave Stella alone: he'd promised Stratton that he'd take care of her, and that's what he was going to do. He had to either take his chances with the police or try to strike a deal with Jordan.

"Listen Jordan," he said. "Is there no way we can sort this out between ourselves without involving the police."

"I don't see how we can," said Jordan. "Short of killing you, there's no way to resolve it."

"But your brother was a sick bastard. He preyed on little girls. You've got a family haven't you?" he pleaded. "I believe you've got two girls. Imagine if someone did something to them. What if your brother had done something to them?"

A flash of anger lit Jordan's face then quickly disappeared. "My brother would never have touched my children," he said emphatically.

"Maybe not," said Oggi. "But he was encouraging people that would. He was dealing in child pornography. He was dealing in little girls. He was a massive part of the problem. People like him need to be dealt with - I know it and you know it."

"It doesn't matter now," said Jordan. "The police are already on their way. You'll just have to explain yourself to them."

Oggi leapt out of his chair and made a break for the door, but the doorman had anticipated his move. With cobra-like speed he let fly a kick to the back of Oggi's right knee. Oggi fell to the floor in crippling pain.

"You're not going anywhere, so just sit down and be quiet," said Jordan. "Next time it'll be a bullet not a kick."

Oggi pulled himself up and limped back to his chair. He had to accept the inevitable.

Five minutes later there was a knock on the office door, followed by: "Police! Open the door!"

Jordan's henchman opened the door and six armed-police filed into the room: four uniform and two plain clothes. Jordan pointed to Oggi. One of the plain clothes officers produced his warrant card. "Oswald Grimshaw," he stated. "I'm arresting you on suspicion of the murders of Frank Jordan and Steve Hurworth, anything you say…"

"I know my rights thank you very much," said Oggi. He held

out his hands. "Just cuff me and let's go."

Stella watched helplessly as they led him away. She would have to find Stratton on her own.

Chapter 54

There were days when Scott Grady just couldn't be bothered, and this was one of them. He'd had enough of Britain; he'd had enough of politics; and he'd had enough of Miles. All he wanted to do was go home. Too fed up to devise a fancy plan, he was going to take the bull by the horns and rip Miles apart until he called off the hounds. He knew it wasn't good to tackle a delicate situation with fire in your belly, but he was at the end of his tether.

He reached the hotel suite and hammered on the door. "Room service!" he shouted.

The door opened and gun in hand, he breezed past a submissive Jennings. Miles was sitting at the dining table eating breakfast with Grant Romano. He looked up at Grady, his eyes conveying fear and surprise. "What are you doing here?" he said. "Jennings! Do something!"

Jennings shrugged and shut the door. "Not much I can do," he said. "He's an armed man. I think we'd better let him make the decisions."

Miles glowered at him and said, "What about your gun? Don't just stand there, get it out."

"I'm afraid it might exacerbate the situation," said Jennings. "My priority is your safety Professor Miles. If I draw my gun it's possible he might shoot you." He turned to Grady. "Isn't that right?"

"You're damn right, it's right!" said Grady staring coldly at Miles. "In fact I don't know why I don't just shoot you right now you snake in the fucking grass." He pointed the gun at Miles' head.

Miles raised a pacifying hand. "Now now Scott," he said. "There's no need to be like this. You know how these things work. Sometimes people have to be sacrificed for the greater good."

"What fucking greater good?!" screamed Grady. "The only good that you seem to be serving is your own. I don't think anything you're doing is for the good of the United States government or the American people. You're in this for yourself and nobody else."

Miles kept his calm. "Look Scott," he said. "I'm really sorry it's come to this. You're right of course - I have behaved rather badly, but I'm under a lot of pressure at the moment. I can understand how you feel, but I didn't think I had any other choice. If I'd admitted to the fact that I'd sent you back into the fray, then the British would have kicked up an almighty stink and we'd have lost our chance to get our hands on the box - which was our aim in the first place."

"You're damn right we would have kicked up a stink!" exclaimed Jennings. "I knew you were up to something. From what I can make out you've been leading everybody a merry dance, including your friend Grant here."

Miles thought for a moment and then said, "Look, I'm sure there's some way that we can settle this amicably without resorting to violence."

"Yes there is," said Grady, still training his gun at Miles' head. "You can ring up the authorities concerned and tell them to leave me alone. All I want is to get back to the States. You need to come clean and get me off the hook."

"If only it were that simple," said Miles. "If I do that then I implicate myself, and bang goes our chance of getting hold of the box. You have to understand how important it is."

Grady inched closer to Miles and said, "It's important to you - not to me. Like I said, all I want is a safe passage back to the States."

"Well then, we seem to be at an impasse," said Miles. "Of course, there is one way to sort it all out."

"And what's that?" asked Grady.

Miles cleared his throat and said, "You find me the box."

"And how the hell am I supposed to do that?"

"With the help of Jennings here. The pair of you seem to be in cahoots anyway, so why not find the box for me? That way, I can get you off the hook, and Jennings will avoid me having to tell his superiors about the danger he put me in by teaming up with a rogue agent." He paused for thought. "Yes, with the exception of Grant, there's no-one in this room who isn't in trouble." He let the words hang as a threat.

Grady lowered his gun and put it back in his shoulder holster. Shooting Miles wasn't going to help his cause. He grabbed a seat at the table and helped himself to some scrambled eggs and bacon and coffee. Jennings joined him.

"Ok," said Grady, in between mouthfuls. "So we're all in the shit. But you're the one who got us into it Professor. So I suggest that you think of a way to get us all out of it."

"I told you Scott, there is only one way out - and that is to find the box."

Grady sipped his coffee and eyed Miles over the top of his cup. "That's easier said than done. Jennings here tells me that there's no news on this Yoshima guy: no-one's seen him - he's disappeared."

"It seems that way," said Miles. "But I have an idea how to narrow down your search. Grant can…"

At that moment Jennings' phone rang. He apologized to the company and took the call to the bathroom.

"Like I was saying," Miles continued. "Grant can help us with this."

"How so?" asked Grady, looking sceptical. "Is he going to make a nationwide appeal in the name of Hollywood?"

Romano laughed.

"No," said Miles. "Grant can see things that you and I can't. He's got an amazing sixth sense. He's a psychic."

"Get outta here!" said Grady. "Grant Romano a psychic, I

don't believe it."

"Well it's true. And I think he might be able to give us a location." He turned to Romano. "What do you think Grant?"

Romano hesitated for a moment. "I'm not sure to be honest. I've not really done this type of thing before. My area is mainly dreams. I guess if you gave me something associated with the guy I might be able to give it a go."

"I thought you might say that," said Miles looking concerned. "The problem is, I don't think we're going to be able to get hold of anything that belongs to him. Maybe if we got you something associated with the box then that might work."

Before Romano could answer, Jennings returned to the room with a smile on his face.

"What is it?" asked Grady.

"I think we might have a lead."

Chapter 55

Jennings buzzed the intercom to Stella's flat. He'd hurried over there from the Dorchester as quickly as he could. Grady had stayed behind to guard Miles. They both agreed that he couldn't be trusted.

Stella activated the door release and Jennings entered the hallway. He walked up the stairs to her flat. He was glad that she'd phoned.

"That was quick," she said as she let him in.

"It sounded urgent."

"It is," she said, walking into the living area and gesturing for him to sit down. "And it has been for the last two days. I'm sorry to have bothered you, but I've got nowhere else to turn. Now that Oggi's been arrested I'm not sure what to do. I thought you might have some ideas. You weren't busy on a job were you? I don't want to get you into trouble."

Jennings laughed. "I'm already in trouble," he said. "I don't think a little more is going to hurt." He briefly explained the situation with Grady and Miles.

"Wow!" said Stella when he'd finished. "You've certainly gone out on a limb. Brennan will go spare if he finds out what's going on. I can't believe you'd do something like this. You're in danger of becoming reckless."

"I can't believe I've done it either. Something's just flipped inside me. I've spent years toeing the line and I think it's all been building up to this. I've forgotten how good it feels to be bad."

Stella lit a cigarette. "So, what do you suggest we do?" she said.

"I'm not sure. You said on the phone that Oggi got arrested while you were chasing a lead?"

"Yes. But the lead turned out to be nothing. Just a trap to lure Oggi. All I know is that Stratton may have been abducted by someone in a grey Mondeo."

Jennings shook his head. "Not much to go on then," he said. "The only thing I can suggest is that we give Miles' idea a try."

"And what's that?" she asked.

"Well," he said awkwardly, "you're probably going to think this is a bit mad, but he wants to use a psychic. He reckons that if we give this guy something connected with the box then he'll be able to give us an idea of its location. Of course, now that Stratton's gone missing, I suppose it might be easier to get a piece of his clothing or something like that. After all, we can probably assume Yoshima, the box, and Stratton, are all at the same place."

"Yes they probably are," agreed Stella. "And I don't think using a psychic is entirely mad; after what I've experienced in the last week I don't think anything could surprise me."

Jennings grinned and said, "There is one thing that might."

"What's that?" she asked.

"The identity of Miles' psychic. It's Grant Romano."

Stella stared at him eyes wide. "What? *The* Grant Romano?"

"Yes, *the* Grant Romano," nodded Jennings. "Apparently he's a good friend of Miles'. He's been staying at the Dorchester with him. He's quite a cool guy actually - really friendly. We watched a film together yesterday afternoon."

Wow! Grant Romano, thought Stella. She'd had a crush on him ever since she'd seen him in 'Wheels of Steel' back in the late 1980s, when she was ten years old. She remembered sneaking into the cinema with her friends, lying about their age because of the film's 15 certificate. And now, all these years later, there was a chance of meeting him; of seeing him in the flesh; of speaking to him. The thought of it made her flush.

"Are you ok there?" asked Jennings, noticing Stella's faraway look.

"Yes, sorry, I'm fine," she said. "Just daydreaming, that's all. He's a bit of a hero of mine."

Jennings got out of his seat. "Well then, let's not waste any time. We need to get something of Stratton's and get over to the Dorchester. Do you have anything of his here?"

"No. We'll have to go to his flat at the Angel and pick something up from there."

Stella slipped on a pair of trainers and they left the flat.

It was eleven am and the traffic across town was light. Jennings chatted away with Stella, giving her a more detailed rundown of all that had happened since he'd last seen her.

"I don't know," said Stella. "Disobeying orders; teaming up with psychotic agents; putting yourself in danger. Sounds to me like you're having a midlife crisis."

"Christ!" said Jennings. "I hope not. I'm only 34."

"It can happen at any time."

They reached the Angel just before half eleven. Jennings parked up out back and they walked round to the front entrance. Jennings hesitated at the door.

"What's wrong?" asked Stella.

"Well, if you remember, the last time I went in there I wasn't exactly welcomed with open arms."

Stella laughed. "Oh yeah," she said. "Don't worry though, I'm pretty much ok in there now, through association with Oggi."

The bar was fairly busy for the time of day and it was five minutes before Stella managed to get Lenny's attention. After giving Jennings a suspicious look he handed Stella the spare set of keys to the flat. They walked through to the back stairs, Jennings self-consciously avoiding eye contact with the customers. Even though Stella was confident, he wasn't going to give the locals an excuse to kick off.

"Nice flat," said Jennings in half surprise, as he entered Stratton's quarters. "It's certainly a lot better than downstairs."

"Could it be worse?" said Stella.

Jennings looked on as Stella hunted the flat for a suitable object. His feelings were bitter-sweet. She was beautiful. Even now, doing a mundane search in jeans and a T-shirt, she stirred something inside him. Her mere presence felt intoxicating. He felt like a sailor lost in the Sirens' call. But he knew that this was one woman who would never, could never, be his. Her heart was somewhere else, with somebody else, and neither time nor distance would change it. He smiled to himself sadly.

Stella looked across at him. "Are you ok?" she asked.

Jennings shook away his reverie. "Yeah, I'm fine," he said. "I was just wondering what the best thing to take would be. Probably an unwashed piece of clothing that he's worn recently I would imagine."

"That's what I thought as well," she said. "I've found a T-shirt, boxer shorts and socks. Which do you think?"

"The T-shirt will be best won't it? I can't imagine Grant Romano wanting to handle smelly socks or boxer shorts."

"You're right," said Stella. "I didn't think of it like that. The T-shirt it is."

They left the flat quickly and dropped the keys back to Lenny at the bar.

As they walked into the car park Jennings suddenly stiffened. Something was wrong. He felt his stomach twist. He stopped and barred Stella's way with his arm.

"What's wrong?" she asked.

"I don't know," he said. "I've just got a strange feeling in my guts. A bad feeling - like we're being watched."

They scanned the car park and surrounding buildings for prying eyes, but no-one was there.

"Are you sure you're not being paranoid?" said Stella.

"Maybe," he admitted. "I hope so anyway. Let's get out of here and over to the Dorchester."

He unlocked the car and they both got in. He turned the key in the ignition but there was no response. He tried it again. Again there was no response. "Fucking hell," he muttered, and made a third attempt. It was unsuccessful. He hit the steering wheel in frustration.

"Calm down," said Stella. "It's probably nothing serious."

Jennings was about to reply when a gloved hand flashed out from the back seat and chopped him at the base of the neck. He slumped forward. Stella tried to grab the hand as it shot back, but her seatbelt restricted her movement and she was too slow. The next thing she knew, another hand was clamped over her mouth. In the hand was a piece of material. The smell of chloroform hit her nose and she passed out.

Chapter 56

Jennings came round with a sore head. He opened his eyes and shook himself to restore his vision. He turned to say something to Stella but she wasn't there. His watch indicated that it was twelve thirty: he had been out cold for over half an hour.

After releasing his seatbelt, he got out of the car and walked around the car park in an attempt to clear his head. Things had gone from bad to worse. He cursed himself for not listening to his intuition. The signs had been there but he'd ignored them. That feeling in his stomach was rarely off target. Now Stella was missing as well, and it was his fault. He had to find her.

His first instinct was to call Brennan and ask for help. But this wasn't an option anymore. He'd cut himself off from official operations as soon as he'd let Grady into the hotel suite. Any conversation with Brennan would inevitably involve some sort of explanation of the current situation, and that would leave Jennings heading for the dole office. Whatever happened from now on he had to keep it between himself, Grady, Miles and Romano.

He gave the car a cursory search and found nothing apart from Stratton's T-shirt. Then he tried the key in the ignition one last time. To his surprise the engine purred to life. He shrugged his shoulders in bemusement and headed for the Dorchester.

When he got back to the room Miles and Romano were sitting on the sofa. Grady was watching them gun in hand. They all looked up at him expectantly. He sat down and explained what had happened.

"Do you really think it's Yoshima who's taken them both?" queried Miles.

"I imagine so," said Jennings. "Stella said that Stratton had something that Yoshima needed. I'm guessing that Stratton's stayed tight-lipped, and the only way Yoshima's going to get anything out of him is by threatening Stella. Besides, who else is going to want to take them?"

"Good point," said Grady. "But what are we going to do about it?"

"We've got no choice but to go with the professor's idea," said Jennings. "Luckily we still have this." He held up Stratton's T-shirt. "And hopefully Grant can get a vibe from it."

"I'll have a go," said Romano. "But, like I said, I haven't done anything like this before; so don't expect too much."

Romano took the T-shirt and went to his bedroom for some peace and quiet. He needed to give his full concentration to the matter in hand. He sat down on his bed and tried to clear his mind. He held the T-shirt between his palms and closed his eyes.

The others stayed where they were.

"So Professor," said Grady. "All this is going way above my head. What exactly is it that Yoshima needs from Stratton?"

"I'm not too sure myself, as it goes," admitted Miles. "But it looks like Stratton removed some vital information from the box before Yoshima stole it from him. I imagine what he took was a key to the symbols. The box is covered in symbols, but they're of no use whatsoever if you don't know what they do or how to activate them. In Reiki you have to be attuned to the symbols to use them - without the attunement they do nothing. It's like having a computer with no power source."

"Okay, I sort of get it," said Grady. "But is it worth all this shit? You offered me two million bucks just to find it for you. It seems a lot just for a little wooden box."

"Not when it holds the secrets of the universe, Mr Grady. That box is a link between us and the cosmos. It's the key to the evolution of mankind. I'm absolutely sure of it."

"I hope you're right," said Grady. "Because I'd hate to think that we're going through all this crap for nothing."

Grady got out of his chair and walked around the suite to stretch his legs. He was tired, wearier than he had been in a long time. Not only that, he was stuck in a room with a bunch of fruit loops.

All this psychic nonsense was doing his head in. Even Jennings seemed to be getting caught up in it. Power of the universe, my ass, he thought. The only power in that box was the power of suggestion. He had a degree in psychology for Christ's sake! He knew all the tricks that these so called psychics used. If somebody was desperate enough to believe in something then they would, regardless of logic or reason. He was only going along with the whole thing because he wanted to get back home. Home. That reminded him.

"Are your men still watching my girlfriend?" he asked Miles.

"They never were," said Miles. "It was just a bluff to get you to play along. Of course, we knew where she was if we'd needed her."

Grady grunted. At least she was safe.

"How about some lunch?" suggested Miles. "It's nearly one o'clock. I can order something from room service."

Grady looked at him suspiciously. "Lunch sounds good," he said. "But I'll do the ordering. I can't have you trying to raise the alarm. What do you want?"

Miles told Grady what he wanted and poured himself a large brandy. He was a prisoner, but at least his cell was mink-lined. He couldn't blame Grady for being suspicious: his conduct hadn't exactly been honourable. There had been a time when he wouldn't have dreamt of being so underhand; he'd always prided himself on his honesty. But working for the government had changed him. He'd soon realized that the only way to keep his research going was to play ball with the powers that be. And if that meant the occasional deception, then so be it. His work was important; too important to let his conscience jeopardize it.

After having been in his room for over half an hour Romano finally emerged. He was still holding the T-shirt. He looked despondent.

"Any luck?" asked Miles.

Romano shook his head. "Nothing," he said. "I can't get any reading from it at all. I didn't think I'd be able to do it."

Jennings addressed the room. "What are we going to do now then?"

Chapter 57

Stella woke with her head spinning and pounding. She was lying in pitch dark. Rope was coiled round her body and bound her arms at her side. The last thing she remembered was a hand stifling her mouth. She struggled to loosen her bonds but soon realized that it was a hopeless cause. "Fuck!" she said aloud.

"You're alive then," said a familiar but strained voice. It was Stratton.

"Yes, just about," she said. "But I'm beginning to wish I wasn't. My head's throbbing like God knows what."

"That's the chloroform I expect. They used the same thing on me."

"They?" questioned Stella. "I thought it was Yoshima that took you."

"It was," said Stratton. "But it turns out he's working for someone."

"Who's that?"

"Augustus Jeremy. He's the Jeremy that my grandfather spoke about in those transcripts."

"Fucking hell! He must be getting on a bit," said Stella. "Why's he suddenly turned up looking for the box? You'd think he'd forgotten about it after all these years."

"I don't know what rekindled his interest," said Stratton. "All I know is that he's prepared to do anything to get hold of the secrets of the box. He's certainly put Yoshima to work on me."

"I was going to say. You sound awful."

Stratton choked. "I'd hate to see what I look like - it can't be pretty. I've been punched and kicked within a millimetre of my life. My face must look like a balloon."

Stella shuffled herself along the floor in the direction of Stratton's voice. She reached him quickly and nestled at his side. She found it comforting to have their bodies touch. "What does he want with me?" she asked.

"He's using you to get to me," said Stratton. "I thought it might happen, which is why I left Oggi specific instructions not to let you out of his sight. I even attuned him for protection against Yoshima. So what happened?"

Stella went through the events of the previous day.

"Jesus!" said Stratton. "I didn't realize Jordan still thought it was Oggi. It's been so long I thought he'd turned his attention elsewhere. And handing him over to the cops as well - what a rat."

"Whatever you think of him Stratton, he did kill two people. And whether they were paedophiles or not, it's still murder."

She was right of course, he thought. Murder was murder however you dressed it up. From the cognizant act of sadistic homicide, to the unconscious act of self-defence; from the merciless slayings of a deranged paedophile, to the noble actions of a brave soldier defending the rights of the vulnerable. One factor connected them all: a life had been taken. And justified or not, it was never truly right. It was a symptom of what mankind had become.

Stella broke into his thoughts. "What do you think Jeremy's going to do to me?" she asked.

"It'll be Yoshima that does it," said Stratton. "And I really hate to think. I don't think it'll come to that anyway. I've got no choice now - I'm going to have to give him what he wants. There's no way I'm going to let you go through the same thing as I have."

"Don't be such a chauvinist pig!" she said angrily. "Don't think just because I'm a woman that I can't take it. I'm ex-Special Branch, with years of experience in the field. You don't do what I did without being tough. If you tell him anything I'll never forgive you."

"Calm down will you. It's not because you're a woman, and I don't think you're weak. I don't want you to get hurt because..."

"Because what?"

Stratton thought about what he was going to say, he wanted to tell her how he felt but it didn't seem right. Eventually he said, "Because I don't. I don't want anybody to get hurt on my account. If you were a total stranger I wouldn't want you to be punished because of me."

Stratton heard the familiar rattle of keys. The light came on. Jeremy walked in. He immediately noticed that Stella had moved.

"Ooh very cosy," he said. "Keeping each other warm are we? How touching."

"Get fucked," Stratton muttered.

Jeremy cupped his hand to his ear. "What was that?" he said. "I didn't quite catch it. Mind you I am getting a bit old. I don't suppose it was that important." He paced about in front of them. "Now then, have you given any more thought to your situation? Are you going to let me have the information?"

Stratton wanted to say yes, he wanted to save Stella from the pain that would be inflicted upon her. But before he could answer she spoke: "No he's not. He's never going to give it to you, no matter what you do to me."

Jeremy gave a perverse smile. "You're very brave my dear, but ultimately very stupid. You really don't know what you're in for."

Jeremy left the room. A minute later he returned with Yoshima. "Do what you will Yoshima," he said.

Stratton closed his eyes and concentrated. Stella was being headstrong, but he could help her out. He traced the Master Symbol in his third eye, the sixth chakra, between his eyebrows. Then he traced the Power Symbol; and then the Long Distance Symbol. Lastly he pictured Stella and drew around her a symbol he'd seen on the box. A symbol he knew would protect her.

Yoshima went to work with enthusiam. He started, as he always did, with kicks to the stomach, just to knock the wind out of his victim.

Stella lay on her side and braced herself as the first kick flew in. But instead of the winding blow she expected, there was only a slight tickle. Was Yoshima playing games with her? Was he psyching her out? Before she could think a second kick hit her. Again, she felt nothing. It was as if Yoshima's feet were bouncing off her.

Yoshima looked down curiously at his target. The girl hadn't even flinched. True, he hadn't kicked her that hard, but even so he expected some reaction. He kicked again, this time putting all his weight behind it. Still she didn't move. He moved up to her head.

Stella winced as she saw Yoshima's boot fly towards her face. But although he connected and her head jerked back, she still didn't feel anything. She appeared to be surrounded by an invisible shield. What the hell was going on?

Yoshima had another couple of goes and then stopped. Perplexed, he turned to Jeremy and said, "Something's wrong. She's not feeling any of this. He's done something to her." He pointed accusingly at Stratton.

Jeremy put a meditative finger to his lips. "Interesting," he said. "I wonder what he's done." He turned to Stratton who was grinning through his broken teeth. "What have you done to her?"

Stratton kept his silence.

"Okay then," said Jeremy. "We'll have to get serious. Yoshima, go and get your knife."

A minute later Yoshima returned holding his slim dagger. He dragged Stella up from the floor and held the knife to her throat.

"Do you think that you can protect her from steel?" said Jeremy.

Stratton stared into Jeremy's cold eyes. He wasn't bluffing. Would the shield work against weaponry? He doubted it very much. He was amazed that it had worked so well against Yoshima's kicks. He looked at Stella. He looked at Jeremy. He looked at Yoshima. He looked at the knife. He looked back to Stella. She was outwardly calm, but there was fear in her eyes.

He loved her. "Okay," he said. "You win; I'll let you have the parchments."

"No!" shouted Stella. "Don't let him have anything!"

"Sorry," he said. "I've got no choice."

Jeremy signalled for Yoshima to let Stella go. He pushed her to the ground beside Stratton.

"Well then Stratton, where are the parchments?" asked Jeremy.

Stratton answered with distaste, almost spitting the words out in annoyance. "They're in my flat," he said. "They're in a safe under the floorboards in the kitchen. I'm the only one who knows the combination. You're going to have to let me get them."

"Really," laughed Jeremy. "Do you think I'm stupid enough to do that? As soon as you're untied you'll try and pull a fast one on me."

"You can keep Stella as collateral."

Jeremy thought for a moment. "No. I don't think so. You can give me the combination of the safe and I'll send Yoshima to get them."

"He'll never get in there," said Stratton.

"I think if he can bypass security at a stately home then he's more than able to break into a shoddy old building like the Angel. Isn't that right Yoshima."

Yoshima nodded.

Knowing he was in no position to make bargains, Stratton gave Jeremy the combination to the safe. He was loathe to do it, but Stella meant too much to him to sacrifice. He knew the importance of the documents that Yoshima would collect, and that they were bigger than one life. However, a person was a person, a sentient being, a soul, and how could you quantify the value of that? It wasn't for him to make the decision; it was in the hands of a higher power. His only hope was that Yoshima might get caught.

"Is there any chance of making us more comfortable?" asked

Stratton. "And how about some food and water?"

"I'll make you more comfortable when Yoshima returns with the scrolls," said Jeremy. "Until then you're going to have to stay tied up I'm afraid. But I will fetch you some water and a bit of food to keep you going. I can't have you dying on me yet. I may still need your help."

Jeremy and Yoshima left the room but this time the light was left on. Stella turned her head towards Stratton. His face was in a terrible state. He looked like he'd gone twelve rounds with George Foreman. With everything else going on she hadn't really registered how bad he was, but now as she gazed at him in the cold, harsh light, her eyes welled with tears.

"What's wrong?" Stratton asked.

Stella hung her head. "It's your face. I can't believe what they've done to you."

"Don't worry, it's probably worse than it looks," he joked.

Stella smiled. "What just happened anyway?" she asked.

"What do you mean?"

"I mean, what just happened with me? Yoshima was laying into me big time but I didn't feel anything. His blows kept bouncing off me. It was like I had a force field around me."

"Oh that," said Stratton. "It was something I had to try. I used one of the symbols from the box and projected it onto you. I had no idea if it would work or not. I just had a hunch that it might."

"Well, it was a good hunch. I still don't understand how it all works though. How did you know which symbol to use?"

"Inside the box, in the compartment, there was a key to all the symbols. There were two pieces of parchment inside. If you join the pieces together they replicate the grid of symbols on the top of the box, except with drawings where the symbols should be. Each drawing represents what the corresponding symbol can do. Some of the drawings are clear as to their purpose, but some are not."

"What do you mean?" she asked.

"Some of them are drawings of people with arrows pointing to a specific part of the body. If, say, a symbol is mirrored by a drawing of a man with an arrow pointing to his heart, then it's pretty safe to assume that the symbol can be used to help diseases of the heart. Some of them are more obscure and I really didn't get a chance to go through them properly."

"What about the one you used on me?"

"That one had a picture of a warrior attacking an unarmed man. The man was surrounded by a line with rays emanating from it. He was repelling the assault. Obviously I took it to be a symbol of physical protection. And luckily I was right." He turned to her and smiled. "I wouldn't have wanted you to end up looking like this."

"But why didn't you use it on yourself?" said Stella.

"I don't know. It didn't even enter my head. Yoshima started on me so quickly that I couldn't think. And also, I wasn't that worried about myself. I don't know why - perhaps I'm just self-destructive by nature; or maybe subconsciously I wanted to be a martyr. Who knows? What I do know is that I didn't want you to get hurt, and I was willing to try anything to prevent it."

"But now Jeremy's going to have access to the symbols," said Stella. "Who knows what he might do."

"I don't know," said Stratton. "But he assured me he only wanted it for healing purposes. And funnily enough, I believed him. There's a specific reason for his interest in the symbols, but I don't know what it is yet. The main thing is that, whoever's got them, the symbols and the key have been found. It's a massive discovery." He paused for a moment and then said, "Do you play computer games?"

"Not a lot, but I do have an X-box," she answered. "Why? What's that got to do with anything?"

"I just want to explain to you about the importance of the symbols and how they work: you said just now that you still didn't quite understand. Think of life being a computer game. In nearly all games there are cheats right? Hidden weapons and moves and suchlike that can be activated by pressing buttons in a certain order." Stella nodded. "Well the symbols are those hidden cheats. Drawing a symbol in the air or picturing it in your mind is a way of activating concealed parts of the program, areas that most people can't see. The symbols are the key to tapping into the mysteries of the game. A gift from the programmer for all those who can think outside the box. Those with the vision to see further than what's in front of them."

Stella digested what he'd said. She understood where he was coming from yet it was all still a bit fantastical to comprehend. But how could she doubt any more; twice she had witnessed the startling effect of the symbols, once when Yoshima had disabled her, and just now when Stratton had protected her. Both times she had felt an unseen energy enter her body. Both times she had felt the presence of a higher being. In the face of this power she felt helpless and scared.

Chapter 58

Stella woke in the dark. She didn't know the time of day but her body clock told her it was morning. She had been asleep since Jeremy had given her and Stratton some bread and water the night before. She wondered if Yoshima had succeeded in his mission. She wondered what the day would bring.

"Stratton," she said softly. "Stratton."

She heard a groan and then: "What?"

"I was just seeing if you were awake."

"Well, I am now," he said.

Five minutes later the door opened, the light came on, and Jeremy and Yoshima entered. Yoshima walked over to them and drew a knife. He cut through Stella's ropes, and then did the same for Stratton. Both stretched their limbs, trying to regain some feeling. Stratton winced with pain as he tried to move.

"There you go," said Jeremy. "There's no need for any more torture. Yoshima's got what I want. And I don't think you're going to be so much of a threat anymore are you?" He gave Stratton a stern glance.

Stratton tried to stand up but his legs buckled underneath him and he fell to the floor.

"Take it slowly," said Jeremy. "You've been tied up for almost three days now."

"What the hell do you care?" said Stratton. "It's your fault I'm in this state."

"Actually it's your own fault. If you'd told me where the scrolls were in the first place then all of this could have been avoided."

After pacing up and down the cellar a couple of times Stella turned her attention to Stratton. She took a good look at his face and was amazed at how much the swelling had gone down overnight. His eyes, previously almost closed, were now wide open, and his bruises had all but disappeared. "You look better," she said. "Well, less like the Elephant Man anyway."

"Thanks," he said. "It's a pity my legs don't agree."

Stella turned to Jeremy. "Are you going to let us out of here now and give us some proper food? He needs to eat."

"Of course my dear. You've played the game, so I will reward you both. And besides, I may still need his help. But don't be fooled by this act of his. He may be weakened but he's got more strength in him than you imagine." He turned to Stratton. "Haven't you?"

"I don't know what you mean," said Stratton innocently. "I can hardly stand up."

Jeremy rolled his eyes. "Keep up the pretence if you must," he said. "But don't think for one second that I'll be letting my guard down too much. Yoshima will be watching you like a hawk. Any funny business and your beloved here will be the one to suffer."

Jeremy led them out of their damp cell and up a flight of stone steps. Yoshima followed behind keeping a close eye on Stratton, who was leaning on Stella for balance. At the top of the steps was a narrow, dimly-lit passageway with a white door at the end. They passed through the door and into the farmhouse kitchen.

Stratton felt a surge of emotion. After being locked up in the dark for three days, his senses deprived, the sight of a homely kitchen was more than welcome. There had been moments when he'd doubted that he'd ever see daylight again. The shadows played tricks with your mind.

Outside the dawn was only just breaking. Stratton looked at the clock on the wall which told him it was half past six. At Jeremy's invitation, he and Stella sat down at the large oak table that dominated the room. Jeremy boiled the kettle and made them hot drinks. Stella had coffee; Stratton had green tea. The warm liquids coursed through their veins, sharp and invigorating. Stratton felt life returning.

After a hearty farmhouse breakfast of bacon, sausages, eggs and mushrooms, Jeremy produced a tattered brown book. Stella recognized it as the one Stratton had been obsessed with when they lived together.

"What the hell are you doing with that?" asked Stratton. "That's my own private notebook. It's got nothing to do with the box. Give it back."

Jeremy sat down next to Yoshima, opposite his captives. "Well, you say it's got nothing to do with the box, but that's not exactly true is it?"

Stratton remained clear. "It's just a collection of personal notes. It's of no worth to anyone else."

"I disagree," said Jeremy, opening the book. "For a start it has the Power Symbol emblazoned on the front. And it's full of references to ancient healing techniques." Catching the look on Stratton's face he added, "Oh yes, I can read Sanskrit my boy. I'm sure your grandfather must have mentioned my interest in archaeology."

"So what if you can read Sanskrit, there's nothing in there that you need. All you need are the parchments, which I assume you have as well."

"Yes I have them," said Jeremy. "And they will serve their purpose. But what I've read in this little book of yours has been a real eye-opener. It was prudent of Yoshima to take it as well."

He removed three loose sheets and unfolded them. They were just under A4 size, yellowy-brown in colour, and fraying badly at the edges. Stella thought they must be hundreds, if not thousands, of years old.

Stratton sighed loudly.

"How long have you had these?" asked Jeremy.

"Long enough."

"Where did you get them from?"

"Kerala, India. I came across them on a research trip."

Jeremy raised his eyebrows and gave Stratton a look. "On a research trip? You make it sound very everyday. You don't just stumble upon documents like this. I don't expect someone was selling them on the street. There must be a story behind it."

"Yes there is," said Stratton. "But it's a long one, and I don't want to go into too much detail at the moment. Let's just say that I was in the right place at the right time. I don't even know if they're genuine."

"Haven't you had them carbon dated?" Asked Jeremy.

"Yes - and they check out. But you can never be totally sure."

Stella leant forward and interrupted. "What exactly is it that's so important? What do they say?"

"I'll read it to you," said Jeremy. "I'll make the translation as coherent as I can and stick to the relevant bits." He put on his glasses, picked up the sheets from the table, and began to read.

"... and when the guards had left and we were able, we removed his lifeless body from the cross. At Peter's direction we took him to the secret cave and laid him on the floor. We cleaned his wounds and dressed him in new robes of white. I wept for his passing. Peter rested his hand upon me and said, 'do not be sad my friend, for this is not the end. The Master foresaw his fate and has left me instruction. He will rise again. We can breathe life into him once more. We can bring him back.'

'But only the Master can perform miracles,' I said. 'We are but human beings - the Master was divine.'

Peter smiled at me, 'We are all divine,' he said. 'Or have you not listened to his teachings.' I took comfort in his words but I was in grave doubt that we could bring the Master back.

Peter bade us stand in a circle around the Master's body. He told us to join hands and create an energy. He told us to remember what the master had taught us, and to fill our heads and hearts with a love of all things.

Peter covered the Master's body with a shroud and stood next to it, drawing symbols in the air above him. Then he knelt down beside him and muttered an incantation. It was not intelligible to the rest of us. He laid his hands on the Master's head. I could see vapour rising from the point of contact. Then Peter moved his hands to the Master's heart.

Again, steam began to rise. The Master's body started to glow with an aura of blue and white. Peter began to shake, his body trembling with the power that surged through him. The whole cave was bathed in a light so bright that it hurt to look. It got brighter and brighter until it peaked with a blinding flash. I was overwhelmed by its force and fell back against the wall of the cave. I hit the floor and darkness took me.

I was awoken by a soft hand on my forehead. I opened my eyes. I gasped in disbelief. Kneeling over me was the Master, smiling with a kindness that only he possessed. 'Yes, it is I,' he said. 'You have brought me back. You, Peter, and the rest of our brothers. I am reborn. Thank you.'

I still thought I was seeing things. I grabbed his hand to make sure it was real. It was. I wept with joy."

Stella was open-mouthed. "Is that saying what I think it is?" she said. "That the Apostles brought Jesus back from the dead."

"Exactly," said Jeremy.

"But who wrote it? It must have been one of the apostles. Which one?"

"All in good time my dear," said Jeremy. "There's more to come yet. Much more." Again, he started to read.

"...And that evening we brought a great feast to the cave and sat down with the Master to eat. He wouldn't leave the cave for he did not wish to be seen. We were in high spirits due to his return, but our merriment was to be brief.

At the end of the meal the Master spoke. 'I am afraid this is the last time that I shall sit with you. Tomorrow I must travel east to the land of my education.'

There was a hush in the cave. Then Peter spoke. 'But why must you go Master? Surely there is much still to be done. When the people see that you are alive, they will truly know you as the Son Of God.'

The Master smiled. 'Yes they will my brother. Or at least that is what they will think. It will go against everything that I have been trying to teach. There is no singular Son Of God; we are all sons and daughters of the power. Every being on Earth is capable of doing what I do. The kingdom of heaven is within everybody, not just me. You have proved that to yourself by bringing me back. All my healings and miracles were nothing compared to what you have done. You and our brothers here have performed the ultimate miracle. Do you not see?'

'Yes Master,' said Peter. 'But without your guidance we could never have done it. We still need you here to teach us further.'

'You need me no longer. Each of you knows enough to help others realize their potential. We must all go our separate ways and take the knowledge far and wide. You must show people that if they search hard enough everything they need is within themselves. You must teach people the basic principles of healing.'

'But I am no teacher. I do not hold sway over people's minds. They will not listen to me. They will only listen to you Master. They look to you for guidance. They worship you.'

The Master sighed. 'And therein lies the problem dear friend. I have spent my time here telling people about the hypocrisy of the church, and that being good does not require great shows of piety. But it seems they have jumped from one object of worship to another. Soon they will be selling statues of me in the street - and that is exactly what I don't want. There is no need to worship me. If the people want enlightenment they have to look to themselves. "Peace comes from within. Do not seek it without," as the Buddha said.'

'I understand. But you are my brother and I will miss you.'

The Master clasped Peter's hand in his own and said, 'We will meet again brother. In our next life.'

The next day the Master made ready to leave. He took each of us aside in turn and gave us instruction on where we should go to carry on his teachings. Lastly he came to me. 'I come to you last Didymus because, like myself, you must go east to India. We will travel together for a while. Then I will take the road across country and you shall take to the sea.'

We journeyed together for two weeks until at last we reached the port from which I was to sail. I was filled with sadness at the thought *of our parting. 'Don't be sad Didymus,' the Master said. 'Because we too will meet again in another life. But now in this one we must go our separate ways. You must take the teachings to new people.'*

'But I am no teacher,' I pleaded. 'I will not be able to show people the path. They will not listen to me.'

The Master smiled gently. 'Always full of doubt my brother. You doubt yourself. You couldn't believe that I had come back from the other side. Cast aside these doubts; these fears. Because they will eat away at you as surely as the sea erodes the rocks. Doubt and fear are the devices of evil, do not succumb to them; be always brave.' From his bag he produced a large white cloth, with a shadowy image upon it. 'Take this Didymus. It is the shroud used to cover my body at my reawakening. It will remind you of what happened and what you, and all men and women, are capable of. If ever you doubt yourself, take heart with this.'

We parted then. He taking the road to northern India, and myself taking a boat to the south."

Stella looked incredulous. "So Jesus survived the crucifixion and went to India? I thought he ascended to heaven."

"That's what the Bible would have you believe," said Jeremy. "But it's been suspected amongst scholars for some time that he went back to India."

"Went back to India?" questioned Stella.

"Yes," said Jeremy. "Went back. There is little or no record of Jesus' life between the ages of 12 and 30. But there is record of a spiritual teacher in India at this time. There is a school of thought that believes the historical Jesus spent these years in India, learning ancient healing methods and then teaching them. He returned to his homeland of Israel briefly, attempting to teach them a peaceful path. It is this time of his life that is recorded in the Bible. But although the Bible declares his ascent to heaven, there is evidence that he returned to India. His tomb is in the town of Shrinagar in Kashmir." He held out the documents. "These writings seem to prove that theory."

"I guess so," said Stella. "If they're genuine that is. Who is Didymus? I've never heard of him."

"Didymus is another name for St Thomas," said Jeremy. "It is well-known that he travelled to India after the crucifixion. He took Christianity to Kerala state in the south west of the country. That is where Stratton found these. St Thomas was even on an Indian stamp in 1972.

"Not only that, but the story of the shroud fits in as well. The relics of St Thomas were returned to Edessa in Mesopotamia by an Indian king. Edessa is where the Turin shroud was found in 544AD. So these writings back up many theories."

Stella turned to Stratton and said, "How long have you had these?"

"Long enough."

"Why haven't you shown them to anybody? Surely people deserve to know all this."

Stratton shrugged. "I didn't know if they were genuine for a start. And also, how do you think people would react to it? The Church would denounce them as fake, like they do with anything that conflicts with their domination of people's minds. There's no way they'd let it be known that the very being they encourage people to worship didn't want to be worshipped. The Church is a complete paradox, but it makes money, which equates to power, so it will never fall. Not until people wake up. I'm sure Jesus would be sickened by the wealth of the Catholic Church."

"That's a bit harsh," said Stella.

"Yes, maybe it is," admitted Stratton. "The Church does do a lot of good, and I'm sure it's heart is in the right place. But ultimately it's a religion, and religions can only lead to one thing, and that's war. Mass religion goes against everything that Jesus believed in. If he had one message for us it was to forget about religion and get on with being nice to each other."

"Okay," said Stella wearily. "I don't want to get into a theological debate about it. All I really want to know now is, what has any of this got to do with the box?"

"I don't know," said Stratton coolly.

Jeremy got out of his chair and looked down at him. "I think you do my lad," he said. "I think you suspect the same thing as I do. That Jesus was a Reiki Master and used the symbols to heal people. That the symbols on the box hold the secret to his power. Thomas spoke of Peter drawing symbols above Jesus before they brought him back; it's obvious they were using a powerful form of Reiki."

"Maybe," said Stratton. "I hadn't really thought about it," he lied.

Jeremy poured himself a glass of water. "Do you know how old the box is?" he asked Stratton.

"No idea. I didn't get a chance to have it dated."

"Well I did," said Jeremy. "And carbon dating tells us that it was made between 30 - 60 AD. Suggesting that there's a possibility that we know its maker."

Stella stared at Jeremy with wide eyes. "You don't mean…"

"Yes my dear, I mean exactly that. Think about it - who else but a skilled carpenter could have carved the symbols. A carpenter with a deep knowledge of healing and the spirit world. We can't prove it, but it's a real possibility. The dates fit. The geography fits. So why not?"

Stratton shook his head in disbelief. "You're off your rocker," he said.

"I don't think so," said Jeremy. "It's something I've suspected for a long time. I just needed some evidence to back up my theory. And you've provided it. So, armed with this knowledge, I can get on with my plan."

"And what's that?" said Stratton. "World domination?"

"No, not world domination. I have something far more interesting in mind."

Chapter 59

Romano stood in the mild morning mist. He was in a large field. In front of him, about two hundred yards away, was a farmhouse. In the window he could see a man and a woman. Their fists banged against the glass. Behind them he saw the ninja approaching, knife in hand. He waved his hands in an attempt to warn them. They paid no heed. The ninja raised his knife and stabbed wildly, first at the man, then at the woman. Blood spattered the window. Romano watched helplessly. It was murder; it was a bloodbath; it was a slaughter. The word echoed in his mind - 'slaughter...slaughter...slaughter...' Then, with a jerk, he woke up.

After a quick shower he joined the others for breakfast in the main hotel suite. He sat down and grabbed himself some coffee from the cafetiere.

He took a sip and said, "I think they're dead."

"Who's dead?" asked Jennings, not certain he wanted to hear the answer.

"Your friends Stratton and Stella. I had a dream about them. They were in a farmhouse being stabbed to death by a ninja, that Yoshima guy I assume." He bowed his head. "I'm sorry."

Jennings felt deflated. A week ago he would have laughed it off as just a dream, but his view of the world had changed since then. He sensed the gravity in Romano's voice, and it sickened him to the core.

Miles picked up on Jennings' solemnity. He finished a mouthful of bacon and said, "Now now Grant, let's not jump to conclusions about this dream of yours. It may not mean that they're dead, it could be telling you something else."

"What?" piped Grady. "Like they're sitting on a beach in the Caribbean."

Miles ignored the comment and continued. "Tell me exactly

what you saw Grant."

Romano described the dream. "But what about feelings you had? What about sounds? It's all important," Miles pressed.

"I'm not too sure," said Romano. "I felt kind of helpless I guess. I tried to warn them about the attack but they couldn't see me, or they ignored me. As for sounds - I don't think there were any."

Miles gave him an earnest look. "Are you sure?"

"Yeah, pretty sure," nodded Romano. "Although just as I was waking up I remember thinking it was a slaughter, and the word kept ringing in my head. It was probably because I was traumatized."

"Slaughter," Miles muttered to himself. "Interesting. What could it mean?"

"It means they've been fucking slaughtered, for Christ's sake," said Grady. "What else could it mean?"

"Dreams are there to be interpreted," insisted Miles. "They are not always meant to be taken literally. We need to look for clues as to where they are."

"As a wild guess, may I suggest a farmhouse," said Grady facetiously.

"Yes, obviously a farmhouse," sighed Miles. "But where? England's hardly short of them is it?"

An idea popped into Jennings head. "There's an area called the Slaughters just outside Stow on the Wold," he suggested. "I know it's a bit of a long shot, but I can't think of anything better."

Miles got up from the table and paced the room in thought. "Good thinking Jennings," he said. "That's exactly the sort of thing we need to be looking at. But how do we go about verifying your theory. Is there any way of checking whether a farmhouse has been recently rented out in the area."

"Yes there is," said Jennings. "It's called going up there and looking for ourselves. I can ask someone at Scotland Yard to ring round letting agents in the area, but that's going to take time. And we haven't got that luxury. I vote we leave right now. Unless anybody has a better suggestion."

Miles and Romano agreed. Grady however was sceptical. "What if your idea is completely out of whack," he said. "Shouldn't we think about this for a while? Maybe let your guys at the Yard check it out first. If we head up there on a wild goose chase then we waste valuable time, and may well be signing their death warrants."

"Listen Grady," said Jennings. "We're wasting time talking about it. We have no other leads."

Grady finally agreed and within ten minutes they had left the Dorchester and were heading for the Cotswolds. Jennings phoned a friend at Scotland Yard and asked her to make discreet enquiries in the area.

Once they were free of the city Jennings put the car through its paces. The thought of Stella being butchered had hit him hard. It was his fault that she was in this situation. If he'd listened to his instincts then maybe she would still be safe. If anything happened to her he would never forgive himself.

Grady gripped the sides of the passenger seat. "Whoa! Slow down there Schumacher," he said. "You're going to get us killed driving like that."

Jennings ignored his protestations and drove even faster. Grady made the sign of the cross on his chest.

By ten o'clock they had reached Stow on the Wold. Jennings' phone rang. He answered on loudspeaker. It was Scotland Yard. They could find no record of a recent farmhouse letting in the area.

"Fuck it," said Grady. "What do we do now?"

"We carry on up to the Slaughters," said Jennings. "We'll ask about in the villages. If someone's rented a house in the area then it'll be known."

Jennings drove slowly along the lanes that led to Lower Slaughter. He asked Romano to keep an eye out for anything familiar from his dream. Romano looked carefully but he saw nothing recognizable.

The sun lit up the village of Lower Slaughter. It was well-kept and even in the depths of winter looked stunning. Jennings imagined that in the full bloom of summer it would be postcard perfect.

The road through the village appeared deserted. Jennings crawled along looking for signs of life. A hundred yards ahead he saw an old man pushing his bike. He drove up to him and pulled over. The man stopped. Jennings wound down his window. "Excuse me sir," he said. "I'm with the police." He flashed his warrant card. "I'm looking for a farmhouse in the area. Is there one that's been let out recently?"

The man eyed Jennings inquisitively. "Let me think," he said. "There is one. Between here and Upper Slaughter. Old Jeffries let it out about a month ago, to some bloke from the city apparently. It's called Honeybee Farm. It's about half a mile down the road on your right. Just keep going as you are."

Jennings thanked the man and sped off.

As they reached the entrance to the farm Jennings slowed down. He parked the car out of sight and he and Grady got out. They forced Miles and Romano to stay in the car. An unseen approach would be almost impossible with four of them.

The house was two hundred yards from the gate. Access was via a dirt track. It was surrounded by open fields. Whichever way they approached they would be sitting ducks. The only cover they could see was an old rusting roller, about halfway down the track. They decided to make their advance in two stages.

Jennings looked to the house and, when he was sure that no-one was watching, he ran, keeping as low as he could. Grady followed in his shadow. They reached the roller and sat with their backs to it.

"Did you see anything?" asked Jennings, gasping for breath.

"No, nothing," said Grady, and then added, "A bit out of

shape aren't you? That could only have been a hundred yards."

"All right. Don't go on about it. I've been too busy working to stay fit. I have a full-time job - unlike some people, Mr part-time freelance."

Grady poked his head over the top of the roller and scanned the windows for life. The curtains were still. "If there's anybody in there, they aren't watching us," he said. "Let's go!"

Jennings took a deep breath and sprinted for the house. Grady stayed close behind. They reached the side wall and stood flat against it.

"The door must be round the other side," whispered Jennings.

Grady nodded and crept his way round, crouching to avoid the windows. There was still no sign of life.

"What's the plan then?" asked Jennings when they reached the front door.

"I suggest a good old-fashioned kicking down of doors," said Grady. "Followed by a lot of shouting and shooting."

"Ok."

Grady moved away from the wall and faced the door. He hit it with a crashing back kick. The lock broke away immediately. Gun in hand, he shouldered his way into the house, carefully checking at every step. "This is the police!" he shouted. "Come out with your hands up!"

The house was silent.

"I don't think he's listening to you," said Jennings.

"Go figure."

They made their way through to the kitchen. "Somebody's been here," said Jennings. "Look at the plates on the draining board."

Grady went over and felt them. They were still wet. "They're either here or they've just left."

They searched the house. Grady took the upstairs and Jennings the ground floor. There was nobody about. There was no sign of a struggle. They met back in the kitchen.

"What shall we do then?" said Grady. "Do we wait for somebody to get back or what?"

"I don't know," said Jennings, opening what he thought was a pantry door. "Shit!"

"What's up?" asked Grady.

"There's a passageway back here. We'd better check it out."

Grady paused for a moment. "Has it occurred to you that this might be the wrong place? I mean, all we have to go on are the ramblings of Jonny film star back there. How do we know he's not way off the mark? How do we know your interpretation isn't way off the mark?"

"This is the place. I'm sure of it," said Jennings grimly. "I can feel it in my bones."

He flicked the light switch at the start of the passage and walked slowly along, gun outstretched. Grady did likewise and also kept his eye on the door behind.

At the end of the short corridor was a set of stone steps. They led down to a heavy wooden door bolted on the outside. Jennings slid the bolt across and carefully opened the door. "Hello," he said. There was no answer.

To his right he found a light switch. He turned it on. He looked in. His eyes fixed on the far corner. His heart froze.

Chapter 60

The security van was on its way to the Old Bailey. Alex Goddard sat in the passenger seat casually munching on a Double Decker chocolate bar. His partner Tom Dury was at the wheel. Together they were the newly-formed D&G Security. The name had two purposes: the first being that it bore their initials; the second being that it was easily confused with Dolce & Gabbana, and nobody was likely to attack a clothes van. Of course, there might be some copyright infringement, but who was to know.

They were on their last job of the morning. It was also their biggest. Their charge was the man who had been accused of the murder of 'cop hero' Steve Hurworth. It was a high-profile job, but Alex was relaxed about it. All they had to do was deliver him to the Old Bailey, he would enter his plea, and then they would take him off to the Scrubs. It would take an hour at the most. Then they could stop for lunch; a long lazy lunch with a couple of pints. Alex pictured the lunch in his head. It took his mind off Tom's lecture on the benefits of leasing a car.

Up ahead the traffic lights turned red. They slowed to a stop five cars back. Alex shoved his sweet wrapper into the glove box, dusted off his hands, and gazed out of the side window. Tom continued to waffle on, but Alex's attention had wandered. His eyes were drawn to the wing mirror. Two men got out of the car behind. They wore balaclavas and were carrying shotguns. His heart started to thump.

"Fuck!" he shouted.

"What's up?" said Tom calmly.

"Guns!"

Tom looked desperately for an escape route in the traffic, but all he saw was a sea of cars. The sound of breaking glass hit his left ear. He was regretting having skimped on the van's body armour. He was regretting starting up his own security firm.

A man stood at the window pointing a gun at his head. "Stop the fucking engine!" he commanded. Tom did as he said. "Now, get out and open the back doors. And don't try being a fucking hero!"

Tom looked into the barrel of the gun and decided against heroics. He got out, went to the back of the van, and unlocked the doors. The gunman pushed him to the ground. The guard in the back came out with his hands up. The handcuffed prisoner followed.

"Let's go!" the gunman shouted.

The prisoner and the two gunmen fled to a side alley, leaving their vehicle in the middle of the traffic jam. They raced up the alley and into a quiet residential street, where another car awaited them. They got in, removed their balaclavas, and sped off. Oggi had escaped.

Chapter 61

"What is it?" said Grady, noting Jennings' look of horror.

"Blood," said Jennings.

Grady entered the cellar and looked around. The pools of blood he expected turned out to be small puddles. "Jesus Jennings," he said. "It hardly looks like there's been a massacre. I've seen worse at a football match."

"Maybe. But the blood looks fairly fresh to me. Who knows what happened in here?" He walked over and bent down to take a closer look. He dabbed his finger in the blood. It was dry. Next to the blood were two sets of rope. They had both been slashed. He picked them up and examined them. One set contained traces of blood; the other was clean.

"What do you make of it?" asked Grady.

"I don't know," said Jennings. "It looks like there were two people tied up. But it appears that they were set free. There's not a lot to go on is there? Some blood; some rope. All I can say is that we're on the right track. I'm sure it was Stella and Stratton who were the captives."

"Well, whoever it was has gone now," said Grady. "Are they coming back? I doubt it."

A voice hollered from the top of the stairs. "Hello!… Jennings!…Grady!" It was Miles.

"Christ!" said Grady. "What's he doing here? I thought you told him to stay in the car."

They left the cellar and went up to the kitchen. Miles and Romano were both there.

"I thought I told you two to stay in the car," said Jennings.

"You did," replied Miles. "But you'd been so long we thought we should come and see what was going on. We thought you might be in trouble."

"Thanks for your concern," said Grady. "But as you can see,

we're all right. What were you going to do if we were in trouble? Get Grant Romano to offer them signed photos in exchange for our safe return?"

"Look," said Miles. "We just thought we ought to come down. There's no harm done so let's leave it. More to the point, have you found anything?"

Jennings told him about the cellar.

Miles paused for thought. "So you're pretty sure it was Stratton and Stella who were tied up?"

"Yes," nodded Jennings. "Well fairly sure. That's what my gut instinct tells me. I couldn't tell for certain, not without forensics. But there's no time for all that, we need to get on their trail ASAP. They might have been alive when they left, but who knows how long that will last? We need to search the house for clues. Names, addresses - anything really. Anything that'll tell us where they're headed. I'll search down here with Grant. And you and Professor Miles can take the upstairs Grady."

Grady gave him a disapproving look. Being paired up with Miles wasn't what he wanted at all.

Jennings started to search through the kitchen drawers. He knew that there was little or no hope of finding anything. The chances of a professional like Yoshima leaving clues were slim to say the least. But he had to try. He'd come too far to give up now. He'd gone out on a limb and put his career on the line. They were closing in on Yoshima, he could feel it. All they needed was one more break; one last sign from the heavens; one last lucky throw of the dice. He thought of Stella and Stratton and prayed that something would turn up.

Romano took the living room. He was relieved that no bodies had been found. Thankfully Miles had been right in his interpretation of the dream. But what use had it really been? True, they had found the house, but it was empty. They were no closer to finding the box than they had been two hours ago. He gave the room a cursory search and found nothing.

He looked to his feelings for inspiration. If they were to locate the box and save Jennings' friends, then the answer would come from intuition, not physical evidence.

He walked back through the kitchen and down to the cellar. Standing in the corner, on top of the blood and ropes, he tried to tap into the energy of the room. He closed his eyes. A wave of power surged through his body. Visions of torture flashed in his third eye. He could feel their anguish; he could feel their pain; he could feel the frustration of their captor. But there was no death. Whatever had occurred in that dank basement, a life had not been taken. Where were they now though? He tried to visualize them in his mind, but all he could see was blackness. While he was awake the visions wouldn't come. Only in the arms of Morpheus would he find them.

Grady, Miles and Jennings were all in the kitchen when he came back up. None of them appeared to have found anything.

"Where have you been?" asked Jennings.

"Down in the cellar," Romano replied. "I thought I'd see if I could make a psychic connection with them."

Jennings looked at him expectantly. "And?"

Romano shook his head. "Nothing I'm afraid. I just don't seem to be able to do it when I'm not asleep. Maybe I'm not switching off enough. Maybe I'm trying too hard. It's frustrating, that's for sure."

"You're telling me," said Grady. "This is ridiculous. We're going nowhere fast." He turned to Jennings. "You've only got one option my friend. You've got to call your boss and get some more people on this. You don't need to tell him the whole story, just that you've stumbled across a lead. You need all the police in the vicinity looking for this guy."

Jennings thought about what Grady had said. He was right of course, they did need a concentrated search of the area, but Jennings was still loathe to involve Brennan. There would be a hell of a lot of explaining to do before Brennan agreed to anything. He couldn't just say he'd stumbled across a lead; Brennan would want to know exactly how he came by it, and exactly how much evidence there was of Yoshima having been at the house. He would then have to explain why he hadn't phoned earlier. It would be complicated. But how could they go on without outside help? There were no more clues to be had; no more hunches to follow. He had to make a decision one way or another. He felt it in his heart. Time was running out.

Chapter 62

Dr Brian Russell was nervous. What he was doing would be frowned upon as extremely unethical. He told himself he was furthering science. In reality he was receiving a tidy sum of money that would pay off his gambling debts and see his kids through college. He tried to dispel the moral dilemmas from his mind. Right or wrong he was doing it and there was no going back now.

Dr Russell was head of research for the Cryonics Institute in Michigan. He had been approached two months previously by a man whose son was frozen at the site. The man wanted to bring him out of his suspended state. Dr Russell had told him that the technology wasn't available for such a process. However, the man had been most persuasive, and Dr Russell had eventually offered to try and return his son to a post-mortem condition.

Russell thought about it. In order to successfully store a person for future reanimation they had to be attended to straight after death. First they were lowered into an ice bath, and then circulation and breathing were artificially restored with a CPR machine. Next, medications were administered to the brain to protect it from lack of oxygen. After this the patient's blood was replaced by a cryoprotectant solution, to stop injury whilst freezing. The patient was then immersed in alcohol to cool their body to -79 Celsius (the temperature of dry ice). The last part of the process was gradual freezing over a two week period to bring the body temperature to -196 Celsius (the temperature of liquid nitrogen). Theoretically all he had to do was reverse this procedure. Many had tried and failed, including himself, but with two million dollars looming on the horizon it was worth trying again.

So two months later here he was. Over the period of three weeks he'd brought the body slowly back to temperature. He was now attempting the difficult task of extracting the cryopro-tectant and replacing it with blood. He was using a standard heart lung machine with a few clever alterations of his own, and it seemed to be working.

He looked at his watch. He had ten minutes before Jeremy came for the body. This was about the time it would take for the remaining cryoprotectant to leave the bloodstream. Perfect. All he had to do was wait and take the remainder of his money.

Ten minutes later the doorbell of the rented house rang. Jeremy was exactly on time. "Hello Doctor Russell," he said. "I hope that everything's going well."

Russell led him through to the makeshift theatre. "It seems to be," he said. "But there's no real way of telling. Who knows what's going on inside the body?"

"You've managed to get the blood back into him though?" Jeremy pressed.

"Yes I have. I didn't think I'd be able to, but it's done. I can't make him breathe again though. All you've got is ostensibly the shell of a recently-deceased human being. Which I believe is all that you asked for."

"Exactly!" said Jeremy with exuberance. "You've done a fantastic job, doctor. You should be very pleased with yourself."

"I am," admitted Russell. "And I shall be equally pleased when I receive my cheque."

Jeremy approached the body and laid a hand on his son's cheek. He smiled and his eyes moistened. "Don't worry my boy. You'll be back with me soon. I've found the way."

Russell looked down and shuffled his feet, feeling that he was intruding on an intensely private moment. What did Jeremy mean - he'd "found the way"? What in God's name was he up to?

"There's just one more thing I need you to do," said Jeremy, addressing the doctor once more.

"What's that?" asked Russell, not liking the sound of it. He'd done his job; he wanted his money.

"I need you to come with me for a couple of hours. I'm going to need a medical man on hand in case there are complications."

"Complications in what?"

"In what I'm about to attempt," said Jeremy. "It will only be a couple of hours I promise. After that you can take your cheque and go wherever you please."

"What if I refuse?"

"Then I'm afraid I'll have to keep hold of the money."

Russell cursed himself. He knew he should have insisted on part payment up front. This situation had been inevitable. "Okay. I'll come with you then. It seems I have no choice."

Russell removed the tubes from the cadaver, and he and Jeremy wheeled it out of the house. A white Mercedes van was parked in the driveway. Jeremy steered round to the back doors. He opened them and, with Yoshima's help, they manoeuvred the trolley into the van.

Doctor Russell's fears began to grow. In the back of the van, handcuffed to the side rails, were a man and a woman. They didn't look in the best of health.

Jeremy saw Russell's concern. He pulled out a gun. "Have you got a problem doctor?" he asked.

"No. Of course not," Russell replied meekly.

"Good. Let's go then. You can ride up in the front with Yoshima and I."

Chapter 63

Stratton and Stella looked at each other with bemusement. They were both thinking the same thing. What the hell was going on? Slowly and independently they reached an identical conclusion: Jeremy was going to attempt a resurrection of his own.

"Fucking hell!" said Stratton, thinking aloud.

Jeremy turned his head. "Something wrong in the back there?"

"You're fucking mad," said Stratton. "If you're going to do what I think you are, then you're stark raving mad. You're fucking certifiable!"

Jeremy laughed. "Am I really?" he said. "Why's that? I'm only doing what they did two thousand years ago, and they pulled it off then."

"That was just a bit of text. It didn't prove anything. We don't know that it actually happened."

"Maybe not," said Jeremy. "But we're about to find out."

Stratton looked at the body and wondered who it might be.

As if reading his mind Jeremy spoke: "It's my son," he said. "He died two years ago from leukaemia. He was frozen and put into suspension at the Cryonics Institute in Michigan. Now he's going to get his life back."

Stratton gave him an incredulous look. "You really think so? He's been dead for two years, not three days. There is no way on earth that this is going to work."

"I suggest you try and be a bit more positive," said Jeremy. "Because you're going to help bring him back. If you don't, then your beloved here dies." He pointed to Stella.

"Why can't you do it yourself? You've got the information. You don't need me."

"I think I do. It took eleven of them to bring Jesus back didn't it? I don't think the energy of one person is enough."

Stratton shook his head. "He's crazy," he whispered to Stella.

"Are you sure?" she whispered back. "I mean, from what I've seen so far nothing is impossible. Why's he waited all this time though? His son died two years ago."

Jeremy turned his head back to them. "It's rude to whisper you know," he said angrily.

"Sorry," said Stella trying to placate him. "But I was just wondering why it's taken you all this time to try and bring your son back?"

"Because my dear, I had no idea he was dead. We had a big falling-out ten years ago and hadn't been in contact since then. I lived in a remote area of Japan and he lived in New York. Three months ago I decided it was time to make my peace with him. It was only then that I found out that he'd died. His wife explained about the leukaemia and that he'd had his body frozen. I was distraught as you can imagine."

"Why did you fall out?" asked Stella.

Jeremy smiled ironically. "Because of our beliefs," he said. "My son was an eminent oncologist and all he believed in was medication and chemotherapy - basically anything scientific. He had no time for my ideas on Reiki and alternative therapy."

"But that's no reason for an ongoing feud," countered Stella.

"No, it's not," admitted Jeremy. "But his mother's death was. She was diagnosed with stomach cancer but refused to have chemotherapy. She wanted to try and heal it with a mixture of Reiki and herbal remedies. My son attempted to persuade her to go down the more conventional route. I incurred his wrath by siding with her. When she died he came to the funeral and that was that - he never spoke to me again."

"Do you blame him?" asked Stella. "You stopped his mother from having a chance to survive."

"It looks like that on the surface, but it's not strictly true. I don't think that she'd have consented to chemotherapy whatever I'd said. She was a very spiritual woman, my wife. It was her belief that she was being called to the other side. If she didn't get better it was because she didn't want to, not because she couldn't. Even though my son was brought up in a spiritual household, he never really understood or believed in our ideals."

Stella began to feel anger. "If you're so spiritual why don't you just accept that your son's dead and leave him to rest in peace? Why have you let innocent people die on the off chance that you'll get him back?"

"Two good questions," said Jeremy. "And I don't think I can answer either of them satisfactorily. I constantly ask myself exactly the same thing. My higher self wants to let it go; it knows that killing is wrong and that I will see my son again in the next world. Unfortunately like everybody else I am a human being, and I haven't advanced far enough to override the primal instinct to look after my seed. The chance of bringing him back holds too much sway over me.

"Not only that, I also wish to see if it can be done. We are on the brink of the greatest discovery ever. If these symbols work then it paves the way for a whole new era. We will finally have the secrets of the universe at our disposal. Surely that is worth a couple of lives?"

"For fuck's sake," spat Stratton. "Don't pull that greater good shit on me. You haven't done any of this for the furthering of mankind; you've done it because you're a power-hungry egomaniac just like your friend Mulholland. Mankind isn't ready to control the energy yet: there's too much fear and bitterness and hatred in us. Those symbols were kept hidden for a good reason. They need to go back to their keepers."

Jeremy stared coldly at him. "I'm sorry you feel that way my boy. I know you don't agree with my methods, but killing to bring life is a paradox that you must accept. Faith, religion, and the universe are full of double standards."

Stratton said no more. Jeremy disgusted him. And yet at the same time his words contained a basic truth. Existence *was* full of paradoxes. In fact if you thought about it long enough and hard enough, it was one big paradox. Who was to say that Jeremy was wrong? Who was pure enough and wise enough to judge him? There were no real answers, only questions. Since the beginning of time man had questioned the essence of being.

Through the ages, from Socrates to Sartre, the greatest minds had reasoned and debated in an attempt to find solutions. But still there were none, and until there were, right and wrong were just a matter of perspective.

The van trundled along steadily. Stella tried to catch a glimpse of passing signposts to see where they were headed; but there was only a small window between the front and back, and it was impossible to make out any place names. She looked at the body in front of her and shuddered. Whatever Jeremy said, what he was about to do was wrong. She wouldn't have been able to articulate why, but her whole body right down to every last nerve ending was screaming it at her. She felt a sickening in her stomach. If there was a God, then he didn't want this to happen, she was sure of it.

She looked up at Jeremy. He was deep in conversation with Dr Russell. She took the opportunity to have a quiet word with Stratton. "I don't like this," she whispered. "I feel horrible. I feel sick to the pit of my stomach. He shouldn't be doing this."

"I know," said Stratton. "I feel the same. But at the moment we've got no choice - we have to go along with him." He touched her cheek with his free hand and gave her a reassuring smile. "Don't worry, nothing will happen to you." There was a pause. "Not while I'm still alive anyway."

His last words hung like a portent. Had he foreseen his own demise? Stella wondered. Or was she reading too much into it. Perhaps the eerie chill pervading her soul was inducing paranoia. She didn't know; she could no longer be rational. Uncertainty was overwhelming her. She looked across at Stratton. Her eyes welled up. She didn't want to lose him.

Chapter 64

It was approaching nine o'clock in the evening. Jennings watched the forensics team finish off their search of the house. Apart from the blood in the cellar nothing of note had been found. There had been fingerprints, but none that matched any on the computer. There were no clues as to where the hostages had been taken.

Earlier that afternoon he had taken the bold decision to phone Brennan, who had been surprisingly good with him considering. There had been no dressing down, no pointed remarks, only a "why didn't you call me sooner". Jennings suspected it was all an act, that Brennan was just being professional, and that his barracking would come once they were back at Scotland Yard.

Grady, who had been outside smoking a cigarette, walked back into the kitchen. "Any joy?" he asked Jennings. "Any word from the traffic cops?"

Jennings shook his head. "No, Nothing," he said. "And I don't expect there will be either. Basically, we're fucked. I might as well not have bothered phoning for help. We're no further than we were, and on top of that I'm probably going to lose my job."

"I admire your optimism," said Grady. He put his hand on Jennings' shoulder. "Listen man, you did the right thing. You had no choice but to call this in. We were going nowhere fast. We might not have got any further, but at least you tried."

Grady's words were cold comfort. He'd risked everything for nothing. He felt impotent. Stella and Stratton were in danger, he could sense it, and all he could do was stand around and wait for something to happen. He was helpless and lost. Anger and fear suffused his body. He smashed his fist into the refrigerator in frustration.

Grady grabbed him by the arms. "For fuck's sake man, save it. You've got to chill out. Getting angry isn't going to help anyone."

"I can't help it Grady. Everything's gone to shit. I've been falling ever since this investigation started. It's like a parasite's worked its way inside me and spread its seed. Something horrible's growing inside my body and I need to get rid of it. I don't know who I am any more."

Grady put an arm around Jennings' shoulder. "Hey man, there's nothing growing inside of you. You're just tired and frustrated. I'm feeling it as well. You've got to have faith. Something will turn up, believe me. Your friends are still alive, and we're going to find them."

Grady couldn't quite believe what he had said. The words had definitely come out of his mouth, but where they originated he had no idea. He wasn't in the habit of comforting people. He really needed to get out of the field. His new-found compassion would get him killed.

Miles and Romano wandered into the room. They had been to the local pub for a bite to eat. Miles had suggested it, his thinking being that better inspiration was had on a full stomach. They had returned in hopeful spirit.

"Anything?" asked Miles expectantly.

Jennings replied in the negative.

"Damn!" said Miles. "I was sure you would get something. I could feel it."

Jennings shrugged. "Sorry. There's nothing doing." He pulled out a knife from the block on the sideboard and flicked it about aimlessly. Curbing a secret desire to drive it straight into Miles' stomach out of sheer, pent-up, annoyance.

Romano's eyes followed the knife as it turned this way and that. Its movement was almost hypnotic. He drifted into his subconscious. His mind went blank. He could feel Jennings' irritation; and sensed his urge to lash out. A picture entered his head of Miles with a knife sliding across his throat. But it wasn't Jennings holding the weapon; it was the man from his dream. And suddenly it hit him. He knew where they had to go.

Chapter 65

It was near midnight and a light mist hovered over Salisbury Plain. Barry Dean walked around the edge of Stonehenge, directing his torch slowly and deliberately. His German shepherd stiffened, sniffed the air, and pricked its ears. Then, satisfied with the absence of scent, it continued with the patrol. Dean was used to the dog stopping and starting in this manner, it no longer worried him, it was just one of the animal's quirks.

Man and dog finished their half hour circuit of the Stones and returned to the warmth of their little room at the entrance to the site. Dean's colleague, Alan Drew, was waiting to take his turn on watch.

"All quiet," said Dean, taking off his coat.

"Good," said Drew, putting his on. "I'll see you in half an hour." He left with his own dog in tow.

Dean boiled the kettle, made himself a cup of tea, and sat down to drink it. The dog lay at his feet. He would be pleased to get the shift over with. It was December 22nd, the winter solstice, a significant date in the pagan world. Apparently it was an even more powerful event than midsummer. There had been a celebration at the site the previous evening. But there was still a good chance that a few weirdoes would want to hold their own unofficial rituals tonight. He didn't believe in all that druid crap himself, but he knew that some people put an awful lot of stock in it. Consequently he and Drew had been especially thorough with their patrols.

He picked up his copy of the *Telegraph* and had a look at the crossword. At his feet the dog started to growl. "What is it boy?" he said aloud. The dog pricked his ears then settled back down again. A false alarm.

The crossword proved tricky and, after getting just four or five clues, Dean laid the paper down and checked his watch. There were two minutes until Drew came back. He put his coat on in anticipation.

Five minutes later Drew still hadn't returned. It was most unlike him. As a rule his patrol would be half an hour to the second. He buzzed him on the two-way. "Hello Alan." There was no reply. He tried again. "Alan? Are you there? Come in Alan."

No reply.

Dean walked out into the cold night. The mist had drawn in and his vision was restricted to less than twenty feet. His dog started to bark ferociously. Dean shone his torch into the blanket of fog but saw nothing. The dog continued to bark.

Dean headed down the underpass that led to the Stones. His dog strained on its lead, maddened by an unseen foe.

At the end of the underpass the dog stopped abruptly. His barking ceased and he sniffed the ground. Dean shone his torch down. Drew and the other dog lay motionless on the concrete. Dean checked for a pulse. His colleague was still alive.

The dog started to bark again. This time even more wildly. Dean shone his torch around in blind desperation. "Who's there?" he shouted. "Come out or I'll let the dog loose."

Suddenly the dog went silent and fell to the ground. Two seconds later Dean joined him.

Chapter 66

Yoshima and Dr Russell wheeled the trolley through the underpass. Jeremy went ahead, leading the way with his torch. Stratton and Stella walked next to him, handcuffed to each other. Neither had a coat and both were bitterly cold.

At the end of the underpass they neatly avoided the prostrate guards and dogs, and headed up the inclined walkway to the Stones. The dense fog made it slow going.

At the top of the walkway Yoshima lifted Jeremy's son from the trolley and put him over his shoulder. Jeremy led them confidently onwards.

"How the hell does he know where to go?" Stella whispered to Stratton.

Jeremy overheard the comment. "Because my dear, like all good soldiers, I have checked and rechecked my terrain beforehand. I know exactly where the Stones are - I could do this blindfold. In about five paces we'll be coming up to the perimeter rope. Mind that none of you trip."

They all navigated the rope successfully and continued slowly on. Seconds later Stella caught her first glimpse of the legendary Stones. They rose ominously out of the mist, great megalithic giants, watching and waiting. Stella felt the back of her neck tingle. She shuddered and clasped Stratton's hand.

Inside the ring the air was clear. There was mist around it and above it, but whether through magic or science, the fog would not penetrate the Stones. Stratton felt a surge of power as he entered the circle. Much like he had experienced at Rollright, but stronger and more foreboding. He looked to Stella and saw fear in her eyes. He mustered up some courage and gave her a reassuring smile. "It's ok," he mouthed silently.

Stella was amazed at how close together the Stones actually were. She had seen them in pictures and on TV, and they had appeared to make one large circle of pillars and lintels with a big space in the middle. In reality the circle was quite small, and the centre was strewn with boulders of various size. If the fog settled in the ring then it would be nigh on impossible to navigate, she thought.

Jeremy stood on a patch of clear grass towards the centre of the monument. From his pocket he removed a tape measure and began to measure distances between the rocks.

"What are you doing?" asked Stella. "Thinking of building a holiday home?"

Jeremy carried on with his task. "No. I'm finding the most powerful position in the circle," he said. "Outside the circle there are two boulders called the Station Stones. There's one either side. Years ago there were another two Station Stones. Where these four stones intersected was the epicentre of spiritual force. Stonehenge is built on a spider's web of ley-lines. Where the stones intersect, the ley-lines do as well. This creates an overwhelming amount of energy. I intend to tap into this to help with our little experiment."

Satisfied he'd found the correct spot, Jeremy beckoned Yoshima over and they laid the body down on the soft grass. From a rucksack he produced five large candles. He positioned them around the body and lit them.

"Right then," said Jeremy with purpose. "Now is the time I shall need your help Stratton. You and I are going to bring my son back to life."

Stratton waved the handcuffs. "There's not a lot I can do with these on is there?"

"Don't worry, they can come off. But any trouble and your little sweetheart here dies."

Yoshima removed Stratton's wrist from its cuff, and used it to secure Stella's hands behind her back. He sat her on a stone and positioned himself next to her. Stratton walked towards Jeremy. Dr Brian Russell looked on nervously.

"Ok then," said Stratton. "What exactly do you want me to do?"

Jeremy pulled out a yellowing piece of paper and unfurled it; then he produced the box. "This is the key to the symbols. There's a picture here of a man rising up from his body. It doesn't take a lot of imagination to guess that the symbol it corresponds to on the box is the one for resurrection. We're going to use that one along with the Master Symbol and the Power Symbol. Together with the power of this place and the added impact of the winter solstice, I believe that we can do this."

Stratton didn't like it. What he was being asked to do felt wrong. Too many lives had been taken for this to end up in anything other than disaster. Even if they did manage to bring back Jeremy's son there would be a price to pay. Jeremy's heart was too black for any good to come from the situation. Stratton felt an unseen force watching them and he felt sick. He couldn't let Jeremy go through with it. But how could he stop him without sacrificing Stella?

"Come on then Stratton," Jeremy pressed. "Let's get on with it. You take his head and I'll take his feet. Draw the Master Symbol over him first, then the Power Symbol, and then the Resurrection Symbol. I'll do the same. Then we'll lay our hands on him and let the energy run through. Okay?"

Stratton nodded reluctantly. Until he could think of something, he had to accede to Jeremy's wishes.

As he made the signs over the body Stratton felt his body shiver. Not through the cold, but because of the might he was rousing. The slumbering leviathan of the cosmos was awakening and flowing through his body. He was so overcome his eyes began to water and his body shook.

Across from him Jeremy was having the same experience. They looked at each other in an awe-filled acknowledgement. Then they knelt down and began to channel the energy.

Stratton placed his hands on the crown chakra at the top of the head. Jeremy placed his at the feet. Immediately Stratton felt a rush of electricity run through him. He juddered involuntarily. His whole being became part of a huge circuit.

Stella looked on intensely. A blue steam rose from Jeremy, Stratton, and the body. Something was happening. She wanted to look away but found herself helplessly compelled to watch. Whatever power was at work, it was drawing on all their auras. Her body tightened. Her throat constricted. She struggled for breath. The earth around her began to vibrate. She closed her eyes and prayed for deliverance.

Chapter 67

Out of the mist Jennings caught sight of a white van parked ten yards ahead. He stopped the car and the four of them got out. They had two torches between them. He gave one to Grady and kept one for himself.

He gathered them round. "Professor, you stick with me. Grant, you stick with Grady. And stay close because you don't want to be lost in this without any light." He saw the sign pointing to the entrance and followed it.

Visibility was down to almost nothing. Jennings trod carefully towards the gate. The lock had been broken. He edged his way through. Miles followed; then Grady and Romano. He led them down the underpass directing his beam this way and that, expecting an attack at any moment. None came.

At the start of the incline Jennings stumbled. "Shit!"

"What is it?" whispered Grady.

Jennings shone his torch down. "Two security guards. Two dogs." He bent down and felt one of the guards for a pulse. "Alive thank God."

They continued up the walkway with extreme caution. At the top Jennings stopped and gathered them again. "Listen, from what I can remember, the Stones are over there." He pointed. "Be as quiet as you can."

He led them blindly into the fog, which was now so close he could hardly see his hand in front of his face. Miles held on to the tail of his jacket. After about twenty paces he hit the floor.

"Fuck!" he said under his breath.

Miles reached down to find him. "What happened?" he whispered.

"There's a rope here. I tripped over it."

Jennings got back to his feet. The rope would be there to cordon off the Stones from the public. They must be getting near.

Dominic C. James

He carried on forward.

At the back of the group Romano had the jitters. The mist and the Stones were all too familiar. He was right in the middle of his dream. It was fast becoming a self-fulfilling prophecy. He hoped that Miles would take heed and be wary.

As he walked on Jennings felt the ground begin to rumble. Then, without warning, he stepped forward into the Stones. In the centre, lit up by candles, he saw Stratton and an old man with their hands on a lifeless body; blue smoke surrounded them. Stella was nearby sitting on a boulder; Yoshima was next to her. Ten feet to their right, on a different boulder, another man sat trembling.

Jennings stopped himself at the edge of the ring. Nobody had noticed his presence. They were all caught up in whatever was going on. Miles came up next to him, followed by Grady and Romano.

"What the...!?" exclaimed Grady, forgetting to keep his silence.

Yoshima turned round and saw them. With his customary speed he leapt from the boulder and attacked. Jennings drew his gun. Before he could act Yoshima had kicked it into the air. Then Grady tried to grab the wily Japanese, but he too was found wanting, and ended up with a sharp jab to the throat. He fell to the ground clutching at his windpipe.

Jennings jumped on Yoshima's back forcing him to the floor. Romano joined in and the three of them struggled and fought in a writhing heap.

Miles, meanwhile, had picked up Jennings' gun and was making his way to the centre of the circle. The earth shook violently beneath his feet. Stratton and Jeremy stayed ensconced in their ritual. Stella and Dr Russell were unable to look away.

On the grass, next to a rucksack, Miles caught sight of the box. With everyone's attention elsewhere he decided to make his move. He took one step forward then froze, paralysed by the unseen energy, and swept up in its inescapable path.

Stratton was lost to the world. Weightless and electrified, he was at one with the universe. Lightning bolts crashed up and down his spine. His head was a whirlwind of light and colour. He felt himself being lifted higher and higher, twisting and turning in the torrential throes of a titanic tornado. He had to stop this madness.

They'd roused a dragon that should have been left to sleep. It was going to swallow them all. "No! No! No!" he screamed in his head. "No! No! No!" he repeated, desperately trying to break free of the spell. Still the dragon held him in its grip. Then, with one almighty act of will, he screamed "No!" out loud, and threw himself backwards to the ground. He lay there gasping for breath.

Stella felt the earth go still. She opened her eyes. The storm had subsided at last. She cast a grateful glance to the heavens then turned her attention to the centre of the circle. Stratton and Jeremy were lying on the ground. Alive or dead, she couldn't tell. Miles stood above them, gun in hand. "Stratton!" she warned.

Stratton lifted his head and saw Miles creeping towards the box. He was too exhausted to stop him. The experience had left him completely drained.

Miles bent down and picked up the box. Jeremy, who was also shattered, made a half-hearted lunge for Miles' legs, but to no effect.

Miles backed away keeping them covered. "Sorry chaps, I hate to spoil your party, but I think this belongs with me now."

Stella got off the boulder and tiptoed up behind the reversing Miles. With her hands still out of action she had to rely on her legs. She let fly an almighty side kick at the back of Miles' left knee. He fell to the ground yelling with pain. The box dropped from his grasp, but he held the gun firmly.

He rolled over and looked up at his assailant. "You silly little bitch," he hissed. Pointing his gun at her he scrambled to retrieve the box. He dragged himself to his feet and put the gun to Stella's head. "Don't try anything else or you're a dead bitch." He hobbled backwards to the edge of the ring.

Jennings and Romano were beaten. Even two on one they had been no match for Yoshima. They lay on the ground barely conscious. Romano saw Miles limping out of the ring. He tried to warn his friend. "Sharlo!" he said weakly.

If Miles heard him he didn't acknowledge it. Instead, he picked up his pace and headed for the cover of the fog.

From the shadows of the Stones Yoshima appeared. Romano saw him draw a knife from his pocket and go after Miles. Romano raised all the strength he could.

"Sharlo!" he shouted. But it was too late; Yoshima had already pounced. With one swift stroke he slit Miles' throat straight across. Romano closed his eyes. He felt sick.

Yoshima removed the box from Miles' dead clutches. He held it with reverence. In his hands he had the secrets of life. He felt a sudden urge to take it and run. True, Jeremy had paid him for his services, and perhaps he should hand the box back to him. But Jeremy already had the knowledge he needed, and Yoshima had far exceeded his remit anyway.

Leaving the box in the West would ultimately spell disaster. Eventually someone would misuse its power and leave a trail of destruction, it was inevitable. He made his mind up: he would take it to Japan where it would be safe from occidental greed. He walked into the fog.

Two paces later he slumped to the floor; a single bullet in the back of his head. Grady had regained his composure and, seeing Yoshima escaping, had had no reservations about shooting him. "Little Japanese fucker," he said as he stood over the body. "Nobody fucks with Scott Grady and gets away with it."

He bent down and rolled Yoshima over, expecting to find the box underneath his body. It wasn't there. He searched around on the grass but found nothing. Where the hell had it gone?

Chapter 68

Stratton opened his eyes and lifted himself to a sitting position. Jeremy was stooped over his son's body looking for signs of life. He checked for breath and then for a pulse. Both were negative. Dropping his head on his son's chest he began to cry.

Stratton got to his feet and walked over to Stella. He put his arms around her and held her tightly. "It's ok," he said. "It's over now." He drew back and kissed her softly on the lips.

"What happened?" she asked. "It felt like the end of the world."

"I don't exactly know," he replied. "All I do know, is that we tapped into something we shouldn't have. The symbol we used was too much. I felt like I was going to explode. If I hadn't pulled myself away I don't know what would've happened."

"My son would be alive. That's what would've happened," spat Jeremy from behind. "I knew you'd stopped it, you arrogant little prick. You think you're bigger than the Power don't you?"

Stratton turned to face him. "No I don't, because nobody is. The reason I stopped was because it overwhelmed me."

Jeremy sneered. "Rubbish," he said. "You stopped it because you thought it was wrong. Always making moral judgements in your head. All you've done though is stop the greatest break-through mankind is ever likely to see. And more to the point, you've stopped me from seeing my son again."

"I don't care what you say," sighed Stratton. "Your son was never coming back."

Jeremy reached down to his belt and pulled out the gun that was lodged there. "I'm afraid I disagree. You may as well have murdered him." He aimed the weapon at Stratton's chest.

Stratton put his hands up defensively and said, "Listen Jeremy, there's been enough death already; don't you think? It's over now. Just put the gun down and let's all walk out of this in one piece."

"Listen to the man," said a voice from the side: it was Grady. He had his gun trained on Jeremy. "Put the gun down and nobody gets hurt."

Jeremy didn't flinch. "I'm not putting anything down," he said firmly. "As soon as I do you lot will have me arrested. And don't threaten me - I'm not scared of dying. I'm nearly 90 years old. I've had a long life. I've just lost my son, and I've got nothing to lose." He paused. "Of course, if you hand me back the box then I'll leave without hurting anyone."

"I'd love to," said Grady. "But I'm afraid it's disappeared."

"Don't give me that rubbish. I wasn't born yesterday," laughed Jeremy.

"It's true," said Grady. "That little ninja fucker took it. When I searched him it had gone. If you want to go out into the fog and look for it old man, then you're very welcome."

"If I go out there you'll shoot me in the back," sneered Jeremy. "You. Stratton. You go out there and get it for me. If you do then I won't shoot your young lady here." He turned his gun on Stella. "Go on then, hurry up."

Stratton made his way to the edge of the Stones where Yoshima's corpse lay half in the mist. He checked the body and the area around it but found nothing. He extended his search to a ten foot radius, which he guessed was the maximum distance it could have flown; still he found nothing. He came to the conclusion that someone, or something, had taken it.

Jennings and Romano were back on their feet. Stratton looked hopefully at them as he walked back into the circle. Both shook their heads and shrugged.

Stratton approached Jeremy. "Grady's right," he said. "It's not there."

"Don't mess with me you lot. I'm not stupid," said Jeremy angrily.

Stratton tried to calm him. "Nobody's messing with you Augustus. It's lost."

Jeremy thrust his gun at Stella with intent. "You're taking me for a fool!" he screamed.

Stratton continued to speak slowly and softly. "No. We're telling you the truth. It's not here."

Jeremy began to shake. "Don't patronize me you little shit!"

His eyes flashed at Stratton. Then his voice dropped. "You've had your last chance," he said grimly. "It's time for you to suffer."

To Stella the next few seconds were a blur. Stratton dived in front of her. A gun fired. Stratton hit the floor. Another gun fired. Jeremy dropped to the ground. Blood poured from his temple. Her heart stopped.

The next thing she knew Jennings was in front of her, kneeling over Stratton who was face down in the grass. "Stratton," he said. "Stratton. Are you all right mate?"

There was no answer. Stella felt her stomach twist.

Jennings rolled Stratton onto his back. In the limited light he could see no injuries. Lifting up Stratton's jumper he saw where the problem lay. There was a small black hole in his chest, with a river of red running out of it. He felt for a pulse. There was none.

He looked up at Stella and shook his head.

Stella dropped to her knees and leant over Stratton's body. "Come on Stratton," she said. "Stop messing about. It's not funny."

Jennings gave her a grave look. "Stella. He's dead. I'm sorry."

"No. He can stop his pulse, remember?"

Jennings put his hand on her shoulder. "Not this time. He's been shot through the heart. He's gone. I'm sorry."

Stella looked down at Stratton lying peacefully beneath her. Part of her expected him to open his eyes at any moment. But deep down in her heart she knew he was gone. Unable to caress his face because of her cuffed hands she bent over and kissed him on the forehead.

And then it hit her: Stratton was dead. He wasn't coming back. She turned aside and vomited violently.

Dominic C. James

Chapter 69

It was Christmas Eve. Stella lay curled up in her bed, as she had done for most of the day. Her holiday having fallen through she was supposed to be visiting her mother. The festive spirit had escaped her though. All she could think about was Stratton. She still couldn't believe he was dead.

For the fourth time in five minutes the intercom buzzed. Whoever was there wasn't getting the message. She reluctantly heaved herself up and answered her caller. It was Jennings.

"I'm a bit busy right now," she said. "Can't you come back another time?"

"No I can't. Let me in or I'll call the fire brigade to break the door down."

Stella gave a half smile and released the door.

Jennings stood at the door carrying a plastic bag. He was wearing jeans, trainers and a smart black leather jacket. Apart from the comedy wear he'd got from the hospital, it was the first time she'd seen him out of a suit. "Not on duty today then?" she said.

"No," he replied. "And probably not for the foreseeable future. I'm officially resting. Which means they're holding an enquiry into my conduct. It doesn't look good."

Stella invited him in and put the kettle on. They sat down in the living room.

"What happened then?" she asked. "You caught the killer and his boss; surely you should be a hero."

"If only," he laughed. "Unofficially I think that the PM and Brennan are pleased at the result. But you know what it's like. I'm in trouble because Miles got killed and I was supposed to be protecting him. And I'm in trouble for not calling for back-up at Stonehenge. I explained that a large scale operation would have caused more deaths, but it fell on deaf ears. I expect I'll keep my

403

job but to be honest I don't really care any more. I've decided that maybe a change of career might be in order. These last ten days have changed my perspective."

Stella smiled. "I'm not surprised," she said. And then: "What's happened to Grady? Is he off the hook? And what about Grant Romano? I know he was there at the Stones but it's all a blur to be honest. I can't really remember a lot."

"Grady and Grant flew back to the States this afternoon," said Jennings. "I helped get Grady out of the shit by giving the dirt on Miles. Shooting Yoshima and Jeremy helped his cause as well. In fact, if anyone's going to come out of this a hero it's him. It's ironic after all he did to us." He smiled to himself. "But you know what - I don't begrudge him it at all. Between you and me, in a weird way I kind of like the guy."

Stella went to the kitchen and made them both a cup of coffee.

"Anyway," said Jennings when she returned with the drinks. "Enough about what's happened. How are you? I've been ringing and texting for two days and you haven't answered."

She lit a cigarette. "I've been lying in bed. I haven't answered the phone to anyone so don't take it personally. I just don't feel like talking to anyone at the moment. The only reason I answered the door is because you wouldn't go away."

"I know. It was the only way I could think of getting to you. I've been worried; I didn't know what you'd do."

Stella understood the inference. "Don't worry, I'd never do that however low I got. I'm just trying to get my head round everything."

"You really loved him didn't you?"

Stella's eyes filled with water. "Yes, I did. I spent five years trying to forget it, but it was always there. And then, just as I was coming to terms with it again, this happens. I just don't know what to do. I feel empty and lost." She paused. "To tell the truth, I can't quite believe he's gone. I know it sounds stupid but I didn't think he could die. He always had this magical quality about him, even when we first met. He's always seemed almost invincible to me. Whenever he was around I felt like nothing bad could happen. He made me feel safe."

"I'm sure he wouldn't want you moping around the flat," said Jennings.

Stella put out her cigarette and lit another. "I know," she agreed. "I know exactly what he'd say. He'd be all philosophical to start with and give me all that rubbish about how life has to go on. Then he'd tell me that death isn't final, that people move on to other worlds, that they meet again in parallel universes etc."

"Don't you believe that? After recent events I thought you might give it some credence."

"Maybe. But it really doesn't help me at the moment. At the moment I'm stuck in this world without the man I love. All I really want right now is for him to walk through that door. I didn't even get to say goodbye or tell him that I still loved him. One minute he was there and the next..."

"I'm sure he knew how you felt," said Jennings sympathetically. "It was pretty plain to see."

"I guess so," said Stella. "I just wish I'd said it, that's all."

She looked away in thought. A silence hung in the air.

Jennings reached in to the plastic bag he'd brought and pulled out a flat rectangular object in wrapping paper. "Look. I know you're probably not in the Christmas mood but I got you this." He handed her the package.

Out of politeness she thanked him and opened it. She allowed herself a smile: it was a photograph of Grant Romano signed 'To the beautiful Stella'.

"Thank you," she said. Her mood lightened a little. "What about the box? Did anybody find that?" she asked.

"No. We searched in the morning when the fog had lifted but there was no sign of it whatsoever. It's a complete mystery. It seemingly vanished into thin air."

"What about Grady or Grant Romano, couldn't they have taken it?"

Jennings shook his head. "No. We checked everyone leaving the site, including that Dr Russell. I felt sorry for the guy; he was still trembling hours afterwards. The whole thing affected him quite badly."

Stella sipped her coffee. "Oh well," she said. "Maybe we'll never know. To be honest I'd be quite glad if it was lost forever."

"I think Stratton was right, as a race we're just not ready for that kind of power. You just have to look at our society, we're a nation and a world full of wannabes, all people want nowadays is fame and fortune. The majority of people don't care about spiritual growth or discipline; they want the clothes, the cars and the mansions. Kids want to grow up to be one of the 'beautiful people'; they want to be 'Brad and Angelina', 'Posh and Becks', or 'Wayne and Coleen'. They aspire to be what they see on TV and in the papers. And what's worse, they want to do it without any effort. They think that fame and fortune are a birthright. Stratton told me that people like Yoshima wanted to keep Reiki away from the West. I can understand why."

"But what about the healing powers?" said Jennings. "Apparently Brennan's wife has made a miraculous turnaround after Stratton saw her."

"I'm glad. But I stand by what I said - we're just not ready."

Jennings chuckled.

"What's so funny?" asked Stella.

"You know who you're beginning to sound like don't you?"

"No. Who?"

"Stratton," said Jennings.

Stella gave a half-hearted laugh. "Yes I suppose I do. It's exactly what he'd say. He must have brainwashed me."

"I think he's had an effect on all of us," admitted Jennings. "My attitude's certainly changed. The world seems a lot smaller, and the universe a lot larger, if you know what I mean."

Stella let the memory of Stratton wash over her like a warm breeze. "I know exactly what you mean," she said.

Epilogue

I

The corridors of the mortuary were eerily silent. Rick Allenby had worked there for five years and he still hadn't quite gotten used to it. There was an atmosphere about the place that only death could bring. The night shift was the worst; he could almost feel the corpses reaching up from below clawing at his feet. He shivered at the thought.

To cheer himself up he got out his wallet and gazed fondly at the photo of his wife and children he kept there.

The kids would be sound asleep by now and his wife would be filling their stockings with presents. Soon she would be tiptoeing into their bedroom and depositing the goodies at the end of their bunks, keeping the magic of Father Christmas alive. He looked forward to the morning when he would return to see their wide-eyed wonder.

The mortuary toilet was positioned at the end of a cold and sterile passageway. As usual Rick had stayed his bladder until he could hold it no longer. He hated the walk there and back, much as he had hated the midnight trip to the bathroom as a child. There was an unseen presence in the building that made his skin crawl. He needed to get another job, he told himself. But he'd been saying that for five years and he knew he wouldn't.

As he hurried along the hall he thought he heard a noise behind him. He stopped abruptly and spun round: there was nothing but open space. He carried on at speed, keeping his eyes front.

He pushed open the toilet door and then locked it quickly behind him. He relaxed slightly, feeling safe behind the bolted wood. He relieved himself gratefully. Then, from the hallway, he heard a squeaking noise. He stiffened and pricked his ears. The noise came again. There was somebody or something out there.

Slowly and quietly he slid back the metal lock and opened the door ever so slightly. He peeked into the corridor.

Before he had a chance to see anything somebody kicked the door open and Rick was sent flying back against the wall. He slid down onto the tiled floor. Standing in front of him were three masked men, dressed from head to toe in black and brandishing shotguns. Rick felt his bladder squeeze.

"Get up!" ordered one of the men pointing his weapon at Rick's head.

Rick did as he was told. The men led him back to his desk and tied him to his chair.

The lead man held a piece of paper in front of Rick's face. It had a name on it. "Where's the body?" he barked.

"D-d-downstairs," Rick stammered. "In n-n-number f-forty two."

The men taped Rick's mouth, took his keys and headed downstairs.

Five minutes later they were back up. The largest of the three was carrying a body bag over his shoulder.

He shouted "Merry Christmas!" and they left through the front doors. Corpse number 42 was gone.

II

Whilst families ate their Christmas dinner and the Queen gave her annual speech, four men stood around a marble altar. They were in a small church, in a small village, on the border of Warwickshire and Oxfordshire. The church was built upon a network of ley-lines that looked like Spaghetti Junction. It was for this reason they had chosen it.

On top of the altar lay a naked body, cold and blue and lifeless. The leader of the group, a large bearded man, made several signs in the air above the cadaver. His colleagues followed in turn. Then each of them laid their hands on the corpse and closed their eyes.

Thick blue smoke engulfed the men. Each of them straightened as if hit by an electrical surge. The church shook from its foundations. Under immense strain the men continued to hold their contact with the body. The smoke grew denser.

The dead body started to glow. White sparks jumped unpredictably in the air around it. A rush of lights swirled above them. The men shuddered and swayed violently in the ferocious current, barely holding themselves together.

At last, when they could stand it no longer, the rumbling of the earth hit a peak and sounded its climax with a clap of thunder. At the same time an unendurably bright flash swallowed the church. The men were thrown back from the body. The church fell silent.

For five minutes the men lay still. Then, mustering all his strength, the bearded man opened his eyes and pulled himself to a sitting position. Gradually, one by one, his cohorts did likewise.

He got to his feet and looked down at the body on the altar. It was motionless. He shook his head and sighed with resignation. "Oh well old friend," he said regretfully. "I tried. I'm sorry."

He turned away defeated, not noticing the reddening of the

skin and the absence of the bullet wound.

At that moment a wide smile spread across the face of corpse 42. He opened his eyes and breathed in deeply, savouring the blast of oxygen to his lungs. Life streamed through his rejuvenated veins, stronger and deeper than ever.

Stratton was born again...

Reader Information

The Reiki Man is the first novel in a trilogy. For more information on the next two books please go to www.dominiccjames.com

BOOKS

0 is a symbol of the world, of oneness and unity. In different cultures it also means the "eye," symbolizing knowledge and insight. We aim to publish books that are accessible, constructive and that challenge accepted opinion, both that of academia and the "moral majority."

Our books are available in all good English language bookstores worldwide. If you don't see the book on the shelves ask the bookstore to order it for you, quoting the ISBN number and title. Alternatively you can order online (all major online retail sites carry our titles) or contact the distributor in the relevant country, listed on the copyright page.

See our website www.o-books.net for a full list of over 500 titles, growing by 100 a year.

And tune in to myspiritradio.com for our book review radio show, hosted by June-Elleni Laine, where you can listen to the authors discussing their books.

MySpiritRadio